ART AT AUCTION 1976-77

ART AT AUCTION

The Year at Sotheby Parke Bernet
1976-77

Two hundred and forty-third season

SOTHEBY PARKE BERNET

© Sotheby Parke Bernet Publications Ltd, 1977

First published by
Sotheby Parke Bernet Publications, Philip Wilson Publishers Ltd,
Russell Chambers, Covent Garden, London WC2E 8AA

First published in the USA by
Sotheby Parke Bernet Publications Ltd, c/o Biblio Distribution Center
81 Adams Drive, Totowa, New Jersey 07512

Edited by Anne Jackson
Assistant editors: Diana Lucas (UK) and Barbara Evans (USA)

Production by Peter Ling
Layouts by Martin Ashley

ISBN: 0 85667 040 5

Printed in Great Britain by Jolly & Barber Ltd, Rugby, Warwickshire and
bound by Webb Son & Co Ltd, Glamorgan, Wales

Frontispiece: The dining room at Mentmore

The publishers would like to acknowledge Agence Top for their permission
to use the views of Mentmore by Roger Guillemot reproduced on the
frontispiece, prelims p ii, and on p 12. These photographs first appeared
in *Connaissance des arts*, May 1977.

Endpaper illustrations: A repeating pattern of Liverpool delftware tiles
printed in black by J. Sadler, *circa* 1758-75. From a collection of over one
hundred similar tiles belonging to the late Sir William Mullens, DSO, TD, DL,
which was sold in London on 22 February 1977 for a total of £5,205
($8,848).

Contents

One of a pair of Venetian marble
busts of blackamoors, second half
of the seventeenth century,
height 31in (78.5cm)
Mentmore £32,000($54,400).
18.V.77

These Blackamoor figures stood
in the Great Hall at Mentmore.
For a view of this figure in
its original setting see p 12

Contents continued

Note:

The prices given throughout this book are the hammer prices, exclusive of any buyer's premium or sales tax which may have been applicable in any of the salerooms.

Conversion rates between different currencies have been averaged out over the season. While providing an adequate guide, the sterling or dollar equivalents in brackets after the actual sale prices do not necessarily conform with the exact exchange rate applying on the day of the sale.

The following rates in relation to the pound sterling have been used throughout: US dollars 1.70; Canadian dollars 1.70; Hong Kong dollars 8; French francs 8.40; Swiss francs 4.30; Dutch gilders 4.30; South African rand 1.50; Italian lire 1,500.

The way to the sale: first view of Paxton's little-known masterpiece in festive dress

Dealers and collectors came from all over the world: old friends meet just before the sale

A section of the principal marquee a quarter of an hour before the opening sale. All seats were reserved

A hitch! The auctioneer's microphone turns temperamental seconds before the first sale session is due to start. Lord Rosebery to the rescue

The world's press, there in force, make the most of the occasion

Photographs by the author

We're off: Peter Wilson in the rostrum after an agonising delay. Exit the loud hailer, right

Infinitely memorable

a view of the sale at Mentmore

Frank Herrmann

Recollected in tranquility there can be no doubt that the sale of the contents of Mentmore in Buckinghamshire in May 1977 will become a milestone in the social history of our time. From the moment that the proposed sale became public know-ledge in January of this year, people began to realise in growing numbers that it crystallised the threat to great houses when they are caught in the conflict between punitive death duties and a faint-hearted government enfeebled by economic con-straint. Conservationist lobbies launched a crusade of unprecedented ferocity to preserve the house and its contents intact, and what had virtually been an unknown nineteenth-century mansion suddenly became a national *cause célèbre*. The press had a field day. Parliament debated it both upstairs and down. Ministers made countless statements on the subject. The one figure in the whole *contretemps* to emerge with dignity and with grace was Lord Rosebery who, with his advisers, had been patient, generous in spirit and ultimately shrewd and common-sensical. The long drawn out controversy had been fuelled by a series of letters in *The Times*, but here again it was a letter from Lord Rosebery's sixteen-year-old daughter, Lady Jane Primrose, that stands out in the memory as refreshingly sane:

> 'For several generations', she wrote about the house, 'it was lived in, in that incredibly dazzling life style, and now that it has to go – can it not die in some semblance of the dignity in which it lived?'

To most of us who attended the sale it seemed that her wish was granted. In the superbly beautiful setting of Buckinghamshire in a late, seemingly reluctant spring, the ten days at Mentmore were like a long outing into cloud-cuckooland. The results of the magnificent and ostentatious collecting activities of Baron Mayer Amschel de Rothschild and his successors were bound to be a magnet for buyers from all over the world, when the dominant attraction in the art market today are objects of a spectacular kind in the £3,000 to £12,000 price bracket. And Paxton's enormous – and surprisingly elegant – neo-Elizabethan/Jacobean stone pile contained these in apparently unlimited quantities. Genuine boulle and marquetry mazarins appear in the London saleroom perhaps once every two years. Here were *nine*, some dating from 1690, and some not so markedly different, produced in 1850. (In retrospect some of the early marquetry ones may well have been bargains at £6,500 to £9,500.) Of elaborately decorated French clocks there were no fewer than thirty-two in the first two furniture sale sessions. The catalogues, a triumph of their kind, and universally

Three generations of the Rosebery family attended diligently right through the sales

The highly organised porters' teams worked miracles of transportation. Almost every piece was shown at the time of the sale

admired, became best sellers and went out of print nearly three weeks before the sale started. Although the press had thought them expensive at £30 for the set of five, they were reported to be changing hands on the opening day of the sale at £180 a time.

The morning of the first sale session, which was devoted to the pick of the French furniture, was as brilliantly sunny as an opening day at Wimbledon, and the atmosphere of mounting anticipation was not dissimilar. Cars streamed in early: the parking controlled with decorum by the estate staff. 'I want to see his Lordship make a lot of money today', a retired gardener confided. A host of different languages could be heard on the lawns around the house as little huddles of dealers made last-minute checks on the notes in their catalogues. The most opulent arrived by helicopter on a specially marked pad at the front of the house. The degree of organisation became apparent as one approached the gigantic sales marquee: sign posts pointed the way to the bar and cafeteria, information offices, telephones, press office, cashiers' office and removal firms.

Entry was by reserved ticket. Shortly before 11 a.m. most of the 1,000 seats were occupied. One whole section of the vast tent had been taken over by television cameras and swarms of photographers. It became increasingly warm. Lighting on the raised dais was fierce. Eleven microphones decorated the front of the auctioneer's rostrum. Someone gave the microphone of the loudspeaker system in the marquee a little tap. Silence. Subsequently it refused to respond to every form of coaxing or electronic blandishment. Lord Rosebery, jacketless as always, rushed to the rescue. Peter Wilson, about to take the first sale, smiled uncertainly. After an agonising few minutes he apologised for the delay. Lord Rosebery scurried back and forth. The delay heightened the very tangible sense of drama. Someone produced a loud hailer from the cark park to see if that could be used instead, hand-held by the chief cashier, but at that very moment the faulty microphone squealed back into life. We were off. And in the first two minutes it became clear which way the sale was going to go. Lot 1 (out of a total of 3,739), 'a fine Louis XV Leather Travelling Trunk', jumped up to £13,500 ($22,950). The estimate had been between £4,000 and £8,000. Lot 2, 'a Louis XVI Ormolu-mounted Mahogany Console-Desserte' with a similar estimate, moved

Four old men who've seen it all before: some items among the general contents of the house

Some of the lesser items on view in the stable: the degree of competition for them was totally unexpected

even more speedily to £17,500 ($29,750). Bidding was not initially at the Bond Street pace and bid-callers, specially brought over from Sotheby Parke Bernet, New York, due to the size of the marquee, helped the auctioneer to make sure that no potential buyer was overlooked.

The first real buzz of excitement was caused by lot 24: 'a rare Louis XVI Ormolu-mounted Parquetry Writing Cabinet'. The bidding started at £5,000. It almost ceased at £8,000; then in rapid staccato form it moved to a final one from Mallett at £32,000 ($54,400). The estimate had been £8,000 to £14,000. The next lot, 'a Louis XVI Royal Ormolu-mounted Mahogany Secretaire' made for Marie-Antoinette and stamped with the magic name, J. H. Riesener, had been found by Sotheby's in the cellar, unused for generations. Although in 'distressed condition', it was now bought at more than twice the top estimate by the Palais de Versailles for £51,000 ($86,700). The total at the end of the first day reached a staggering £1,749,970 ($2,992,449). By the second day it had increased to £2,776,930 ($4,748,550). By the end of the third day, which included a large collection of Limoges enamels, one of the splendours of the house, it had shot up to £4,175,655 ($7,140,370). Even the general contents – the china, the glass, the fire irons, hot-water cans, coat hangers, the furniture from the kitchen and servants' bedrooms – saw the most spirited bidding. After a Sunday break, the tortoiseshell, the amber, the ivories and rock crystals again made the headlines. And by the end of the eighteenth session on the ninth day no less than £6,389,933 ($10,926,785) had been raised, probably the highest total in any similar continuous series of sales.

There was relief and gratitude. For the staff at Sotheby's it had been the most enormous job of work, at times in highly dispiriting conditions because of the initial uncertainties. But the brilliance of the organisation had not gone unnoticed by buyers, sellers, the curious public or the press, and the greatest achievement of all was that an event which could have been funereal or merely unprepossessing had, in fact, been imbued with an enormous sense of fun and style, and was crowned with stunning success.

Collectors contrasted

Baron Mayer Amschel de Rothschild and the 5th Earl of Rosebery at Mentmore and elsewhere

Sir Francis Watson

For nearly a century the Hamilton Palace sale of 1882 has been a touchstone: 'the greatest sale of all time' as it has often been called. Over a seventeen-day period the sale produced £397,562. Now all that is changed. The Mentmore sale of 1977 broke all records for the disposal of a single art collection and realised £6,389,933 in nine days. Henceforward it must take its place as one of the grand climacteric moments in the history of the saleroom.

Not only were the collections at Hamilton Palace and Mentmore remarkably alike but they had been assembled in a very similar manner. At Hamilton Palace the basic collection had come from William Beckford of Fonthill whose daughter had married the 10th Duke of Hamilton. To this collection the 11th Duke made extensive additions. The 5th Earl of Rosebery married Hannah, daughter of Baron Mayer Amschel de Rothschild, and thus inherited Mentmore and the vast art collection he had assembled there. Rosebery, likewise, proceeded to make considerable additions to the collections his wife had inherited at Mentmore as well as in his other houses.

Mayer Amschel de Rothschild was the youngest of the four sons of Nathan Mayer de Rothschild and had been sent to London in 1797 to found a branch of the family bank there. More significantly he appears to have been the earliest and one of the most enterprising of the many great collectors that the Rothschild family has produced.

Baron Mayer's mother bought the first parcel of land which eventually constituted the Mentmore estate in 1836. To this her son added the rest of the estate piece by piece as it came on to the market. Within the next two or three decades brothers and cousins were to buy estates and build or restore imposing mansions in the same area of the vale of Aylesbury; Anthony and Lionel at Aston Clinton and Halton, Leopold at Ascott and other members of the family at Waddesdon and Tring, so that the whole neighbourhood came to be known as 'the Rothschild country'. But it was Mayer Amschel who bought the most beautiful estate and built on it the first, the largest, and the most architecturally distinguished of these palatial residences, Mentmore Towers.

It was perhaps his impending marriage to Juliana Cohen as much as the need to house adequately his growing art collection which prompted the Baron to construct a mansion on the Mentmore estate. The style adopted, based on Wollaton Hall outside Nottingham, was, according to a contemporary issue of *The Builder*, entirely Mayer Amschel's own choice. In selecting Joseph Paxton as his architect he was not only employing the creator of one of the greatest architectural monuments of the age, the

The Great Hall at Mentmore

Crystal Palace, but one who had spent much time with his first employer, the 'bachelor' Duke of Devonshire at Hardwick Hall ('more glass than wall'), a house very similar in conception to Wollaton. Paxton's most personal modification of the chosen style, was his use of extensive areas of plate-glass both inside and outside and the creation of the vast glass-covered Great Hall, an Elizabethan courtyard transformed into a conservatory. Paxton had already taken the first steps in his chosen profession of architect by building conservatories at Chatsworth for the Duke.

His greatest ingenuity was displayed in adapting the 'Jacobethan' design of the building to its function of housing the Baron's growing collection of objects of very different periods. Like so many other rooms in the house the Great Hall (illustrated p 12), 48 ft long by 40 ft wide and 40 ft high, was clearly designed with some of the more monumental works of art in mind. Such were the huge black and white marble chimneypiece said to have come from Rubens' house at Antwerp or the three huge Venetian lanterns, the largest 12 ft high, which hung from the roof and were claimed to have come from the *Bucintoro*, the Doge's state barge, but were more probably designed for one of the greater Venetian churches. The Venetian throne-chairs (probably by Corradini rather than Brustalon as claimed) would have overwhelmed any room smaller than this where even the twelve Gobelins tapestries of the Lucas Months around the walls seemed little larger than pocket handkerchiefs and the unusual Louis XVI orrery clock, over 8 ft high, was completely dwarfed.

Other rooms in the house were likewise clearly designed with the display of the Baron's collection in view. The dining room (illustrated p ii), for example, was planned not only to take the magnificent panelling but also to provide for the display of his Renaissance and baroque silver. The *boiseries* themselves, masterpieces of the *Régence* period, came from the hôtel de Villars in the rue de Grenelle where they had been in the *galerie*, a room of which a contemporary guide-book records, 'il passe pour le plus beau de Paris'. No doubt the owner of Mentmore acquired the panelling when the huge hôtel was sold in lots and partially pulled down in 1845. The carving surrounding the panels is of an extraordinary richness and was the work of Nicolas Pineau, one of the greatest masters of the early rococo in France, and Bernard. The Baron's study, later Lord Rosebery's, was likewise designed around a smaller and rather less-distinguished set of Louis XV panelling. The same also applies to the so-called 'Austrian Dressing Room' to which the architect seems to have adapted a remarkable pair of *armoires* by Charles Cressent, though their form was considerably modified in the process to enable them to be used as hanging wardrobes.

The style and richness of the interior of Mentmore with its use of Sicilian, Rouge Royal and other coloured marbles, as well as the general splendour of the collections, drew an interesting comment from one of the early visitors. Lady Eastlake wrote: 'I do not believe that the Medici were ever so lodged at the height of their glory'. A less artistically-minded visitor described the design as a 'stunning circumvention of cosiness'. Palaces, and Mentmore is no less, are not intended for cosy, middle-class life; nevertheless Paxton did provide a great deal of up-to-date comfort for the visitors. From the beginning the house was heated by water circulation at a time when hot-air heating was almost the universal practice for architects. In addition artificial ventilation was installed, though complaints were voiced from time to time that 'it pumped more stale air into the bedrooms than ever it extracted'.

More importantly, Paxton and the Baron, who clearly understood one another exceptionally well, succeeded between them in creating a prototype for housing the

Two carved wood figures of grape-pickers with contemporary silver and silver-gilt mounts, maker's mark *N* over *R* in a shaped shield, Frankfurt, *circa* 1628, height 10in (26cm)
Mentmore £22,000($37,400). 19.V.77

great Rothschild art collections of the period. The châteaux of Ferrières outside Paris and Pregny on the lake of Geneva were both Paxton's work, both built for members of the family and both inspired in the same spirit as Mentmore. When, after Paxton's death, Destailleur built Waddesdon Manor for Baron Ferdinand de Rothschild he likewise followed the principles on which Mentmore was built, though the house is hardly so successful or so distinguished architecturally.

Baron Mayer Amschel's taste in art was eclectic like that of most members of his family, but eclectic in a rather unusual way. In buying Limoges enamels (see pp 240-47 for further discussion), Augsburg silver and the more exotic creations of the northern Renaissance in ivory, amber, tortoiseshell and silver or rock crystal, as well as Italian majolica and other faiences, he was following in the footsteps of his family as well as one of the best traditions of his own day – it was exactly such things as these

A North German amber games board, seventeenth century, 14½in by 14½in (37cm by 37cm)
Mentmore £52,000($88,400). 23.V.77

that the 11th Duke of Hamilton added to the collection inherited from Beckford. But the Baron was also, consciously or unconsciously, linking his collections with another more deeply historical tradition stemming from his native land; that of the *Wunderkammern* and *Kunstkabinette* in which the German princes of the Renaissance and the seventeenth century delighted. The numerous Augsburg cabinets and portable altars, the fantastically carved ivories, the magnificent Augsburg clock with its intricate mechanism, or the grotesque creations of amber, tortoiseshell and other semi-precious materials, are precisely the sort of things that the Emperor Rudolph II assembled at Prague and the Kings of Saxony gathered into the Green Vaults at Dresden.

Onto this historical taste Mayer Amschel grafted another, foreign not only to his day and age but to his family traditions as well. As I demonstrated elsewhere, it was not until the sales of Robert, Earl of Pembroke's Paris collections in 1862 that French eighteenth-century furniture came into fashion. Baron Mayer Amschel's boast (it can hardly have been less) that in the early 1850s he found it cheaper to furnish his guest bedrooms at Mentmore with fine Louis XV and Louis XVI commodes rather than to purchase modern wash-hand stands from Maples is a measure of the degree to which such things had ceased to be esteemed by the rich. It was not until the 1870s that the other members of the Rothschild family, at first in the persons of Baron Edmond de Rothschild, his brother Alphonse, and their cousin Ferdinand, began seriously to collect French eighteenth-century furniture and works of art. By that time the

An Augsburg tortoiseshell, mother-of-pearl and pietra dura quarter-repeating altar-clock mounted in silver and gilt metal, *circa* 1730, height 45in (114cm)
Mentmore £70,000($119,000). 20.V.77

Mentmore collections were long since complete and Mayer Amschel's death was only a few years away.

Unhappily we know very little of when or how the Baron's individual purchases were made. This is particularly the case with the *dix-huitième* furniture and objects, no doubt on account of their very unfashionableness. We do know, however, that he was buying rococo objects in the 1830s, that in the 1840s and 1850s he was buying Venetian art, and by 1860 he was a client of that remarkably discerning collector and dealer Alexander Barker from whose house near Hyde Park Corner so many Old Masters (he was a pioneer of collecting *quattrocento* painting) and eighteenth-century works of art entered the great English collections of the day.[1] He was also making fairly extensive purchases at the great English sales of the period, at Stowe in 1848, at the Bernal sale of 1855, the Clare sale of 1866 and the Ricketts sale of the following year, at all of which he had Lord Hertford as a rival for eighteenth-century French works. His splendid Savonnérie carpets (one from the *Grande Galerie* of the Louvre, another made for Louis XV's father-in-law, the King of Poland) and a *banquette* cover woven for Louis XIV's Queen were in his possession by 1863, for they appear in a watercolour view of the Great Hall of that date. In fact he probably possessed them over a decade earlier, for it was at that period that the Rothschild family began, with great discernment, to purchase large quantities of these most beautiful of all carpets of European weave and in which hardly any other collectors of the period seems to have been interested.

It is doubtful if Mayer Amschel purchased the matching commode and upright secretaire of late Louis XVI date (perhaps by Molitor) at the Watson Taylor sale of 1825 himself. He was hardly old enough. But amongst individual items of French eighteenth-century art which he purchased directly we know that he bought the two Sèvres milk-pails from Marie-Antoinette's *laiterie* at the Château de Rambouillet at the sale of the contents of the Dowager Duchess of Bedford's house on Camden Hill in 1853. They there appeared as lot 1378 and though they were erroneously described as coming from the Trianon and of Dresden porcelain, their identity can hardly be questioned:

> 'A pair of REMARKABLY FINE *DRESDEN CHINA PAILS*, 20 in. high, with goats'-head handles, on stands; formerly the property of Marie Antoinette, and removed from the Swiss dairy at the Trianon'.

The milk-pails at the Trianon dairy were of a quite different form.

We know that the Baron made fairly extensive purchases of works of art confiscated from the Orléans family after the Revolution of 1848, chiefly sculpture and furniture but also paintings. But sadly we rarely know where his best furniture came from, neither pieces such as the BVRB *secrétaire en pente*, the Roentgen commode made for Versailles (sold for a world record price of £63,000 in 1964), and, most magnificent of all, the *bureau plat* made by Joubert, probably for the Dauphin, son of Louis XV. Yet we may be fairly confident that he purchased them cheaply, for such things were always cheap at the period when he must have acquired them. The same problems of provenance arise with the Baron's paintings. We know that a number of his sixteenth-century Old Masters came through Alexander Barker from the Manfrin

---

[1] Such little information as we have about Mayer Amschel's purchases comes from a two volume catalogue, *Mentmore*, privately printed and compiled by Hannah Rosebery and the dealer Charles Davis.

One of two Sèvres milk pails, made for Marie-Antoinette's *laiterie* at Rambouillet, 1787–88, height 19in (48.5cm)
The two were sold at Mentmore for a total of £105,000($178,500). 24.V.77

LOUIS-NICOLAS VAN BLARENBERGHE
The meet of the royal hounds at Fontainebleau
Gouache on canvas, 20⅝in by 39⅝in (52.5cm by 100.6cm)
£11,000($18,700). 25.V.77

Collection in Venice. But there is no record of where his equally splendid Paters originated. The portrait by Drouais of Madame de Pompadour in the last year of her life, was acquired, we know, from the estate of 'old Webb', as the dealer was always referred to by two of his best clients, George IV and Lord Hertford. It had previously belonged to the Marquis de Cypierre, one of the most discerning of the early collectors of *dix-huitième* art who had bought it for a song in the 1830s, when he was buying Watteaus and Bouchers for even less. Some of his huge collection of gouaches by van Blarenberghe (there was an entire room of them at Mentmore) were purchased by Mayer Amschel at the Lord Harrington sale in 1800, but by no means all of them. Yet in buying these rare and beautiful things he was showing almost as much discernment as Cypierre, for it was only two years before the Baron's death that van Blarenberghes took their first tentative steps towards becoming stars of the auction room, a status which they only attained in the last two decades of the nineteenth century. It was equally enterprising at this period to have acquired the two masterpieces by Marguerite Gérard painted in collaboration with her teacher, uncle and lover, Fragonard, even though he did buy them as works by Fragonard himself.

Baron Mayer Amschel's passion for continental furniture of the baroque and rococo periods was even more unusual in mid nineteenth-century England than his interest in French furniture of the same period. It was as early as 1835 that he bought what is perhaps the masterpiece of the collection, the upright bureau-cabinet in the extreme German rococo style attributed with some confidence to Michael Kümmel,

FRANÇOIS-HUBERT DROUAIS
Portrait of Madame de Pompadour
Signed and dated twice: *la tête en avril 1763; et le tableau fini en mai 1764*, 85in by 62in (214cm by 157cm)

Private sale to the National Gallery, London, on behalf of the Executors of the late 6th Earl of Rosebery

A Dresden ormolu-mounted and mother-of-pearl inlaid kingwood parquetry bureau cabinet, attributed to Michael Kümmel, cabinet-maker to Augustus III, King of Poland and Elector of Saxony, *circa* 1755, height 9ft (274cm)

Private sale to the British Government on behalf of the Executors of the late 6th Earl of Rosebery
Now on loan to the Victoria and Albert Museum.

A Franco-Flemish ebony and gilt-bronze cabinet, traditionally presented by the City of Florence to Marie de Medici on her marriage to Henri IV of France, mid seventeenth century, height 5ft 7in (170cm)

Private sale to the British Government on behalf of the Executors of the late 6th Earl of Rosebery

royal *Kabinet-Tischler* at Dresden, and therefore perhaps made, as family tradition claimed, for Augustus III. For this he paid £1,000, a high price for the period and likely to have been a great deal larger than anything he paid for his Louis XV or Louis XVI furniture. But it has the high claim of being considered one of the two or three most remarkable pieces of German furniture outside its native land. There were other pieces of German seventeenth- and eighteenth-century furniture in the house as well as examples of Italian, Netherlandish and even Russian furniture (then as now almost unknown outside Russia itself) as witnesses to the originality and catholicity of his taste. Only one of these, however, can be regarded as a masterpiece comparable to the Saxon piece or his finest French pieces. This was the cabinet of ebony and gilt bronze and silver alleged (with little or no reason) to have been presented by the City of Florence to Marie de Medici on the occasion of her marriage to Henri IV of France in 1600. This he bought in 1855, also for the large sum of £1,000, presumably as an Italian piece. However it appears to date from at least half a century later than the royal marriage and may well be of French origin. Possibly it is one of the Louis XIV cabinets, seemingly vanished today, which were sold from the *Garde-Meuble* as old-fashioned at various times during the eighteenth century and of which Monsieur Verlet wrote 'Who knows if these illustrious pieces are not still in existence in some English country house?'. Although careful study of the piece itself and of the Royal inventories would be necessary before pronouncing on this question, there is no doubt that it resembles certain descriptions of the grandiose cabinets produced at the Gobelins factory in the latter part of the seventeenth century, especially the work of Jean Macé or one of the other Antwerp trained *ébénistes* employed there (incidentally no piece could more adequately illuminate the origin of the word '*ébéniste*', introduced into the French language a few years later). The frieze of spread-eagles, laurel swags and infants around the stand appears on a number of cabinets convincingly attributed to Macé, though they are generally carved rather than applied in gilt bronze as here.

When Mayer Amschel died in 1874 he bequeathed all these treasures, together with a fortune variously estimated as between £2 and £3 million to his only daughter, Hannah, who thus became the richest heiress in England. Four years later she married the 5th Earl of Rosebery, the future Liberal Prime Minister.

Lord Rosebery was himself a well-to-do Scottish landowner with an annual income of over £30,000 inherited on his grandfather's death in 1868. He had already begun collecting in a modest way whilst still an Eton schoolboy. With his marriage, limitless possibilities must have opened up in his imagination. In spite of leaving Oxford without a degree (much commoner then than today) Rosebery was of a scholarly turn of mind. His interests were historical rather than aesthetic and his taste was very different from his father-in-law. He wrote a number of serious historical works, including studies of Napoleon, the two Pitts, Sir Robert Peel and Lord Randolph Churchill. In addition he was an avid bibliophile. It was in these fields that his mark was chiefly made on Mentmore and his other houses. To him, for example, is largely due the series of remarkable portraits of historical and literary figures in the collection which were divided between Mentmore, Dalmeney, Barnbougle and Berkeley Square: the Reynolds portraits of Gibbon and George Selwyn, a version of the Gainsborough portrait of Pitt, the 'second' Lansdowne portrait of George Washington by Gilbert Stuart, David's portrait of Napoleon in his study (now in the National

JACQUES-LOUIS DAVID
Portrait of Napoleon in his study
80¼in by 49¼in (204cm by 125cm)
Formerly in the collection of the late 5th Earl of Rosebery
Now in the National Gallery of Art, Washington, Samuel H. Kress Collection

A Louis XVI royal ormolu-mounted mahogany *secrétaire à abattant*, stamped *J. H. Riesener* and made for the apartments of Marie-Antoinette at Versailles, *circa* 1785, height 4ft 7in (140cm)
Mentmore £51,000($86,700). 18.V.77

Gallery, Washington), the portraits of Marigny, the *maréchal* de Belle Isle, the van Mander portraits of Prince Christian of Denmark and Queen Amalie, amongst them. But there can be no doubt that his principal interest as a collector was in buying books.[2] Bain, the well-known bookseller, declares in his *Memoirs* that Lord Rosebery visited his shop almost every day when he was in London. A detailed account of his library is impossible here and those interested can be referred to two scholarly articles on the subject written by the present Dowager Countess of Rosebery.[3]

As a by-product of Lord Rosebery's interest in Napoleon which resulted in his book *Napoleon: the Last Phase*, he acquired a quantity of Empire furniture from Malmaison and Saint-Helena, a period which seems not to have interested Baron Mayer Amschel at all. Rosebery's more purely aesthetic interests are more difficult to decipher. At the Hamilton Palace sale (where he bought many of his historic portraits) he purchased the splendid Riesener *secrétaire à abattant* which went first to London and subsequently to Mentmore. Probably this was acquired at least as much on account of its alleged historical association with Marie-Antoinette, whose travelling library he already possessed, than because of a particular admiration for French eighteenth-century furniture. In buying the series of early Goya tapestries, which were hung at Dalmeny, however, he displayed a remarkable aesthetic discernment for the period. It was Lord Rosebery, too, who bought the splendid series of Tiepolo sketches[4] which had probably descended directly from the artist's widow (who is said to have staked her entire collection of these things on the turn of a single card) and other Venetian *settecento* paintings at the sale of Edward Cheney's collection in 1883. Whilst Dalmeny (as he then was) was still at Eton he formed a warm friendship with Cheney and engaged in a regular correspondence with this much older man, one of the most interesting of the British expatriates living at Venice in the nineteenth century. At the same sale he acquired, clearly for historical reasons, an object of the greatest rarity, the *cornù* of the last Doge. Only a handful of such *cornù* survive, generally in much inferior condition to the Mentmore example as they have been retrieved from the ducal coffins and tombs.

A love of Venice probably inspired his purchase of some of Canaletto's latest – and finest – drawings, namely those for the *Feste Dogale*[5] (a set of engravings illustrating the principal public functions the Doge carried out each year) buying them at the sale of the Hoare Heirlooms in 1880. But if Lord Rosebery loved Venice he 'adored' (his own word) Naples from the time of his first visit as a young man. 'My God, I've bought a villa at Naples' he exclaimed to his elder son on opening a letter telling him that his modest offer for the Villa Delahante at Posillipo, had been accepted. The interesting *settecento* views of Naples by Vanvitelli (illustrated p 28) and others were doubtless added to the collection on that account.

The contrasting interests of Baron Mayer and Lord Rosebery and the resulting collections are of particular significance for historians of taste. At the time when the sale of the contents of Mentmore was the subject of widespread discussion in the press, a writer to *The Times* described the collection as 'one of the glories of Britain's

[2] See *Art at Auction 1975–76*, p 233.
[3] *See:* 'Unfamiliar Libraries: Barnbougle Castle', *The Book Collector*, Spring 1962, pp 35-44; 'Books from Beckford's Library now at Barnbougle Castle', loc. cit. Autumn 1965, pp 324-34.
[4] See *Art at Auction 1974–75*, p 38 and *Art at Auction 1975–76*, pp 30 and 31.
[5] See *Art at Auction 1974–75*, pp 44 and 45.

GASPAR VAN WITTEL (VANVITELLI)
A fair in front of the royal palace at Naples, 1763
30in by 50in (76cm by 127cm)
Mentmore £13,000($22,100). 25.V.77

peak of greatness'. If that somewhat ambiguous phrase was intended to imply that the collection was in anyway typically British, the comment was very wide of the mark. The strong stamp impressed on Mentmore by Baron Mayer Amschel de Rothschild's taste was wholly continental in character and certainly quite overwhelmed Lord Rosebery's contribution. That was its interest and, in view of its rarity in this country, the justification for wishing to preserve it intact. That a large part of the Baron's collections had their roots in the *Kunstkabinette* of German Renaissance princes has already been stressed. These men were interested in assembling a heterogenous group of exotic, glittering and strange objects of precious materials or of unusually skilful craftsmanship and mechanical complexity, designed to impress by their 'curious' character quite as much as by their beauty.

This traditional nature of Mayer Amschel's taste was widely misunderstood. An exceedingly unhistorical and somewhat sour-minded account of the collections which appeared in the *Times Literary Supplement* on the eve of the sale, described his possessions as 'expensive abominations, objects which had value because they were boastfully singular'. The words 'abominations' and 'boastfully singular' are, of course, heavily loaded and mean little more than that the writer did not like what he saw and made no attempt to understand it. Taste changes. It is questionable if it ever occurred to a Renaissance prince like Rudolph II or Christian IV of Denmark (or even an eighteenth-century one like Augustus the Strong), to consider whether their

A portrait of Baron Mayer Amschel de Rothschild (1867) by George Frederick Watts, OM, PRA

A portrait of the 5th Earl of Rosebery (1887) by Sir John Everett Millais, PRA

possessions were 'beautiful' or not. They were what a great prince was then expected to collect in northern Europe and their spirit still inspired the great merchant princes whom Bode used to build up the Berlin Museum into one of the greatest in the world. A century ago the historical and traditional character of the Baron's taste would have been more widely understood than today. A tired phrase, like 'of exquisite beauty', would more likely to have sprung from the pen of a hack journalist required to write about Mentmore than the 'expensive abominations' produced today. As for the charge of extravagance there is no evidence whatever that the Baron paid above the market value for his possessions (that is rarely a habit with bankers). In the case of those things, such as French eighteenth-century furniture, which are most generally admired for their 'beauty' today, all the available evidence suggests that he bought them extremely cheaply, sometimes, perhaps, *because* they were cheap. The Mentmore sale at least provided evidence that posterity has decided that he bought with considerable discernment.

Lord Rosebery's taste was, of course, more characteristically British than this. But in works of art it was not the taste of his day which was chiefly directed to collecting early Italian masters and French eighteenth-century art. Rosebery was interested in history more than in art and his additions to his wife's inherited collections are marked by an interest in historical association rather than aesthetic value. This was an eighteenth-century taste which goes back to collectors like Horace Walpole, sometimes called the patron saint of English collecting. But it was not the taste of his contemporaries. He probably bought a good deal more extravagantly than his father-in-law had, for so many of his purchases (his portraits of historic personages, for instance) were made at high-price auctions like the Hamilton Palace sale. Or they consisted of things that were already fashionable and therefore costly.

Sir Winston Churchill wrote of Lord Rosebery: 'The Past stood ever at his elbow and was the counsellor on whom he most relied'. This was not least the case when he was buying paintings, works of art and books to add to the inherited glories of Mentmore and his other houses.

Illustrations of other works sold at Mentmore appear in their appropriate sections throughout the book.

Paintings, Drawings and Sculpture

DAVIDE GHIRLANDAIO
The story of Joseph
A pair, on panel, each 16½in by 64¼in (42cm by 163cm)
London £38,000($64,600). 8.XII.76

GEORGES DE LA TOUR
La Madeleine à la flamme filante
$46\frac{1}{2}$in by $35\frac{1}{2}$in (118cm by 90cm)
This painting was sold privately to the Los Angeles County Museum of Art

BARTOLOMEO VENETO
Portrait of a lady
On panel, signed and dated on a cartellino: *1530/Bartolo/mei/Veneti/·F·*, 36¾in by 27½in (93cm by 70cm)
Mentmore £28,000($47,600). 25.V.77

ALESSANDRO ALLORI
Portrait of a collector
On panel, signed: *AS·AL·B·P·F·MDLXXXX*, 52½in by 41in (133cm by 104cm)
Mentmore £35,000($59,500). 25.V.77

AQVI ESTO SIN TEM
Y DELA MVERTE
NO HE PAVOR.

M . D . LX .

Io: Bap. Moronus .p.

GIOVANNI BATTISTA MORONI
Portrait of the 5th Duke of Albuquerque, Governor of Milan
Signed and dated: *M.D.LX. Io: Bap. Moronus. p.,* 44in by 33in (112cm by 84cm)
London £150,000($255,000). 13.VII.77

Fig 1   BAREND VAN ORLEY
The Virgin and Child adored by St Martin
On panel, 27in by 30in (70cm by 76cm)
Amsterdam Fl 760,000(£176,744:$300,464). 9.VI.77

The Collection of Old Master paintings formed by the late Dr Hans Wetzlar

Derek Johns

The greater part of the late Dr Hans Wetzlar's collection of Old Master paintings was sold at the Round Lutheran Church in Amsterdam on 9 June 1977 for the record total of Fl 14,800,000 (£3,500,000; $5,950,000). Dr Ebbinge Wubben, Director of the Boymans-van Beuningen Museum, Rotterdam, wrote in the foreword to the sale catalogue that Dr Wetzlar had been well aware how much he himself owed to the re-emergence of collections from the past, by way of auction sales and art dealers, and wanted to be certain that his own collection would be a future source for the art market. With Sotheby's as his vehicle, he knew that it would be possible for the public to view his paintings internationally before the collection was dispersed, thereby giving collectors from many countries the opportunity of experiencing the delights of acquisition.

Hans Wetzlar lived in Amsterdam for most of his life where he had a successful business career and in his spare time applied his intellectual and critical senses to forming an Old Master painting collection. He started collecting in a traditional manner in the 1930s with a group drawn from the 'Golden Age' of Dutch painting and although his taste subsequently changed, his collection remained strong in these seventeenth-century works. Under the influence of Max J. Friedländer, who had been forced to move to Amsterdam at the beginning of the war and with whom he formed a close friendship, Wetzlar turned his attention away from the seventeenth-century masters and concentrated on the northern and southern Netherlandish painters of the fifteenth and sixteenth centuries. To these early Dutch paintings he also added works by their contemporaries from the German-speaking area, to which Friedländer had devoted particular attention when he was working in museums in Berlin.

Dutch painting has such a distinctive character that it is easy to overlook its ties with the baroque style. However, such painting *can* be considered a part of baroque art, since the latter embraces realism as well as classicism. In the case of Holland, realism is the more important. The Dutch depicted their life with such thoroughness that their painting provides a complete visual record of their environment. It should not, however, be considered as mere reportage. A sensitive feeling for the painterly beauty of everyday life and nature raised their production to the level of great art. The comprehensive realism which developed in the early seventeenth century, coupled with high standards of artistic craftsmanship, may explain the unusual degree of specialisation in subject matter on the part of the individual artist, a striking feature of Dutch painting.

Fig 2   BALTHASAR VAN DER AST
A still life of flowers
One of a pair, on panel, signed,
$6\frac{7}{8}$in by $8\frac{7}{8}$in (17.5cm by 22.5cm)
Amsterdam Fl 380,000(£88,372:$150,232). 9.VI.77

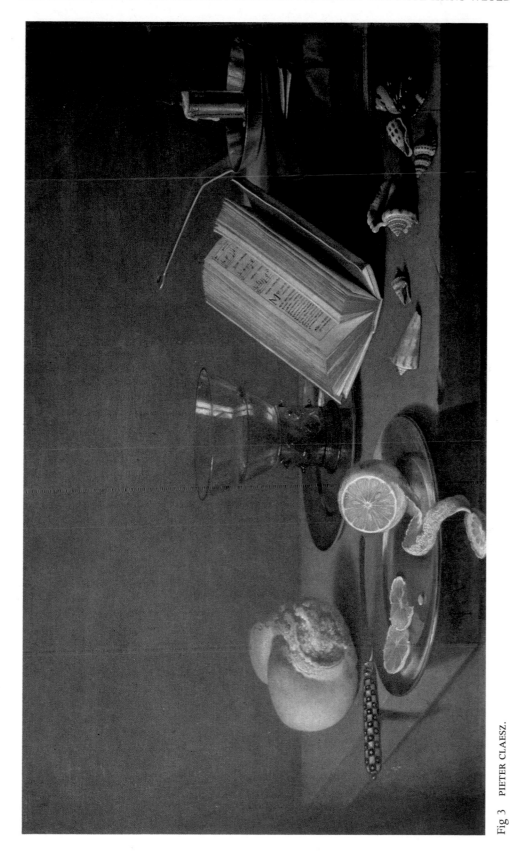

Fig 3   PIETER CLAESZ.
A Vanitas still life
On panel, signed and dated *1629*, 14in by 24¾in (35.5cm by 63cm
Amsterdam Fl 360,000(£83,721:$142,325). 9.VI.77

Hans Wetzlar had the foresight to buy paintings of the Dutch school at an early stage, before they became generally sought after. The most important part of his collection was still-life compositions. It is interesting that our English word 'still life' derives from the Dutch *stilleven*. The Dutch themselves only began to use the term about 1650, and before that time labelled their subjects 'breakfast' (*ontbijt*), 'banquet' (*banket*), 'fruit-piece' (*fruytagie*), *Vanitas* and so on. One of the oldest subjects is the flower-piece, established as a separate category in the late sixteenth century. With the widespread interest in gardening and the cultivation of exotic flowers and herbs during this period, this phenomenon is not surprising for there would have been many amateur gardeners and botanists who would have wanted to possess permanent records of familiar and strange blossoms by the foremost artists of the day. Once established, it never lost its popularity and it is appropriate that today the Dutch are still the most flower-loving people in the world.

The founder of a dynasty of fruit and flower painting is Ambrosius Bosschaert the Elder (*circa* 1565–1621). Hans Wetzlar acquired a mature work by this master in his early days as a collector. Analysis of the flower-pieces made by Bosschaert and other flower painters of the time reveals that their bouquets were seldom painted from life, but were normally assembled from independent studies. The pictures frequently show blossoms which bloom at different seasons of the year and the same specimens often recur. Bosschaert's type of flower-piece remained popular until the middle of the century. His most interesting follower was his brother-in-law, Balthasar van der Ast (1590–1656), who managed to avoid the hard metallic quality of so many others influenced by Bosschaert. The small pair of signed examples by van der Ast in the Wetzlar Collection (Fig 2) was of the highest quality.

A still life by Pieter Claesz. (1598–1661; Fig 3), from his early period and dated 1629, shows a common *Vanitas* composition depicting a snuffed-out candle, a half-empty *roemer* of white wine, an open music-book and half-peeled lemon. *Vanitas* motifs were chosen to make the observer contemplate such philosophical concepts as the brevity of life, the frailty of man and the vanity of wordly things. Finally in the still-life section of the collection, and realising the highest price of the day, was a large exotic bouquet of flowers by Jan Brueghel the Elder (Fig 4), the Flemish contemporary of Ambrosius Bosschaert.

Among the vast production of seventeenth-century Dutch painting the predominant subject is landscape. With landscape, as with still life, there was a great deal of variety and specialisation within the general category. When discovering realism in connection with seventeenth-century Dutch landscapists, it is important to bear in mind that these artists hardly ever painted their pictures out of doors, a practice that did not become common until the nineteenth century. In earlier times landscape paintings were nearly always composed in studios, artists working up their pictures from sketches made in the open. In the Wetzlar Collection there were fine examples of winter scenes, dunescapes, landscapes with animals and street scenes. The Dutch manage to show us that nature in all its varied aspects has a grandeur and intimacy of its own which can be appreciated outside the rigid boundaries of classicism.

Strangely, the large number of winter landscapes painted in Flanders towards the end of the sixteenth century finds no equivalent in the northern Netherlands of the same period. No Dutch winter scenes were painted before 1600 and the earliest such rendering in the Wetzlar sale was by Esaias van de Velde (*circa* 1590–1630), painted about 1620 (Fig 5).

Fig 4   JAN BRUEGHEL THE ELDER
Flowers in a wooden tub
On panel, 25$\frac{1}{4}$in by 19$\frac{1}{4}$in (64cm by 49cm)
Amsterdam Fl 800,000(£186,047:$316,279). 9.VI.77

Fig 5   ESAIAS VAN DE VELDE
A village in winter
On panel, signed, 10¾in by 17½in (27cm by 44.5cm)
Amsterdam Fl 130,000(£30,233:$51,395). 9.VI.77

Fig 6   SALOMON VAN RUYSDAEL
A winter scene near Arnhem
On panel, signed and dated *1652*,
19½in by 27¼in (49.5cm by 69cm)
Amsterdam Fl 680,000(£158,140:$268,838). 9.VI.77

Salomon van Ruysdael was one of the leading artists in the seventeenth century to bring pictorial realism in Dutch landscape to a climax. He was also one of the first to use the suggestion of atmosphere to animate his canvases. The Dutch sky plays a dominant role in his works and in the *Winter scene near Arnhem* in the Wetzlar Collection dating from 1652 (Fig 6), it is possible to see the master using a very fluid, impressionistic style in grey and brown tones. Ruysdael was born at Naarden in Gooiland and during his early years he was known as 'Salomon de Gooyer' and was inscribed in the Guild of Painters at Haarlem in 1623 with this name, working under the influence of Esaias van de Velde. He painted three recorded winter scenes all dated 1627 and it was only after a break of over twenty years from such subjects that he completed this panel, which fetched an auction record. His winter scenes from this late period make use of architectural motifs indicating a strong revival of interest in topography.

A new generation of Dutch artists was soon to emerge, achieving a more monumental landscape, the foremost artist of this phase being Jacob van Ruisdael (1628/9–1682). Born at Haarlem, the son of a framemaker and painter, Isaak van Ruisdael, Jacob became active as an independent master in about 1646 when he was only eighteen years old. At this time he was under the influence of his uncle, Salomon van Ruysdael, and other Haarlem artists. Not a single dated winter landscape by Jacob van Ruisdael exists, but comparison with the dated winter scenes painted by his contemporaries indicates that the Wetzlar example (Fig 8) probably dates from the mid '50s. Another early example by Jacob Ruisdael showing a farm amongst trees, situated in the dunes, dated 1648, the year that Jacob was elected to the Guild of St Luke in Haarlem, realised an auction record of Fl 740,000.

While discussing Jacob van Ruisdael, one other painting by him in the Wetzlar Collection which is well worth mentioning is a marine composition (Fig 9). In Ruisdael's entire oeuvre only thirty seascapes are recorded. The particular type of frothy wave crests which characterises many of his rough seascapes was visible in the Wetzlar painting. Again, no dated seascapes are known but it is safe to assume that none was painted before 1660.

A small panel by Jacob Vrel of Delft (active 1654-62) shows a street scene of great charm and intimate realism (Fig 7). This artist's work was often confused in the last century with that of Pieter de Hooch and Jan Vermeer of Delft.

The earlier south Netherlandish paintings collected during Dr Wetzlar's friendship with Professor Friedländer included the important panel of *The Virgin and Child adored by St Martin*, painted by Barend van Orley (1488-1541) (Fig 1). It is the right-hand wing of a diptych which belonged to the Abbey of Marchiennes, for which it was painted, as the gift of Abbot Jacques de Coene, *circa* 1514, shortly before he was appointed court painter to Margaret of Austria in 1518 (a portrait of the Abbot is on the reverse side of the panel, painted by a follower of van Orley). The left wing, which shows *St Martin knighted by the Emperor Constantine*, is in the William Rockhill Nelson Gallery of Art in Kansas City.

This sale saw the dispersal of the results of over thirty-five years of collecting by Dr Hans Wetzlar and it may be hoped that a large proportion of the paintings finds their way to similar private collections, as I am certain the late Dr Wetzlar would have wished.

Fig 7   JACOB VREL
A street scene
On panel, 14in by 11in (35.5cm by 28cm)
Amsterdam Fl 480,000(£111,628:$189,767). 9.VI.77

Fig 8   JACOB VAN RUISDAEL
A winter landscape
Signed, 12¼in by 7¾in (31cm by 45cm)
Amsterdam Fl 240,000(£55,814:$94,884). 9.VI.77

Fig 9   JACOB VAN RUISDAEL
Vessels in a stormy sea
Signed, 18in by 25¼in (46cm by 64cm)
Amsterdam Fl 200,000(£46,512:$79,070). 9.VI.77

PIETER JANSZ. SAENREDAM
Interior of the church of St Mary, Utrecht
On panel, signed and dated *1651*, 18⅞in by 14⅛in (48cm by 36cm)
Amsterdam Fl 230,000(£53,488:$90,930). 15.XI.76

DAVID TENIERS THE YOUNGER
Peasants playing cards ('Le Bonnet Blanc')
On panel, signed and dated *1644*, 19¼in by 26¾in (49cm by 68cm)
Amsterdam Fl 470,000(£109,302:$185,813). 15.XI.76

GODFRIED SCHALCKEN
A scene in a brothel
On panel, signed, 15in by 12in (38cm by 30.5cm)
London £35,000($59,500). 6.IV.77
From the collection of H. Blaker

PIETER BRUEGHEL
THE YOUNGER
Winter
On panel, 16½in by 19¼in
(42cm by 49cm)
London £42,000
($71,400). 8.XII.76

AMBROSIUS BOSSCHAERT
THE ELDER
A still life of fruit
On panel, signed in
monogram, 14in by 21¼in
(35.5cm by 53.5cm)
London £42,000
($71,400). 13.VII.77

ADAM WILLAERTS
The departure of the pilgrims from Delft
On panel, signed and dated *1620*, 11½in by 18½in (29cm by 47cm)
New York $105,000(£61,764). 16.VI.77

CLAUDE-JOSEPH VERNET
A southern seaport at sunset
Signed *Joseph Vernet/f. Roma 1749*, 43¾in by 63in (111cm by 160cm)
London £115,000($195,500). 13.VII.77
From the collection of the Hon Mrs Aileen Plunket

GIOVANNI ANTONIO CANALE, called CANALETTO
Above: *Venice: the Piazzetta and the Library*
Below: *Venice: the entrance to the Grand Canal and the Salute*
A pair, each 19½in by 39in (50cm by 99cm)
London £150,000($255,000). 13.VII.77
From the collection of Sir Arundell Neave, Bt

ANTONIO JOLI
Above: *London and the Thames seen from the terrace of Somerset House*
Below: *Westminster seen from the north*
A pair, each 17¾in by 35½in (45cm by 90cm)
London £28,000($47,600). 13.VII.77
From the collection of the late Captain R. S. de Q. Quincey

ROBERT LEFEVRE
Portrait of Princess Pauline Borghese
Signed and dated *1808*, 84in by 60in (214cm by 149cm)
Monte Carlo Fr100,000(£11,904:$20,238). 4.XII.76

Pauline Borghese returns home

Mary Henderson

A few days before Christmas 1976 a large van stopped outside number 39 rue du Faubourg St Honoré in Paris. The eighteenth-century *porte cochère* of the British Embassy was too narrow for it to enter, so two burly men carried the large portrait of Princess Pauline Borghese into her former Paris home, the Hôtel de Charost. Even then the picture had to be turned on its side, because it measures 84in by 60in and is in a heavy gilt Empire frame.

In 1803 Napoleon had helped his favourite sister purchase the hôtel from the heirs of the Duc de Charost. Pauline did, however, borrow from her brother Joseph and her sister Elise to make up the full purchase price and to pay for the lavish redecoration. In 1814 she sold the house with all its contents to the Duke of Wellington for the British Embassy. The Duke, as Ambassador to France, acted on behalf of the Prince Regent.

The sale of the painting in Monaco had caused a patriotic flutter in French museums and press circles. The portrait, together with five others of the Bonaparte family, had been carried away as booty from the Château de Saint-Cloud by Marshal Blücher after the Battle of Waterloo, and had remained in his family's possession for more than a century and a half. It is now the latest loan to the British Embassy in Paris, the result of a swift and generous move by the Rayne Trust and Lord Goodman assisted by Sotheby's and Herm Investments in response to the British Ambassador's request for help.

This splendid State portrait by Robert Lefèvre dated 1808 (there is a somewhat inferior signed version at Versailles, dated 1806) shows the Princess in a white Empire satin dress with gold embroidery, wearing the Borghese cameo jewellery, and standing beside a bust of Napoleon.

Born in Bayeux in 1755, Lefèvre made his first journey to Paris on foot at the age of eighteen; later, in 1784, he joined Jean-Baptiste Regnault's atelier and worked for Boze. Although his early pictures were decorative and historical (*Love disarmed by Venus*, 1795, and *The First Consul and General Berthier at Marengo*, in 1801), he soon concentrated on portraits and became the Imperial family's official painter. Under the Restoration he was nominated the King's painter – largely as a result of his portrait of Louis XVIII 'done from memory'. But after the July revolution he was deprived of his royal titles and committed suicide (1830). It is interesting to note that although Lefèvre painted a large number of portraits, the best quality of his paintings is to be found in portraits of his friends, notably that of Carle Vernet (1804), and in feminine portraits – particularly this beautiful portrait of Princess Pauline Borghese which now hangs in the *antichambre* of the British Embassy.

Paulette, as her family called the *gamine* princess, was extravagant and had lovers, but she also had a flair for fashion in dress and decoration. The romantic house she has left to posterity is one of which both the French and the British are justly proud.

BARON FRANÇOIS GERARD
Portrait of Queen Caroline of Naples and her children
84¼in by 66⅞in (214cm by 170cm)
Monte Carlo Fr200,000(£23,809:$40,476). 4.XII.76

Maria-Annunziata-Caroline Bonaparte (1782-1939) was Napoleon's youngest sister. In 1800 she
married Maréchal Joachim Murat who became King of Naples in 1808. They had four children,
Achille (born 1801), Letizia (born 1802), Lucien-Charles (born 1803) and Louise (born 1805).
Like the portrait of Pauline Borghese (see p 56), this painting was taken by Marshal Blücher from
the Château de Saint-Cloud after the Battle of Waterloo

CLAUDE-JOSEPH VERNET
A view of Lake Nemi
Signed and dated
J. Vernet.f.Roma/1748,
24in by 29in (61cm by 73.5cm)
London £19,000
($32,300). 6.IV.77

ADAM FRANS VAN DER MEULEN
Louis XIV in a state coach,
accompanied by his gentlemen
36in by 46½in
(91.5cm by 118cm)
Mentmore £20,000
($34,000). 25.V.77

Van der Meulen entered
Louis XIV's service in
1664. He travelled in the
king's suite during the
French campaign in the
Netherlands, painting
many battles and sieges

LUCA CARLEVARIS
Venice: the Piazzetta
38in by 76½in (100cm by 195cm)
New York $100,000(£58,823). 16.VI.77

ANTONIO CANALE, called CANALETTO
London: Whitehall and Westminster Bridge seen from the Terrace of Somerset House
16in by 28in (40.5cm by 71cm)
London £110,000($187,000). 8.XII.76

Westminster Bridge was not finished until after April 1750 and Canaletto left for Venice in the autumn of that year, but by the summer of 1751 was back in England where he stayed until 1753; he was once again in England from 1754 until *circa* 1756 The picture may therefore have been painted in London in 1750 or a year or so later

VITTORE CARPACCIO
Recto and verso: *Studies of heads*
Pen and brown ink and black and white chalks on blue paper, 9⅜in by 7¼in (23.7cm by 18.4cm)
Now in the Ashmolean Museum

ANDREA MANTEGNA
A study for St James on his way to Martyrdom, baptising the scribe, Josias
Pen and brown ink, 6½ in by 10 in (16.5cm by 25.5cm)
Now in the British Museum

The drawings on this page were sold privately to the British Government on behalf of the Beneficiaries of the Gathorne-Hardy Estate

The Gathorne-Hardy Collection of Old Master drawings

Julien Stock

The Gathorne-Hardy Collection was widely considered to be one of the finest private cabinets to survive in this country. The greater part of it will be familiar to scholars and collectors through the exhibition held recently at Colnaghi's in London and at the Ashmolean Museum, Oxford. In the catalogue accompanying the exhibition, Robert Gathorne-Hardy recounted its history in a delightful introduction. To summarise, Robert's great-uncle, Alfred, married a daughter of John Malcolm (the bulk of whose collection is now in the British Museum) who gave part of his collection of drawings to his son-in-law in the 1860s and '70s. On Alfred's death, the collection passed to his widow, and when she died, to their son, Geoffrey, who in turn left it to his cousin, Robert.

The latter was for many years what one might term 'Keeper of the Collection'. He was passionately interested in Italian art and used to enjoy taking scholars from his home in Stanford Dingley to see the collection which hung in the billiard/hunting trophy room of his uncle's residence, Donnington Priory, Newbury. On these occasions, notes were always kept of any new attributions, and it is interesting to follow the gradually changing opinions offered on the drawings by Sidney Colvin (Keeper of Prints and Drawings at the British Museum from 1883 to 1912), Bernard Berenson and many others.

Robert was also a collector in his own right, and on a very limited budget managed to add three important works to the collection: the Watteau (1684-1721), *Head of Mezzetin* (p 69), discovered in an antique shop in Reading many years ago; the delicate pen study by Piero di Cosimo (1462-1521), purchased at one of Sotheby's sales in 1971 (see *Art at Auction*, 1970-71, p 73) for £650 and sold for £6,500 six years later; and the two fine works by Giulio Romano (1499-1546). These combine to give one an idea of his ability as a connoisseur.

Before putting the collection up for sale by auction, Sotheby's was asked by the Beneficiaries to offer it *en bloc* to the Ashmolean Museum, Oxford, in accordance with the wishes of Geoffrey and Robert. Unfortunately, the museum did not have the necessary funds, and thus the most precious drawings, of 'pre-eminent interest' to the national heritage, were sold directly to the treasury in satisfaction of estate duty. The most important of these are reproduced here on pp 62, 64 and 65. The double-sided sheet of Venetian blue paper with heads delicately executed in black and white chalks by Carpaccio (1460/65-*circa* 1526), surely one of the most enchanting drawings by

REMBRANDT HARMENSZ. VAN RIJN
Tobias and Sara
Reed pen and brown ink,
8¼in by 7⅜in (21.1cm by 18.8cm)

Opposite   REMBRANDT HARMENSZ. VAN RIJN
Group of musicians listening to a flute player
Pen and brown ink and wash, 5¼in by 5⅝in
(13.5cm by 14.4cm)

The drawings on these two pages were sold privately to the British Government on behalf of the
Beneficiaries of the Gathorne-Hardy Estate

this master, has now found a permanent home in the Ashmolean, thus to some degree fulfilling the wish of both Geoffrey and Robert, whose favourite it was, that the collection should pass to their old university. The study by Mantegna (*circa* 1431-1506) of *St James on his way to Martyrdom, baptising the scribe, Josias*, can now be seen at the British Museum. It is of major significance as it is both a preliminary study for the fresco of the same subject in the Church of the Eremitani, Padua, destroyed in the last war, and the only drawing from this period of his activity, *circa* 1456. At the time of writing no final decision has been taken as to the home of the Rembrandts. The *Tobias and Sara*, drawn about 1655, and the wonderfully attentive *Group of musicians listening to a flute player* both show the expressiveness with which Rembrandt used the pen. The same may be said of the tiny study (sold in Amsterdam), of a male actor playing the role of Badelsch (a female) in Vondel's play, *Gijsbreght van Aemstel*, first published in 1637. It is executed with brilliance, displaying the master's grasp of characterisation (p 66).

REMBRANDT HARMENSZ. VAN RIJN
Half-length study of an actor
Pen and brown ink, 3¾in by 2in (9.4cm by 5cm)
Amsterdam Fl 52,000 (£12,093:$20,558). 21.III.77

As the first auction took place on 28 April 1976, drawings from this sale are reproduced in last season's *Art at Auction* (pp 36-39 and p 43). By far the most important of these was the small study of *A bird pecking at some berries* by Mantegna. This once belonged to the Victorian painter William Dyce and soon after the sale we were told by the Walker Art Gallery, Liverpool, that it had once formed part of the collection of the Liverpool banker, William Roscoe. He had acquired it in 1806 for six shillings and in his bankruptcy sale in 1816 it made nine shillings. It is probably a youthful work after the antique and shows the artist's love of sculptural form. The authorship of the *Study of a bearded man* in coloured chalks remained unsolved until 1970, when a young scholar, David McTavish, recognised it as a study for a figure in a very crowded fresco by Giuseppe Porta (*circa* 1520-75) in the Vatican. The truth was established after almost a century. Parmigianino (1503-40) enjoyed an enormous prestige in England in the seventeenth and eighteenth centuries and one can see why when one examines the *Studies of female heads, of a winged lion and of finials*. His drawings are among the most enchanting products of the Italian High Renaissance. The amusing and eccentric Amico Aspertini (1475-1552) was represented by a powerful and horrendous study for a *Massacre of the Innocents*.

The second part of the collection, comprising the Northern Schools, was sold in Amsterdam on 3 May 1976. Although not so rich in masterpieces as the Italian section, it nevertheless contained one of Durer's (1471-1528) earliest-known drawings, *The Holy Family beneath a tree*, dateable *circa* 1491. There was also an interesting assortment of Dutch drawings with artists such as Jan de Bisschop, Nicholas Berchem, Paulus Potter, Jan Fyt, Adriaen van de Velde and a charming study of a camel by Cornelis Saftleven (1607-81). The latter may have been inspired by a travelling circus, since we know of a number of similar animal studies by this artist.

The last of the three sales, held in London on 24 November 1976, provided a big surprise. Michelangelo's (1475-1564) *Study of a male torso*, one of his very late surviving studies of the nude, realised a world-record price for an Old Master drawing. Apart from Berenson, who considered it an early work, all critics agree that it is from Michelangelo's *ultima maniera*, and possibly a study for one of the late *Pietàs*.

MICHELANGELO BUONARROTI
Recto: *Study of a male torso*
A double-sided drawing, black chalk, 9¾in by 6⅞in (24.8cm by 17.5cm)
London £162,000($275,400). 24.XI.76

BARTOLOMEO CESI
A boy playing a viola da gamba
Red chalk, heightened with white chalk, on blue paper, 9¼in by 6½in (23.4cm by 16.4cm)
London £19,000($32,300). 24.XI.76

JEAN-ANTOINE WATTEAU
Head of Mezzetin
Red, black and white chalks on buff paper, 5$\frac{3}{8}$in by 4$\frac{1}{2}$in (13.7cm by 11.6cm)
London £15,000($25,500). 24.XI.76

Other splendid drawings in this last sale were Carpaccio's *Holy Family with saints* (p 70), composed in a charming idyllic spirit and drawn in his characteristic pen manner, Maineri's (1460/70-1540) *Pagan sacrifice* (p 71), a superb example of *quattrocento* Farrarese draughtmanship and thought to be the artist's earliest-known work, *circa* 1485-90, and the gently serene, intensely Raphäelesque *Head of the Virgin* (p 70) by Eusebio da San Giorgio (1470-1550), a study for his painting of *The Adoration of the Magi* of 1505 in Perugia. Bartolomeo Cesi (1556-1620) was represented by the tender study of a *Boy playing a viola da gamba*, used by the artist for an angel in his altarpiece in the church of San Domenico, Bologna.

EUSEBIO DA SAN GIORGIO
Study of the head of the Virgin
Black chalk, 6⅜in by 6⅛in
(16.2cm by 15.5cm)
London £22,000($37,400). 24.XI.76

VITTORE CARPACCIO
The Holy Family with saints
Pen and brown ink, 5½in by 9¼in
(14cm by 23.6cm)
London £78,000($132,600). 24.XI.76

GIAN FRANCESCO DE'MAINERI
A pagan sacrifice
Drawn with the point of the brush in brown, heightened with white,
$16\frac{3}{8}$in by $11\frac{3}{4}$in (41.8cm by 30cm)
London £48,000($81,600). 24.XI.76

CORNELIS SAFTLEVEN
A young man seated on a stool
Black and grey wash, signed and dated *1643*, 11⅝in by 8in (29.5cm by 20.2cm)
Amsterdam Fl18,000(£4,186:$7,116). 18.IV.77

The sale of the Rudolf Collection of Old Master drawings

Terence Mullaly

There was an unexpected sound in the R.W.S. Galleries, recognised by those few tuned in to the right wavelength as a chuckle, when lot 32 had been sold in the Old Master drawings sale on 4 July. Those who were in the know understood it was the shade of C. R. Rudolf, for his beloved Palma Giovanes, thirty-two of them, almost certainly the largest holding in private hands, had fetched £42,170($71,689).

Before the day's proceedings were over the total for the various sales, in London and Amsterdam, of the Rudolf Collection, had been brought to £553,785 ($941,434). Now that the collection has been dispersed, is a matter of history, something to add to all annotated copies of Lugt, it is worth summing up its nature and what it stood for. First, it should be remembered that a permanent record exists in the form of the sale catalogues, and that in the case of the catalogue of the drawings by Palma Giovane and his circle, a contribution to scholarship has been made.

In terms of the history of the collecting of Old Master drawings the Rudolf Collection was not a great collection, but even in these times of inflation, a total of over half a million is a tribute to the interest and quality of the drawings in it. Yet any assessment of the collection based primarily on what it fetched misses the point. A sour note has to be sounded. Rudolf built up one of the last real collections of drawings to be formed in our time, and certainly one of the last that will appear on the market. This need not be the case, but, although today it would still be possible to form a fine collection of Old Master drawings without being a millionaire, there are very few with the inclination to do so, the time to acquire the necessary knowledge, or the sense to take the right advice to seek out what is worth having from an ever dwindling supply.

In a sense Rudolf was lucky; when he began collecting in the '30s it was still possible to go through the boxes at Colnaghi's, and elsewhere, and select fine things for a few pounds. Quite a number of collectors did so, though few with Rudolf's degree of success, for he had those two essential qualities, a natural eye, and unbounded enthusiasm. Towards the end his sense of judgement often alarmingly deserted him, but that was when he strayed away from his main interest, which was Italian and Dutch drawings.

A glance at the illustrations accompanying this essay is enough to show how successful he was in his best days of collecting. Among the Italian drawings there were first and foremost the Palma Giovanes. They covered the whole of the artist's

REMBRANDT HARMENSZ. VAN RIJN
Nathan admonishing David
Pen and brown ink, 5in by 5⅞in (12.6cm by 14.9cm)
Amsterdam Fl 90,000(£20,930:$35,581). 18.IV.77

long working life, from the preliminary study for the monument to Gerolamo Canal, in SS. Giovanni e Paolo, of immediately before 1577, to the drawing dated 1628, the year of his death, and included some of his most beautiful drawings, such as the *Venice crowned by Victory* (p 79), a preliminary study for the painting in the Palazzo Ducale.

That Rudolf had an eye for quality in many different modes of drawing is proved by a comparison of such sheets as Rembrandt's *Nathan admonishing David* and the Castiglione *Adoration* (pp 76 and 77). He responded to the charm of Leoni's *Portrait of a girl* (p 78), and to the Mannerist elegance of Biagio Pupini's *Forge of Vulcan* (p 79). The Rudolf Collection was so much more than just an assemblage of great names; there was a typical Tintoretto, but there were also fine drawings by artists such as Paolo Farinati, Guercino, the Maganzas and Naldini. Rudolf loved them all. It is the kind of collecting we need.

ADRIAEN VAN OSTADE
Interior of a barn with peasants slaughtering a hog
Black chalk, 6½in by 10in (16.4cm by 25.6cm)
Amsterdam Fl 19,000(£4,418:$7,511). 18.IV.77

LAMBERT DOOMER
Two camels by a river
Pen and brown ink and wash, signed, 10½in by 16⅛in (26.8cm by 41.1cm)
Amsterdam Fl 35,000(£8,139:$13,837). 6.VI.77

GIOVANNI BENEDETTO CASTIGLIONE
The Adoration of the shepherds
Drawn with the brush in reddish
paint, with brown wash and grey
gouache, 16¼in by 24¼in
(41.2cm by 61.5cm)
London £23,000($39,100). 4.VII.77

OTTAVIO LEONI
Portrait of a girl
Coloured chalks on blue
paper, 7½in by 5⅜in
(19.2cm by 13.7cm)
London £3,600($6,120).
4.VII.77

PIETRO LONGHI
Recto: *Head of a man*
A double-sided drawing,
black chalk heightened
with white on blue
paper, 9½in by 7½in
(24cm by 18.9cm)
London £4,000($6,800).
4.VII.77

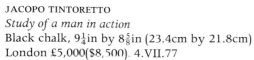

JACOPO TINTORETTO
Study of a man in action
Black chalk, 9¼in by 8⅝in (23.4cm by 21.8cm)
London £5,000($8,500). 4.VII.77

ADRIAEN VAN DE VELDE
Seated female nude
Black chalk, 10½in by 7⅝in (26.5cm by 19.5cm)
Amsterdam Fl 16,000(£3,721:$6,325). 18.IV.77

Left
BIAGIO PUPINI
The forge of Vulcan
Pen and brown ink
heightened with white
on paper washed pink,
$11\frac{1}{2}$in by 8in
(29.3cm by 20.3cm)
London £2,800($4,760).
4.VII.77

GIOVANNI BATTISTA
NALDINI
The Pietà
Pen and brown ink on
paper washed ochre,
$12\frac{3}{8}$in by 9in (31.4cm
by 22.8cm)
London £3,000($5,100).
4.VII.77

Right
PALMA GIOVANE
Venice crowned by Victory
Pen and brown ink and wash, $11\frac{3}{4}$in by $7\frac{5}{8}$in
(29.8cm by 19.3cm)
London £4,800($8,160). 4.VII.77

PALMA GIOVANE
Recto: *Adoration of the shepherds*
A double-sided drawing, pen and brown ink and
wash, $8\frac{1}{8}$in by $8\frac{1}{8}$in (20.7cm by 20.7cm)
London £2,800($4,760). 4.VII.77

FRANS SNYDERS
A fishmonger's shop
Pen and brown ink and wash, signed, $10\frac{7}{8}$in by $16\frac{3}{8}$in (27.5cm by 41.6cm)
Amsterdam Fl 66,000(£15,349:$26,093). 18.IV.77

SIR PETER PAUL RUBENS
Thomyris presented with the head of Cyrus
Pen and brown ink and grey, white and reddish bodycolours, $15\frac{3}{8}$in by $23\frac{3}{8}$in (39.3cm by 59.5cm)
Amsterdam Fl 92,000(£21,395:$36,372). 21.III.77

GIOVANNI BATTISTA TIEPOLO
The Virgin and Child adored by a kneeling saint
Pen and brown ink and wash, 12¼in by 8⅞in (31cm by 22.5cm)
London £14,500($24,650). 7.XII.76

GABRIEL-JACQUES DE SAINT-AUBIN
The entrance of the Academy of Architecture at the Louvre
Black chalk, ink and watercolour, signed and dated *1799*, 6¾in by 5¼in (17.2cm by 13.5cm)
London £7,200($12,240). 4.VII.77

THOMAS GIRTIN
The boats near Mount Edgecombe

THOMAS GIRTIN *Bedgellert*

These two watercolours are from the 'Shepherd' sketchbook which was sold in London on
7 July 1977 for £36,000($95,200).
From the collection of F. W. Shepherd

Girtin's 'Shepherd' sketchbook

James Miller

The only surviving sketchbook by Thomas Girtin first came to light in an auction at Platt Vicarage in Manchester in 1898. It was purchased by a Mr Shepherd, whose descendant consigned it for sale this summer. Although containing only twenty-three drawings these are enough to unfold Girtin's artistic development, travel and patronage during 1800 and 1801 when he was at the zenith of his artistic powers, before his tragic illness and subsequent death in 1802.

At the front is a pen and ink drawing of John Raphael Smith, the engraver, waiting for the mail coach and following it a study for *The White House, Chelsea*, reminding us of Girtin's home in the capital. The rest of the drawings cover his trips around England, in Wales, Yorkshire and Devon. Girtin, like many fellow artists, made these annual pilgrimages to areas famous for their wealth of picturesque and sublime scenery. Unlike his earlier travels, here he concentrates mainly on landscape and clusters of buildings, rather than his former preoccupation with antiquarian ruins.

These personal sketches show Girtin exploring new techniques. Unusual for his time the watercolour of *Bedgellert* must have been executed directly from nature. The colour washes lying adjacent to one another recreate in tonal contrasts the valley and massive mountain with clouds passing up the pass and across the peak. *The boats near Mount Edgecombe* lie calm and balanced with this sensitive modulation of colour subtly stirring the ships in the early morning. The pencil drawings betray their construction even better. In *Bolton Abbey* Girtin laid out the background in blunt pencil strokes. Then sharpening the point he set to work from left to right hatching in the details. The rounded curves of this drawing dated 1800 are replaced in the following year by more angular and forthright strokes as in *The Abbey Mill, Knaresborough*. Here the drawing style becomes more vigorous, not feeling its way round objects but bluntly describing new angular shapes.

The drawings tell also of Girtin's patrons and friends. Girtin was employed by Lord Harewood on whose estate he drew the stables at Plumpton and the villages of Knaresborough, Bolton and nearby Gainsborough, and by Lord Musgrave who entertained him at Middleton Castle. When staying with them Girtin taught drawing and supplied watercolours of local views. His sketchbook also provided a source book from which prospective patrons could choose drawings such as *Sandsend* to be worked up into full watercolours. Notes like 'Bolton Abbey – coloured on the spot. Sold to Mr Rogers 8gn' show that they were also sold straight from the book.

The sketchbook is both an important social document and a group of fine drawings. It was not surprising that it became the most expensive sketchbook ever sold.

JOHN FREDERICK LEWIS, RA
Sir Edwin Landseer, RA, in the act of angling
Signed and inscribed with the original title on the backboard, 19¼in by 25½in (49cm by 63.5cm)
London £8,200($13,940). 7.VII.77

HENRY BERNARD CHALON
*George IV's Persian horses
being taken out for exercise*
Signed and dated *1819*,
39¾in by 55¾in
(101cm by 141.5cm)
London £34,500($58,650).
17.XI.76

George IV (as Prince of
Wales) was presented
with these horses by the
Shah of Persia and
commissioned this
painting of them from the
artist. However he never
paid for the painting
which was subsequently
bought by Major Bower,
an ancestor of the
consignor

WILLIAM SHAYER, SNR
*At the Bell Inn, Cadnam,
New Forest*
Signed, 39¼in by 49¼in
(99.5cm by 125cm)
London £15,000($25,500).
23.III.77
From the collection of
Mrs Norris-Hill

JOSEPH WRIGHT OF DERBY
Portrait of Mrs Ann Carver
50in by 40in (127cm by 101.5cm)
New York $19,000(£11,176). 9.X.76
From the collection of Marietta Peabody Tree and the late Ronald Tree

This portrait was commissioned by the Rev John Griffiths, father of Mrs Ann Carver. According to Wright's account book, he began work on the individual portraits of Mrs Carver and her three children after 1 February 1760

ARTHUR DEVIS
Portraits of Alicia and Jane Clarke
Signed, 36in by 28in (91.5cm by 71cm)
London £26,000($44,200). 6.VII.77

WILLIAM HOGARTH
Portrait of HRH William Augustus, Duke of Cumberland
Dated *1732*, 17¾in by 13½in (45cm by 34cm)
London £65,000($110,500). 6.VII.77
From the Tennant Collection

DAVID ROBERTS, RA
The ruins of the Temple of the Sun at Baalbec
Signed and dated *1842*, 59in by 95in (150cm by 241cm)
London £24,000($40,800). 24.XI.76
From the collection of J. Harper, OBE

GEORGE STUBBS, ARA
Earl Grosvenor's 'Bandy'
Signed, 39¼in by 48½in (100cm by 123cm)
London £60,000($102,000). 17.XI.76
From the collection of Mrs John Nutting

Bandy, so called because of his bent near fore fetlock, was foaled in 1747. He was bred by Thomas Meredith of Easby, Yorkshire and won several important races at Newmarket, Nottingham, York and Lincoln in the years 1752-54. He was purchased by Earl Grosvenor for stud purposes and proved a most successful sire

THOMAS GAINSBOROUGH, RA
A peasant girl gathering faggots
Painted in 1782, 66½in by 48½in (123cm by 169cm)
London £92,000($154,700). 6.VII.77
From the collection of the Beaverbrook Foundation

WILLIAM HOLMAN HUNT, OM, ARSA, RSW
Portrait of Fanny Holman Hunt
Painted 1866-68, 42in by 29in (106.5cm by 73.5cm)
London £22,000($37,400). 14.VI.77
From the collection of Paul A'Court Bergne

This is a portrait of the artist's first wife (1833-66), daughter of George Waugh.
The year after their marriage, in 1865, they set out for Palestine, but were
detained at Florence owing to an epidemic of cholera restricting travel. Fanny died
on 20 December 1866 having given birth to a son, Cyril. This portrait was
apparently begun at Florence and was finished in London in 1868; Hunt was
working on it when W. M. Rossetti saw it in April of that year

SIMEON SOLOMON
Shadrach, Meshach and Abednego
Watercolour, signed with monogram and dated *10.63*, 12¾in by 9in
(32.5cm by 23cm)
London £4,200($7,140). 14.VI.77
From the collection of E. Dobson

This painting shows the three characters in its title preserved from 'the Burning
Fiery Furnace', from the book of David. The figures represented are probably the
two Solomon brothers, their sister Rebeka and, on the left, Algernon Swinburne

THE HON JOHN COLLIER, RA
The laboratory
Signed and dated '95, 61in by 47in (155cm by 119.5cm)
London £4,500($7,650). 14.VI.77
Formerly in the collection of Harry Coghill, 1908

JOHN BYAM LISTON SHAW
'Truly the light is sweet'
On panel, signed and dated *1901*, 15¾in by 11½in (40cm by 29cm)
London £6,400($10,880). 14.VI.77

The title of this painting is a quotation from *Ecclesiastes*, Chapter XI, verses 7 and 8:
'Truly the light is sweet, and a pleasant thing it is for the eyes to behold the Sun. . . .
Yet let him remember the days of darkness; for they shall be many.'

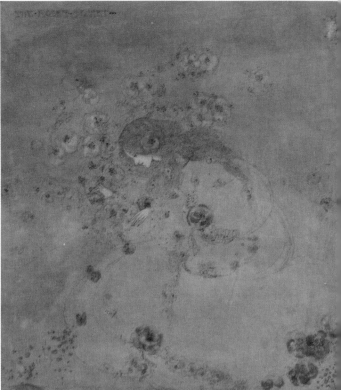

JESSIE MARION KING
The rose's secret
Pen and ink and wash on vellum, signed and inscribed,
$8\frac{1}{4}$in by 7in (20.5cm by 17.5cm)
Glasgow £1,600($2,720). 21.VI.77

JACQUES JOSEPH TISSOT
Waiting for the boat
Watercolour, heightened with white, signed three times,
twice with initials, 20in by $10\frac{3}{4}$in (51cm by 27cm)
London £5,800($9,860). 16.XI.76
Formerly in the collection of N. Ronald

FREDERICK BROWN
Waiting for the boat
Signed and dated *1880*, 22½in by 29½in (57cm by 75cm)
London £2,800($4,760). 16.XI.76

Opposite above
EDWARD SEAGO
Place de la Concorde, Paris
Signed, painted *circa* 1951, 25½in by 35½in
(65cm by 90cm)
London £6,000($10,200). 22.VI.77

Opposite below
SIR ALFRED MUNNINGS, PRA
Daffern Seal, aged 8, on his pony 'Canary' at
Ullesthorpe, Leicestershire
Signed and dated *August 1926*, 30¼in by 41½in
(77cm by 105.5cm)
London £26,000($44,200). 16.III.77

MONTAGUE DAWSON
Chasing the slaver – the frigate 'Acorn' of the West
African squadron chasing the slaver 'Gabriel'
Signed, 39¼in by 49½in (100cm by 125.5cm)
London £13,000($22,100). 10.XI.76
From the collection of H. R. Wilkins

SIR JACOB EPSTEIN
Professor Albert Einstein
Bronze, on a slate base, sculpted in 1933,
height 17¼in (44cm)
London £5,200($8,840). 16.III.77
From the Samuels Collection, Liverpool

CHRISTOPHER RICHARD WYNNE NEVINSON, ARA
The road to Ypres
1915, 19½in by 35½in (49.5cm by 90cm)
London £8,500($14,450). 10.XI.76
From the collection of Mrs Clive Morris

Right
FRANCES HODGKINS
*Still life with flowers,
eggs and lemons*
Pencil and
watercolour, signed,
25½in by 18½in
(65cm by 47cm)
London £1,600($2,720).
10.XI.76
From the collection of
Audrey Withers, OBE

Far right
PAUL NASH
Elms
Blue and black chalk,
pen and ink and
watercolour, signed
and with monogram,
22in by 15in
(56cm by 38cm)
London £2,500($4,250).
22.VI.77

MICHAEL AYRTON
Sir William Walton
Signed and dated *1948*, 24in by 36in (61cm by 91.5cm)
London £2,200($3,740). 16.III.77
Now in the National Portrait Gallery, London

HENRY MOORE, OM, CH
Three standing figures
Bronze, dark brown patina, stamped *Bronze* and *Cire Perdue C. Valsuani,* an edition of six, 1945,
height 9in (22.8cm)
New York $27,000(£15,882). 20.X.76

This piece is the maquette for the large stone sculpture in Battersea Park in London, executed in 1947-48

HENRY MOORE, OM, CH
Mask
Green stone, 1930, height 6½in (16.5cm)
New York $16,500(£9,705). 13.V.77
From the collection of Mrs John Gould Fletcher

FERDINAND GEORG WALDMÜLLER
A view of the Dachstein
On panel, signed and dated *1834*, 12¼in by 10¼in (31cm by 26cm)
New York $50,000(£29,411). 15.X.76

FERDINAND GEORG WALDMÜLLER
A still life of roses in a vase
On panel, signed and dated *1842*, 18in by 14½in (45.5cm by 37cm)
London £32,000($54,400). 4.V.77

BENGT NORDENBERG
The family bible reading
Signed, inscribed *Dusseldorf* and dated *1852*, 37¼in by 49½in (95cm by 126cm)
London £11,000($18,700). 23.II.77

ANDREA APPIANI
Portrait of Angelica Catalani
Signed, 38½in by 28¾in (98cm by 73cm)
Florence L10,000,000(£6,666:$11,333). 3.VI.77

Andrea Appiani (1754-1817) was one of the best-known Italian neo-classical artists and was appointed Official Painter in Italy by Napoleon. Much of his work was executed in fresco in private houses.

At the beginning of the nineteenth century Angelica Catalani was the most celebrated soprano in Europe. She spent the years 1806-13 in London, and subsequently became manager of the Italian opera in Paris. She retired to Florence in 1828

ADOLPH SCHREYER
Bedouins en route
Signed, 32in by 49½in (80cm by 125cm)
New York $25,000(£14,705). 28.IV.77
From the collection of the late Arthur D'Espies

Opposite
GUSTAV BAUERNFEIND
The gate of the Great Mosque, Damascus
On panel, signed, inscribed and dated *München 1890*, 45½in by 35¾in (115.5cm by 91cm)
London £12,500($21,250). 24.XI.76

In the fourth century the Byzantine Emperor Theodosius built, on the site of a heathen temple, a Christian basilica in which the chief relic was the head of St John the Baptist. After the Moslem conquest in 635 the Christian church was shared with the Moslems until Caliph Alb-el-Melchen, a descendant of Omar, deprived the Christians of their share. He altered the church into a magnificent mosque which was considered a wonder of the world. Much of the decoration was destroyed by subsequent conquests. This painting depicts the northern gate called Bab-el-Amara and in the left foreground a dervish is seated with his instruments

PABLO SALINAS
Le vernissage
Signed and inscribed *Roma*, 28¾in by 51in (73cm by 129.5cm)
New York $38,000(£22,353). 28.IV.77

ALFRED VON WIERUSZ-KOWALSKI
Cavalry encamped by a cottage
On panel, signed, 15¼in by 21¾in (39cm by 55cm)
London £6,800($11,560). 23.II.77
From the collection of Eva Schmidt-Bachmann

ALPHONSE MUCHA
Girl in a Moravian costume holding a mirror
Signed and dated *'20*, 22in by 21¼in (56cm by 54cm)
New York $11,500(£6,764). 13.V.77
From the collection of David Frank and Yevgeni Edelman

ANDERS ZORN
Portrait of a child
Watercolour, signed and dated *Luton Hoo*
Nov. 1884, 26½in by 20in (67cm by 51cm)
New York $19,000(£11,176). 15.X.76

HENRIETTE RONNER-KNIP
Studies of long-haired cats
On panel, signed and dated '93,
15in by 18in (38cm by 46cm)
London £6,200($10,540). 23.II.77

JEAN-FRANÇOIS MILLET
The Sower
Signed, painted in 1850, 39¾in by 31¾in (101cm by 80.7cm)
New York $300,000(£176,470). 28.IV.77
From the collection of the Provident National Bank, Philadelphia

Jean-François Millet: *The Sower*

The large exhibition in 1975-76, shown both in London and Paris, offered the opportunity for a reappraisal of Millet's work within the context of a generous cross-section of his oeuvre. In excerpts from the catalogue section entitled *Epic Naturalism* Professor Robert Herbert discusses the importance of *The Sower*.

'Why did Millet's *Sower* become one of the great paintings of the modern era? The answer lies in the painting itself, as well as in the social ideas attached to it.

On an autumn day, at sunset, a young peasant strides diagonally down a slope to our right. The sun comes from the left, catching the cheek, hand, waist and thigh, and seems to push him onward. This thrust of the form and the force of the light are counterbalanced by the rearward motion of outstretched arm and leg and by the harrow being dragged into the sun by bulky oxen, in the right distance. The setting sun gives rich roses, lavenders and grey-blues to the sky, rendering the peasant's face all the darker by contrast, and through that very contrast, evoking ideas opposite those of sunlight: approaching winter, brooding darkness, fatality. From the sky comes another sense of menace, the crows – symbols of darkness – which rattle down to steal the grain.

All of this was seen by Millet's contemporaries, but in a socio-political sense. The peasantry had become a radical force in 1848, or so it seemed, and memories of earlier peasant revolts heightened the awareness of current ills that accompanied the depopulation of the countryside. Conservative reviewers therefore rejected the painting, not wishing to be reminded of social ills, especially when presented with such declamatory power and pessimism.

For liberal critics, the opposite was true. The new literature and the new art were celebrating the peasant as a symbol of oppressed peoples now beginning to loosen their bonds. Courbet's *Stone-breakers* and his *Burial at Ornans* were shown in the same Salon, and overnight these two artists became the heroes of the avant-garde.

Van Gogh's copies are the most famous of many works *The Sower* inspired. It found its way into socialistic movements and into the agrarian revolutions that have so profoundly altered the world in our century. And yet, least it be thought the exclusive heritage of social reform, we need only remember that it has become a symbol of religious devotion to work rather than to political agitation. Millet's power as a form-giver helps explain this dual heritage, as does the fact that he captured what was really an archetype: from the time of the *Trés riches heures du Duc de Berri*, the sower had been given this pose and encharged with weighty symbolism.'

JEAN-FRANÇOIS MILLET
Return of the flock
Signed, painted *circa* 1857-60, 21in by 28in (53.5cm by 71cm)
New York $210,000(£123,529). 28.IV.77
From the collection of the Pennsylvania Academy of the Fine Arts

JEAN-FRANÇOIS MILLET
A peasant grafting a tree
Signed, painted in 1855, 31in by 38½in (79cm by 98cm)
New York $360,000(£211,764). 15.X.76
From the collection of the late Helen G. Clarke

JOHN GULLY   *Mount Cook, New Zealand*
Watercolour heightened with white, signed and dated *1869*, inscribed and numbered *3* on the reverse, 29¼in by 51¼in (74cm by 130cm)
London £5,800($9,860). 1.VI.77
From the collection of Mrs Paulson and Mrs Wade-Gery

THOMAS WATLING   *A view of Sydney*
26in by 53½in (66cm by 136cm)
London £31,000($52,700). 3.XI.76
From the collection of Mrs E. I. Hart

GEORGE FRENCH ANGAS
A young boy collecting butterflies helped by a Maori girl
Watercolour heightened with bodycolour, signed and dated *1844*, 12¼in by 9¼in (31cm by 23.5cm)
London £3,200($5,440). 3.XI.76
From the collection of Mrs F. E. Gubbins

SOUTH AMERICAN SCHOOL, MID NINETEENTH CENTURY
The celebrations outside Santiago on Liberation Day
Watercolour heightened with bodycolour, on buff paper, $27\frac{1}{2}$in by 43in (70cm by 109cm)
London £9,000($15,300). 1.VI.77
From the collection of Henry Lyon-Young

CORNELIUS KRIEGHOFF
Un p'tit coup
Signed, 10½in by 8½in (26.5cm by 21.5cm)
London £5,000($8,500). 1.VI.77
From the collection of F. J. Beimicombe

JACOB MAENTEL.
Michael and Elizabethe Haak: a pair of portraits
Watercolour, *circa* 1835, each 17⅜in by 10¾in (44cm by 27.5cm)
New York $42,000(£24,705). 29.IV.77
From the collection of Edgar William and Bernice Chrysler Garbisch

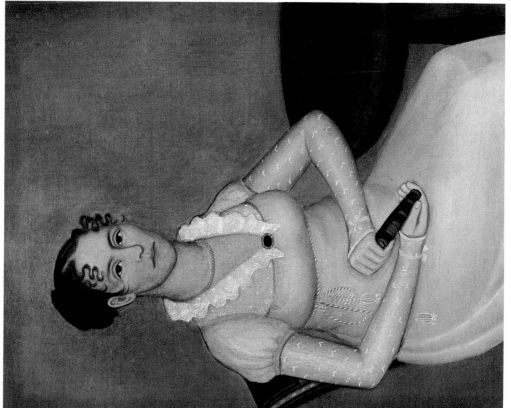

AMMI PHILIPS
Dr and Mrs Crane: a pair of portraits
Painted *circa* 1814-19, each 39in by 32in (99.1cm by 81.3cm)
New York $44,000(£25,882). 21.IV.77

ASHER B. DURAND
Indian rescue
Signed and dated *1846*, 45in by 36in (114.5cm by 91.5cm)
New York $60,000(£35,294). 28.X.76

GEORGE HENRY DURRIE
Winter in the country
Signed and inscribed *N Haven*, 18in by 24in (45.7cm by 61cm)
New York $26,000(£15,294). 21.IV.77

WINSLOW HOMER
The watch, eastern shore
Watercolour on paper, signed and dated *1894*, inscribed *Here you Are – Big Thing*, 15½in by 21½in
(39.4cm by 55.6cm)
New York $120,000(£70,588). 21.IV.77
From the collection of the late Mr and Mrs Edwin S. Webster

This picture was painted at Prout's Neck, Maine. The figure, John Getchell, was a local fisherman
used occasionally by the artist as a model. The inscription on the reverse is to Louis Prang,
lithographer, publisher and friend of the artist who purchased the watercolour in 1895 and made a
few lithographic proofs of it in reverse in 1896

THOMAS MORAN
Point Rubos, Monterey, California
Signed and dated *1912*, 30in by 41in (76.2cm by 104cm)
New York $75,000(£44,118). 21.IV.77

THEODORE ROBINSON
Nettie reading
Signed, painted *circa* 1894, 18in by 22in (45.8cm by 55.9cm)
New York $51,000(£30,000). 28.X.76

WINSLOW HOMER
The croquet match
On board, signed, painted *circa* 1868-69, 9¾in by 15½in (24.9cm by 39.4cm)
New York $210,000(£123,529). 21.IV.77
From the collection of the late Mr and Mrs Edwin S. Webster

EDWARD HOPPER
Hotel room
Signed, painted 1931, 60in by 65¼in (152.4cm by 165.7cm)
New York $200,000(£117,647). 28.X.76
From the collection of the late Nate B. and Frances Spingold

CHARLES DEMUTH
From the garden of the château
Signed and dated *1921*, 25in by 20¼in (63.5cm by 51.4cm)
New York $55,000(£32,353). 21.IV.77
From the collection of the late Mrs William H. Bender

The title refers to the view from Demuth's home in Lancaster, Pennsylvania

THEODORE GERICAULT
The raft of the Medusa
Pencil and watercolour, 1819–20, 4in by 6½in (10cm by 16.5cm)
London £21,000($35,700). 30.III.77

This watercolour was executed by Géricault after the completion in August 1819 of his famous painting. It was one of four watercolours from which lithographs were made by Champion to illustrate the fourth edition of the *Naufrage de la Frégate la Méduse (Relation de Corréard)*. The events depicted took place in 1816 when a French military and naval expedition set out to regain sovereignty over Senegal. In this watercolour, as in the painting, the artist has depicted the raft, and the survivors sighting *The Argus* – the British ship which was to rescue them after ten days of starvation, mutiny and cannibalism. Corréard and Savigny, two of the survivors of this disaster, published an account of it in 1818 and subsequently helped Géricault in the reconstruction of the events for his painting, even persuading the ship's carpenter to make a scale model of the raft for the artist to study

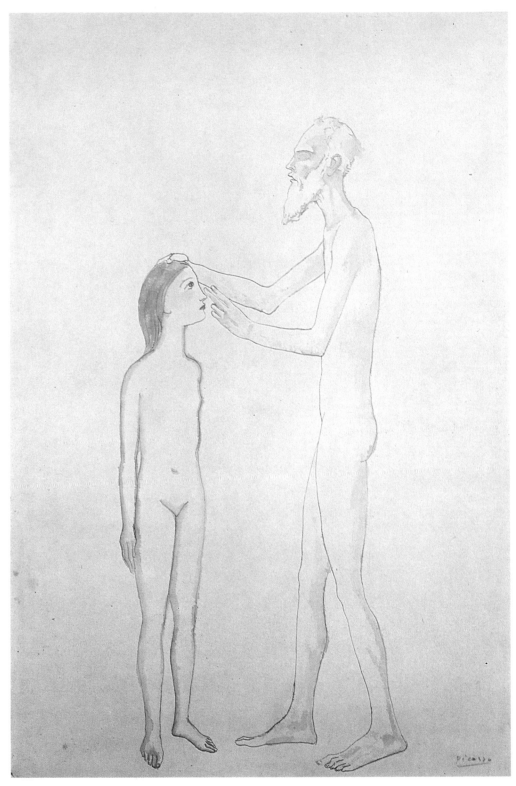

PABLO PICASSO
L'aveugle et la jeune fille
Pen and brown ink and watercolour, signed, executed in 1904, 18in by 12¼in (46cm by 31cm)
London £30,000($51,000). 1.XII.76

JEAN-BAPTISTE CAMILLE COROT
L'odalisque sicilienne
Signed, painted in April 1872, $20\frac{1}{2}$in by $31\frac{5}{8}$in (51cm by 80cm)
New York $220,000(£129,411). 11.V.77

EUGENE DELACROIX
L'arabe au tombeau
Signed and dated *1838*, 18⅝in by 22⅛in (47.3cm by 56.2cm)
New York $130,000(£76,470). 20.X.76
Formerly in the collection of the Duchesse d'Orléans, Paris (in her sale of 1853)

PIERRE-AUGUSTE RENOIR
La promenade
Signed and dated '70, 32in by 25½in (81.3cm by 65cm)
London £620,000($1,054,000). 29.XI.76

Twenty paintings were sold from the collection of the late Nate B. and Frances Spingold, New York,
on 29 November 1976 for a total of £1,450,900($2,466,530)

CLAUDE MONET
La barque bleue – Blanche Hoschedé et Suzanne Hoschedé
Painted *circa* 1887-88, 43in by 50¾in (109cm by 129cm)
London £300,000($510,000). 29.XI.76
Formerly in the collections of René Gimpel and Sir Alexander Korda (sold at Sotheby's on 14 June 1962 for £56,000)

The scene of this painting is the River Epte at Giverny. Blanche Hoschedé was Monet's step-daughter and married the artist's eldest son Jean Monet. Her sister Suzanne married the American painter Theodore Butler. In his diary René Gimpel wrote on 14 June 1926: 'I have bought two canvases from him for 200,000 francs. They are among Monet's masterpieces. They are not actually a pair, but both depict women in boats . . . I don't know which of my two pictures I prefer; they are large horizontals. In the first there are two women in pink; in the second, which is smaller, two women in blue . . . The first is the more poetic in spirit because it's a little sad; the second is at once grave and more tranquil.' The picture is not signed for the reason that René Gimpel gives in the same diary entry: 'Monet asked me for twenty-four hours to sign the canvasses, but I was so afraid that he might change his mind and keep them that I made my escape with them hastily by automobile.'

CAMILLE PISSARRO
La Place de la République, Rouen
Signed and dated *1883*, 18in by 22in (46cm by 56cm)
London £65,000($110,500). 27.VI.77
From the collection of Frank Sinatra

PAUL GAUGUIN
Le jardin en hiver, rue Carcel
Signed and dated '83, 46in by 35½in (117cm by 90cm)
London £98,000($166,600). 27.VI.77
From the collection of Mrs Eva Kiaer, Denmark

Gauguin painted this picture during the time that he was working with Pissarro, an example of whose work of the same date is reproduced opposite

JOHAN BARTHOLD JONGKIND
Vue sur Rouen
Signed and dated *1865*, 16½in by 22⅛in (41.9cm by 56.2cm)
New York $70,000(£41,176). 11.V.77
From the collection of Arthur Murray, Hawaii

PAUL SIGNAC
Concarneau, calme du matin – 'Larghetto'
Signed and dated '91, inscribed *opus 219*, 25¾in by 31in (65cm by 81cm)
London £105,000($178,500). 27.VI.77
From the collection of Henri Lejeune, Saint-Cloud, whose father acquired the picture from the artist
in 1891

Signac sent five pictures to the Exposition des XX in Brussels in 1892, which he had painted in
Concarneau, Brittany, in 1891. To each of the five he gave musical terms as titles ('Scherzo',
'Larghetto', 'Allegro maestoso', 'Adagio' and 'Presto'), as he was at this period studying the
analogies in rhythm and harmony between painting and music. Various critics at the time wrote of
these pictures as symphonies of the sea

EDGAR DEGAS
Quatre danseuses
Pastel, stamped with the signature, executed *circa* 1902, 25½in by 17in
(64.7cm by 43.2cm)
New York $185,000(£108,823). 11.V.77
From the collection of Edgar William and Bernice Chrysler Garbisch, New York

ODILON REDON
La fille aux chrysanthèmes
Pastel, signed, executed *circa* 1905, 26¼in by 21¼in (66.6cm by 53.8cm)
New York $90,000(£52,941). 11.V.77
From the collection of the late Mrs Werner Josten, New York

PAUL CEZANNE
Nature morte – pommes et poire
Painted *circa* 1879–82, 10½in by 13¾in (27cm by 35cm)
London £195,000($331,500). 29.XI.76
From the collection of the late Mrs A. Bonger, Almen, Holland

HENRI MATISSE
Les concombres
Signed, painted in 1907, 15in by 18in (38cm by 46cm)
London £105,000($178,500). 27.VI.77

This painting was sold at Sotheby's in 1970 for £56,500

PIERRE-AUGUSTE RENOIR
Maternité or *Femme allaitant son enfant*
Signed, painted in June 1886, 31⅞in by 25⅝in (81cm by 65cm)
New York $600,000(£352,941). 20.X.76

This painting represents Madame Renoir nursing Pierre, her eldest son, who was born in
March 1885

AMEDEO MODIGLIANI
Fillette blonde en bleu
Signed, painted in 1919, 39¼in by 25¼in (99.7cm by 64cm)
London £120,000($204,000). 29.XI.76
From the collection of the late Nate B. and Frances Spingold, New York

PIERRE-AUGUSTE RENOIR
Le jugement de Paris
Bronze relief, signed, numbered 3 and dated *1914*, 28¾in by 35¾in (73cm by 91cm)
London £27,000($45,900). 30.III.77

Nineteen sculptures and drawings from the Werner and Nelly Bär Collection, Zurich were sold in
March 1977 for £157,500

ARISTIDE MAILLOL
L'été
Bronze, signed, numbered 2 and stamped *Alexis Rudier Fondeur Paris*, executed in 1910-11, height 64in (162.5cm)
$140,000(£82,353).

HENRI MATISSE
Deux négresses
Bronze, signed with initials, numbered 9/10 and stamped *Cire Perdue C. Valsuani*, executed in 1908, height 18½in (47cm)
$100,000(£58,823).

These two sculptures are from the collection of the late Etta E. Steinberg, St Louis, Missouri and were sold in New York on 11 May 1977

JEAN-FRANÇOIS RAFFAELLI
Les buveurs d'absinthe
Signed, 43⅜in by 43⅜in (107.7cm by 107.7cm)
New York $62,500(£36,764). 11.V.77

MAURICE UTRILLO
A la Belle Gabrielle
On panel, signed twice and dated *octobre 1912*, inscribed on the wall: *En face est le meilleur souvenir
de ma vie*, and on the right: *Bien faire et laissez dire-Toto de la Butte*, 29¼in by 41½in (74.5cm by 103cm)
London £62,000($105,400). 29.XI.76
From the collection of the late Nate B. and Frances Spingold, New York

LEON BAKST
Costume design for a bacchante in 'Cléopâtre'
Pencil, watercolour and silver and gold paint, signed and dated *1910*, 11in by 8¼in (28cm by 21cm)
London £5,500($9,350). 25.V.77

NICOLAI ROERICH
Costume design for the clowns in 'Le Sacre du Printemps'
Pencil and gouache, executed in 1913, 9in by 12in (23cm by 30.5cm)
London £3,500($5,950). 25.V.77
From the collection of the late Osborne Robinson, OBE

PABLO PICASSO
Saltimbanque
Gouache, signed and dated *1922*, 6¼in by 4⅜in (16cm by 11cm)
New York $50,000(£29,411). 20.X.76
From the collection of Susan Clark Lefferts, Virginia

JUAN GRIS
Pierrot à la guitare
Signed and dated '25, 51¼in by 35in (130.2cm by 88.9cm)
New York $160,000(£94,117). 11.V.77
From the collection of the late Josef Rosensaft, New York

MARC CHAGALL
Les mariés et le coq
Signed and dated *1939-47*, 35½in by 25½in (90cm by 64.5cm)
London £115,000($195,500). 30.III.77

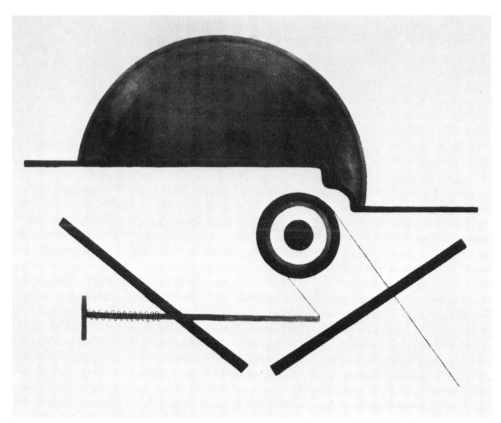

FRANCIS PICABIA
Le broyeur
Pen and indian ink and
watercolour, signed and
titled, executed *circa*
1921-22, 23¾in by 28¼in
(60cm by 72cm)
London £18,500($31,450).
1.XII.76

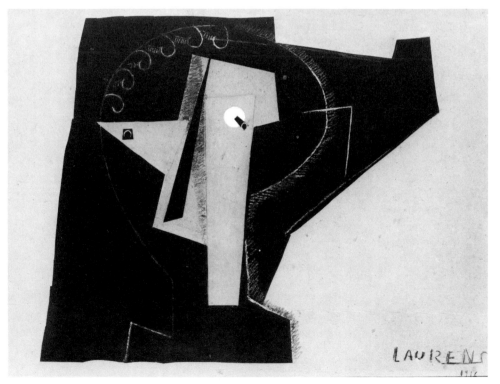

HENRI LAURENS
Tête de femme
Collage, chalk and pencil,
signed and dated *1916*,
21in by 27¼in
(53cm by 69cm)
London £12,800($21,760).
29.VI.77
From the collection of
Douglas Cooper

WASSILY KANDINSKY
Lichte Bildung (Light formation)
Signed and dated '33, $39\frac{1}{4}$in by $47\frac{1}{4}$in (100cm by 120cm)
London £100,000($170,000). 29.XI.76

PABLO PICASSO
Plante de tomate
Signed and dated *6 août 44* on the reverse, 36¼in by 28¾in (92cm by 73cm)
New York $180,000(£105,882). 20.X.76
From the collection of Susan Clark Lefferts, Virginia

PAUL KLEE
Geöffneter Berg
Watercolour with pen and indian ink on paper mounted on board, signed and dated *1914*,
9⅛in by 7⅜in (23cm by 18.7cm)
New York $27,000(£15,882). 12.V.77

JOAN MIRO
La casa della palma
On panel, signed, painted in 1918, 25¼in by 28½in (64cm by 72.5cm)
London £90,000($153,000). 27.VI.77

MAX ERNST
Rêve d'une jeune fille d'un lac
Signed and dated *1940*, 25½in by 32¼in (65cm by 82cm)
London £88,000($149,600). 29.XI.76

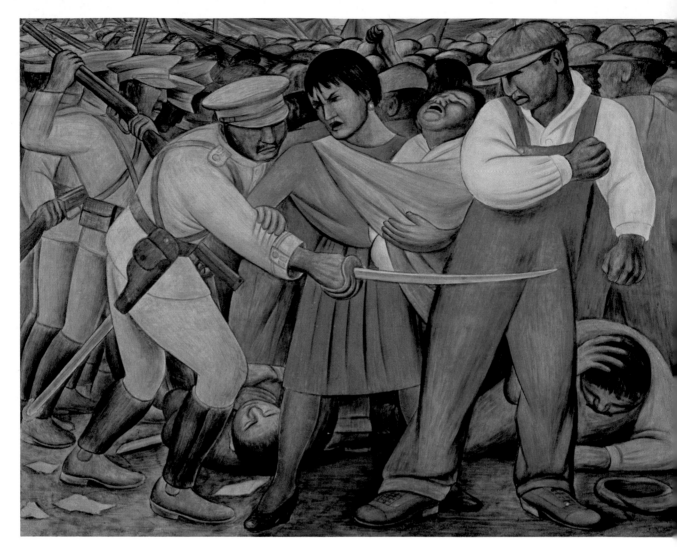

Fig 1
DIEGO RIVERA
Soldiers and workers
Fresco on steel-reinforced concrete,
74in by 94in (188cm by 239cm)
New York $30,000(£17,647). 26.V.77.

Fig 2
DIEGO RIVERA
Cartoon for *Emiliano Zapata, agrarian leader*
Charcoal on heavy paper, executed *circa* 1930, 98¾in by 77¾in
(251cm by 197.5cm)
New York $17,000(£10,000). 26.V.77.

Modern Mexican art and a series of frescoes by Diego Rivera

Mary-Anne Martin

On 26 May 1977 Sotheby Parke Bernet held the first sale of modern Mexican paintings, drawings, sculpture and prints in its history. Included were works by artists familiar to the American and European collector: Orozco, Rivera, Siqueiros, Tamayo, Cuevas, Toledo and Zuñiga. At the same time, works never before seen at auction were successfully offered in a sale designed to encourage buyers from Mexico, America and Europe. The latter group included paintings by Dr Atl, one of the founding fathers of the modern Mexican school; Frida Kahlo, beloved third wife of Diego Rivera and an important painter in her own right; expatriates like Leonora Carrington, Jean Charlot, Pablo O'Higgins and Carlos Mérida, who have worked so long in Mexico that their art has become part of its heritage; and artists like Montenegro, Guerrero Galván, Chávez Morado, Gerzso, Meza and Covarrubias, without whom a survey of Mexican art is hardly complete.

The highpoint of the auction was the sale of four free-standing frescoes by Diego Rivera together with a related group of cartoon designs for a total of $146,250 (£86,029). The frescoes, part of an original set of seven, were painted in New York, on the occasion of the first Diego Rivera retrospective in America, held at the Museum of Modern Art from 23 December 1931 to 27 January 1932. The catalogue of that exhibition describes the commission, indicating that Rivera was to paint them in the style of his Mexican work 'with the possibility that two might be of United States subjects'. Apparently the artist changed his mind, for of the seven frescoes, three, not two, depicted subjects observed in New York. These were *Electric welding* (Fig 4), showing workers welding a boiler in a General Electric power plant, the New York skyline visible on the horizon; *Pneumatic drilling* (Fig 3), depicting labourers drilling through the rock ledge of Manhattan, preparatory to the construction of the Rockefeller Center; and '*Frozen Assets*' (Fig 5), an elaborate political allegory of New York City during the Great Depression. Of the four others in the series, one, *Soldiers and workers* (Fig 1), still remained in the collection of the Weyhe family at the time of this sale and was included in the consignment. Records are somewhat unclear, but it seems that the entire group of seven frescoes were bought in about 1934 by the dealer, Erhard Weyhe, whose Weyhe Gallery has long been a source of Mexican art. Before this date there are some references to 'Mrs Rockefeller's garage', implying that the frescoes were temporarily housed there awaiting their final disposition. According to an old bill of sale, Weyhe sold the fresco of *Emiliano Zapata, agrarian leader* to Mrs Rockefeller on behalf of the museum, and this is now part of the collection of the Museum of Modern Art, New York. This fresco, for which Sotheby's sold the cartoon

Fig 3
DIEGO RIVERA
Pneumatic drilling
Fresco on steel-reinforced concrete, executed in 1931, 94in by 74in (239cm by 188cm)
New York $33,000(£19,411). 26.V.77.

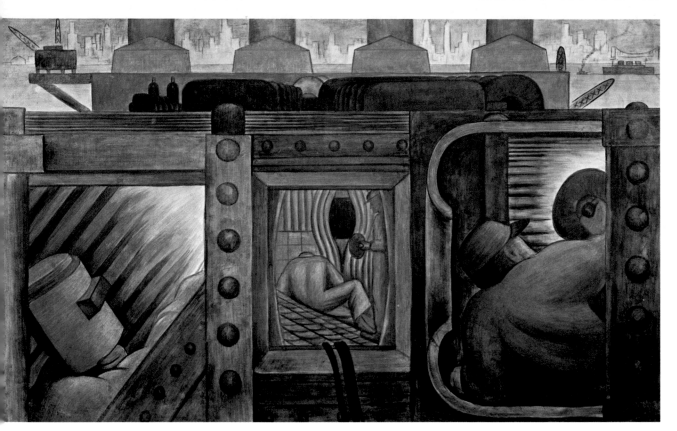

Fig 4　DIEGO RIVERA
Electric welding
Fresco on steel-reinforced concrete, signed and dated *1932*, 58¼in by 94in (147.5cm by 239cm)
New York $15,000(£8,823). 26.V.77.

(Fig 2), was essentially a replica of the famous Zapata fresco in the Palace of Cortés in Cuernavaca, which Rivera completed in 1929. Sometime later, Weyhe was able to sell two more of the frescoes with Mexican themes, *Sugar cane*, also adapted from the Cuernavaca series, and *Liberation of the peon*, based on a 1923-28 fresco in the Ministry of Education in Mexico City. Both of these now flank the main staircase of the Philadelphia Museum of Art. The four others were placed in storage in a Manhattan warehouse, where they remained, unseen, for the following forty-three years.

Removing them from their cell and transporting them to Sotheby Parke Bernet (where they could not get beyond the main lobby because of their weight and size) was a complicated feat requiring the energies of a rigger of 'exotic cargoes', as Diego's portable frescoes weighed a combined total of 5,000 pounds. Once displayed, their freshness and brilliance was astonishing, as the paintings, unexposed to light or weather, were perfectly preserved and in far better condition than any currently to be found in Mexico. Their commercial desirability was quickly apparent as news of their arrival reached the New York press and shortly spread to Mexico City, where they received wide coverage. In fact, all four were purchased in the sale by collectors and dealers who intend to ship them to Mexico.

Even if Erhard Weyhe was unable to find a buyer for it at the time, by far the most historically interesting of the four is '*Frozen Assets*', which achieved immediate notoriety in the 1931 exhibition because of the outspoken indictment of the class system contained in its iconography. Rivera writes on the subject:

'The most ambitious of these frescoes represented various strata of life in New York during the Great Depression. At the top loomed skyscrapers like mausoleums reaching up into the cold night. Underneath them were people going home, miserably crushed together in the subway trains. In the center was a wharf used by homeless unemployed as their dormitory, with a muscular cop standing guard. In the lower part of the panel, I showed another side of this society: a steel-grilled safety deposit vault in which a lady was depositing her jewels while other persons waited their turn to enter the sanctum. At the bottom of the panel were networks of subway tunnels, water pipes, electric conduits, and sewage pipes. A journalist who came to report the show, which opened on December 23rd, baptized this fresco ''Frozen Assets''. . . . The show consisted of 150 pieces, including oils, pastels, watercolours, and black and whites, in addition to the seven frescoes. Although there was embarrassment in some quarters about the frankness with which I represented the current economic crisis in ''Frozen Assets'', my exhibition was well received.'[1]

Bertram Wolfe, Diego Rivera's most sympathetic biographer does not dismiss the controversy so lightly:

'This was the beginning of the third and worst year of the great depression and Americans were very touchy about it. It was distinctly impolite and a little alarming for an invited guest to have noted it, or to have snapped the host when he was not ''dressed for a picture''. There were obscure, disquieting hints in this work of what he might paint if he got to know America better.'[2]

As it happened, '*Frozen Assets*' and the surrounding public dispute portended a far greater scandal in Diego Rivera's American experience, involving the ill-fated mural commissioned three years later by the Rockefellers for Radio City. On this occasion, the critical storm unleashed by Rivera's inclusion of a portrait of Lenin in a mural intended to illustrate '*Man at the Crossroads looking with Hope and High Vision to the Choosing of a New and Better Future*' ended finally with the midnight smashing of the offending fresco into a powder. Rivera's revenge took the form of twenty-one more frescoes, bitterly satyric of American political history and containing devastating caricatures of John D. Rockefeller and J. P. Morgan. These he financed with the commission money he received from the Rockefellers for the destroyed Radio City fresco and donated free of charge to the New Workers' School on Fourteenth Street.

Time has dulled the pain of these controversies and what remains serves principally as a reminder of the impact that the Mexican muralists had upon American art of the '30s, a period when Renaissance *buon fresco* techniques were revived and mural painting again flourished as a means of bringing art and ideas to the public – and work to unemployed artists. The auction of 26 May demonstrated that there is still strong

[1] Diego Rivera and Gladys March, *Diego Rivera, My Art, My Life* (1960), pp 180-82.
[2] Bertram Wolfe, *Diego Rivera, His Life and Times* (1939), p 338.

Fig 5
DIEGO RIVERA
'Frozen Assets'
Fresco on steel-
reinforced concrete,
signed and dated
Nueva York, 1931,
94in by 74in
(239cm by 188cm)
New York
$31,000(£18,235).
26.V.77.

American interest, combined with a measure of nostalgia, in the works of Mexican artists whose history for a decade or two merged with that of the United States. Sotheby's expects that this is only the first of many such auctions designed to expand a market hitherto restricted to Mexican boundaries. Mexican critics, at first concerned that established Mexican prices might not be supported in an alien setting, are now elated to find that Mexican art can hold its own internationally.

CLYFFORD STILL
Untitled
Signed and dated *1954* on the reverse, 117in by 93in (298cm by 236cm)
New York $165,000(£97,058). 12.V.77

ASGER JORN
Il faut les garder
Signed, titled and dated *1958* on the reverse, 45¼in by 34½in (115cm by 86cm)
London £12,500($21,250). 2.XII.76

CY TWOMBLY
Untitled
Oil and crayon on canvas, signed and dated *Roma 1962-63*, 132in by 144in (266cm by 299cm)
London £66,000($112,200). 2.XII.76

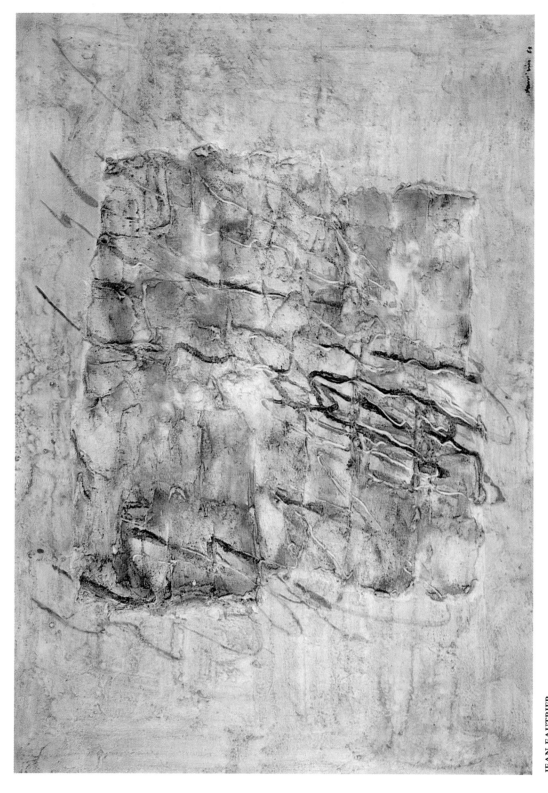

JEAN FAUTRIER
Végétaux
Signed and dated '63, 35in by 51¼in (89cm by 130cm)
London £22,000($37,400). 30.VI.77

MORRIS LOUIS
Beta phi
Acrylic on canvas, painted in 1960-61, 102$\frac{1}{2}$in by 166$\frac{1}{2}$in (260cm by 423cm)
New York $90,000(£52,941). 21.X.76

ELLSWORTH KELLY
Blue, black, red
Signed with initials and dated '64, 91in by 180in (231cm by 274.5cm)
New York $42,500(£25,000). 12.V.77

ROY LICHTENSTEIN
Modern painting with division
Oil and magna on canvas, painted in 1967, 42in by 84in (106.5cm by 213.5cm)
New York $52,500(£30,882). 12.V.77

ROY LICHTENSTEIN
Modern sculpture
Brass and mirror, executed in 1967, height 72in (183cm)
New York $26,000(£15,294). 21.X.76

Prints

PAUL GAUGUIN *Tahitienne accroupie*
Monotype printed in black and orange-brown, 1901-2, 12⅝in by 10in (32.1cm by 25.5cm)
London £17,000($28,900). 27.IV.77
From the collection of Jacques Spreiregen

EDGAR DEGAS
Le client sérieux
Monotype on thin white wove paper, the atelier stamp on the mount, *circa* 1880,
$8\frac{1}{4}$in by $6\frac{1}{4}$in (21.1cm by 16cm)
London £26,000($44,200). 27.IV.77

PABLO PICASSO
Salomé
Drypoint, signed in pencil and inscribed *A Monsieur Delatre*, 1905, 15¾in by 13¾in (40.2cm by 35cm)
New York $40,000(£23,529). 12.XI.76

EDVARD MUNCH
Mondschein
Woodcut, printed in colours on thin japan paper, 1896, 16in by 18⅝in (40.5cm by 47.3cm)
London £13,000($22,100). 27.IV.77

HENRI DE TOULOUSE-LAUTREC
La partie de campagne
Lithograph printed in colours, trial proof before the edition of 100, 1897-98, 15½in by 20¼in (39.2cm by 51.2cm)
London £23,000($39,100). 27.IV.77

PABLO PICASSO
La femme qui pleure
Drypoint, aquatint and etching, dated in the plate
4 Juillet 37, 13¾in by 9¾in (35cm by 24.8cm)
London £31,000($52,700). 6.X.76

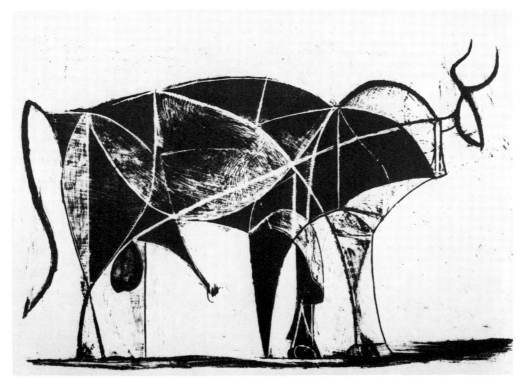

PABLO PICASSO
Le taureau
Lithographs, a sequence
of eleven progressive
states (sixth state
illustrated), 1945-46,
12in by 17½in
(30.5cm by 44.4cm)
London £85,000
($144,400). 27.IV.77

KARL SCHMIDT-ROTTLUFF
Trauernde am Strand
Woodcut, a proof impression, signed in pencil, 1914, 15⅜in by 19¼in (39cm by 49cm)
New York $2,300(£1,352). 10.II.77

GIOVANNI BENEDETTO CASTIGLIONE
David with the head of Goliath
Monotype printed in sepia ink and finished with brush in a darker tone of the
same colour on buff paper, *circa* 1655, $13\frac{7}{8}$in by $9\frac{3}{4}$in (35.2cm by 24.8cm)
New York $16,000(£9,411). 18.V.77

Castiglione is known as the inventor of the monotype. His earliest works in the
medium, primarily nocturnes, were produced by scraping highlights out of a
totally inked surface. The present work is executed in the more elaborate mixed
technique of his later period

PHILIBERT-LOUIS DEBUCOURT   *La main* and *La rose*
Aquatints, a pair printed in colours (*La main* illustrated), impressions of the third and fourth states,
1788, each 14½in by 10⅝in (37cm by 27cm)
London £2,700($4,590). 27.IV.77
From the collection of the Philip H. and A. S. W. Rosenbach Foundation

JAN MULLER
The Adoration of the shepherds
Engraving after Spranger, an undescribed proof before the plate was finished,
$22\frac{3}{8}$in by $17\frac{1}{4}$in (57cm by 43.8cm)
London £800($1,360). 7.X.76

After ROSSO FIORENTINO
The dance of the Dryads
Engraving, an
impression printed in
brownish black ink on
blue paper,
10¼in by 15⅛in
(27cm by 38.3cm)
New York $2,700
(£1,588). 10.XI.76

The relationship of this
plate to two other
known versions of the
subject has not yet been
established

After PIETER BRUEGEL
THE ELDER
The wedding dance
by P. van der Heyden
Engraving, an
impression of the first
state of four, on paper
with an Orb and Cross
watermark,
14⅞in by 16⅞in
(37.8cm by 43cm)
London £2,800($4,760).
27.IV.77

JAN JORIS VAN VLIET
The beggars
Etchings, a set of ten (two
illustrated), impressions of
the first state of four
London £1,600($2,720).
23.VI.77

REMBRANDT HARMENSZ.
VAN RIJN
Student at a table by candlelight
Etching, an impression of
Usticke's first state of three,
on paper with a WK
countermark, $5\frac{3}{4}$in by $5\frac{1}{4}$in
(14.7cm by 13.4cm)
London £1,800($3,060).
7.X.76

WILLIAM BLAKE
Spring and *The shepherd*, both from *Songs of Innocence*
Relief etchings, printed in colours and touched with
black ink and watercolour, on white wove paper,
$1\frac{5}{8}$in by $2\frac{3}{4}$in (4.2cm by 7cm) and $2\frac{3}{4}$in by $2\frac{1}{2}$in
(7cm by 6.5cm)

These two etchings were sold in London on 5 April
1977 for £2,000($3,400) and £2,500($4,250)
respectively

GEORGE STUBBS, ARA
A recumbent lion
Mixed method engraving, signed and dated *1 May 1788*, $6\frac{7}{8}$in by $8\frac{7}{8}$in (17.6cm by 22.5cm)
London £3,400($5,780). 21.VI.77
From the collection of Viscount Ebrington

After DOMINIC SERRES
The reduction of Havana, by P. C. Canot and J. Mason
Engravings, a set of twelve including frontispiece
London £1,500($2,550). 2.XI.76

After JAMES POLLARD
Epsom Races, by Charles Hunt
Coloured aquatints, a set of six published 1 February 1836 by Ackermann
London £1,050($1,785). 2.XI.76

Manuscripts and Printed Books

T. STURGE MOORE
A Brief Account of the Origin of the Eragny Press
Limited to 235 copies, illustrations by Lucien
Pissarro, Eragny Press, Hammersmith, 1903
London £300($510). 3.II.77
From the collection of R. Pissarro

MU'IN
A young prince holding a thin cane
[Isfahan] dated *Shawwal
1063*/November-December 1652
London £40,000($68,000). 2.V.77
From the collection of the Hagop
Kevorkian Fund

*The young emperor Akbar
receiving gifts from his courtiers*
A miniature from the Chester
Beatty *Akbarnama,* [Mughal,
circa 1600-1610]
London £14,000($23,800).
4.V.77

LUFT 'ALI IBN AKA KHAN
Atashkadah (A commentary on Persian poets)
A Persian manuscript with 30 miniatures in a contemporary lacquer binding,
[Qajar] dated *8th Jumada II 1216*/16 October 1801
London £75,000($127,500). 23.XI.77

FIRDAUSI
Shahnama A Persian manuscript by the scribe Muhyi with 42 miniatures, this one
attributable to Siyawush, [Qazwin] dated *Safar 973*/September 1565
London £70,000($119,000). 23.XI.77

BEATVS
VIR·QVI
NON
ABIIT
IN CON
SILIO

impiozum. & in uia peccatozum n stetit.
& in cathedra pestilentie non sedit.
Sed in lege domini uoluntas eius. & in
lege eius meditabitur die ac nocte.
Et erit tanquam lignum quod planta
tum est secus decursus aquarum. quod
fructum suum dabit in tempoze suo.
Et folium eius non defluet. & omnia que
cunq; faciet prospabuntur.

The Harrold Psalter
A Latin manuscript on vellum with over 190 decorated initials, written and illuminated by Simon
the Priest, and with an almost unbroken provenance up to the present day, [Canterbury, Christ
Church Cathedral Priory, *circa* 1173 85]
London £24,000($40,800). 13.XII.76
From the collection of Bristol Baptist College

cirra semitas p quas ele
phantes solito graditur
delitescos. crina corū no
dris alligat. ac suffocans

pimit. Gignitur ī ethio
pia. ꝶ ī india. ī ipo icen
dio rugis estus de belu
a qrie dicitur cetus.

st belua ī mare q̃
dr grece aspido ce
lone lat aut aspido te
studo. Cetus g̃ magnus

est hīs super corrū su
um tanquā sabulū. q̃d
est iuxta littus maris.
hec ī medio pelagi ele

The Bestiary of Humfrey Duke of Gloucester
An illuminated Latin manuscript on vellum with 94 miniatures, a hitherto unrecorded book from the
library of Duke Humfrey, brother of Henry V of England and founder of the library at Oxford
University, [North-Eastern France, last quarter of the thirteenth century]
London £88,000($149,600). 13.VI.77
From the collection of Sion College, London

Book of Hours, use of Rome
Illustrated manuscript on vellum with 16 full-page miniatures, late fifteenth-century
blind-stamped binding, Netherlands, probably Utrecht, *circa* 1400-*circa* 1440
London £36,000($61,200). 13.XII.76
From the collection of Donald J. Wineman
Now in the Royal Library in the Hague

This profusely illustrated Book of Hours was painted in three distinct stages
in the first half of the fifteenth century. The Hours of the Virgin is preceded
by an illuminated title page, one of the earliest surviving examples in any
book. The miniature illustrated, *The Last Judgement*, was painted by the third
artist

Psalter, Litany and Office of the Dead
Latin manuscript on vellum with 12 miniatures (8 full-page), illuminated initials
throughout and over 2,000 decorative line-endings often incorporating animals,
dragons and fish, [Paris, *circa* 1220-40]
London £135,000($229,500). 13.VII.77

The book was made in the court school in Paris and was illustrated by four
painters, one of whom is known from several other manuscripts of the earliest
period of gothic secular book-production. The present Psalter, which was hitherto
unknown and unpublished, was possibly commissioned for the counts of
Burgundy. Its elaborate gilt binding, tooled with flowers, acorns and the star of
David, was made *circa* 1595 also in Paris

LIVY

De Bello Punico Secundo

Latin manuscript on vellum with 11 illuminated initials, and a full page historiated border containing 5 miniatures and a coat-of-arms, written by John of Mainz, illuminated by Marco dell' Avorgo, for Leonello d'Este, Prince of Ferrar and Mantua, bound in eighteenth-century calf, with the arms of Pope Pius VI, [Ferrara, 1449]

London £48,000($81,600). 13.VII.77

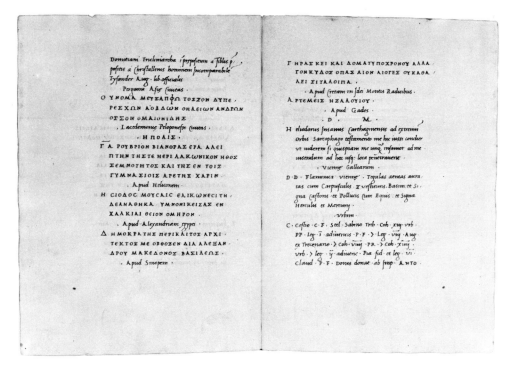

Silloge of Classical Inscriptions
Latin manuscript (a few portions in Greek) on paper, written in an extremely fine italic
script, [Italy, probably Rome, *circa* 1500]
London £11,500($19,550). 13.VII.77
From the collection of Mrs James Wardrop
This manuscript was owned in this century by both Edward Johnston and James
Wardrop and used as the model for the modern revival of italic script in which they
were prime movers

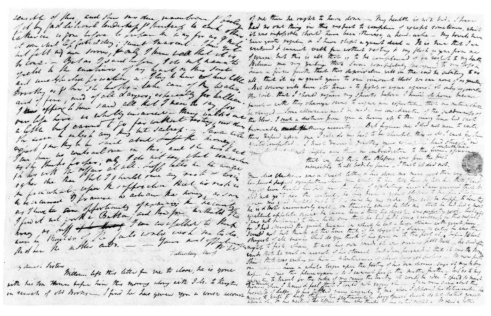

WILLIAM AND MARY WORDSWORTH
A joint letter to Wordsworth's sister Dorothy, part of a large archive of unstudied and
mostly unpublished material relating to the Wordworths, their friends and relations,
[early nineteenth century]
London £35,000($59,500). 6.VII.77

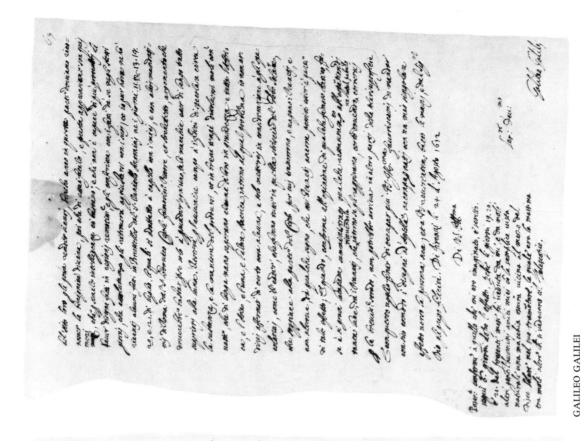

AUGUST STRINDBERG
Svanehvit
An autograph manuscript of the entire play, on 107 pages, probably prepared for presentation to Harriet Bosse, later his wife
London £7,500($12,750). 19.IV.77

GALILEO GALILEI
A page of an important letter on sunspots, mostly in a secretarial hand, but the signature and a seven-line postscript in Galileo's hand, dated
Di Firenzi li 24 d'Agosto, 1612
London £17,500($29,750). 18.IV.77

ERNEST HEMINGWAY
A series of 30 autograph letters and cards to his parents, almost entirely unpublished, written from Chicago, Toronto, New York, Paris, Madrid and elsewhere, 1920-28
New York $65,000(£38,235). 29.III.77
From the collection of Jonathan Goodwin

JANE AUSTEN
Volume the Second
A substantial manuscript of her early works, including Love and Freindship, Lesley Castle, and The History of England, in a vellum album, [circa 1790-93]
London £40,000($68,000). 6.VII.77

This is one of two major Jane Austen manuscripts sold this season, the other, Volume the Third, was sold in London on 14 November 1976 for £30,000

A wooden fan, the sticks decorated with a collection of 25 signatures and portraits of musicians and artists, including Edward Burne-Jones, John Everett Millais, Ludwig Strauss and Charles Hallé, in a contemporary painted satinwood case, 1882-1905
London £700($1,190). 11.V.77
From the collection of the Royal Society of Musicians

JOSEPH HAYDN
The autograph manuscript of the Trio in D major for *Cembalo, Violino and Violoncello*, 21 pages, Vienna, 1785
London £32,000($54,400). 11.V.77

PIETRO ARON
Thoscanello de la Musica
First edition, Venice, 1523
London £3,000($5,100). 8.XI.76

The Vase de Madame Dubarry
A watercolour included in the Beckford archive which was sold in London on
5 July 1977 for £120,000 ($204,000)

The Beckford papers

Roy Davids

'Agate and Onix Cups – in the highest Parisian Gusto.' Thus William Beckford, 'England's wealthiest son' and her 'Kubla Khan', himself described the cups and vases in this watercolour illustration which was in the vast archive of his literary manuscripts, correspondence and personal papers, including designs, architectural drawings, catalogues, inventories, lists and receipts relating to his collection, sold on 5 July.

Crowded watercolour illustrations of this kind, the eighteenth-century equivalents of colour photographs, are known to have been sent by dealers to prospective purchasers. The presence of this one among Beckford's papers strongly suggests that the objects in it were offered to him and may lead to the discovery that he actually owned some of them.

The most prominent piece, a superb *brûle-parfum* made by Charles Ouizille in 1784 with a miniature probably by Jacques-Joseph de Gault, is captioned *Vase de Madame Dubarry*. While the burner is recorded as having been in the possession of Marie-Antoinette from about 1786, its association with a mistress of that ill-fated queen's father-in-law, Louis XV, appears not to have been noted. It was taken from Versailles in October 1789 by Daguerre, the jeweller of 85 rue Saint-Honoré, and its subsequent history is unknown until its auction by Sotheby's on 13 March 1954, at Koubbeh Palace, Cairo, and later by Christie's in Geneva on 28 April 1976.

The archive, which reflected virtually every aspect of Beckford's many interests, also contained drafts and fair copies of his novels, stories, journals, translations, reading notes and musical scores, some 2,500 letters and his invaluable collection of contemporary newspaper cuttings. Included among these was the only surviving fragment of the original manuscript of his fantastic oriental tale, *Vathek*, his translations of the *Arabian Nights* (the first translation from Arabic into English), manuscripts for *Dreams, Waking Thoughts and Incidents* and two printed copies of the book, of which only three other copies are known, both of these being extensively annotated by Beckford in preparation for his *Italy, with sketches of Spain and Portugal*.

Sold by order of His Grace the 15th Duke of Hamilton and Brandon, into whose family's possession the papers came through the marriage of the 10th Duke with Beckford's younger daughter Susan, the archive was one of the largest collections of English literary papers to have been offered for sale as a single lot and it achieved a record price at auction.

RAOUL LE FEVRE

[*Recuyell of the Historyes of Troye*]

The first book to be printed in English, translated by the printer, this copy lacking 16 leaves, [Bruges, William Caxton, 1474–75]
London £40,000($68,000). 13.VI.77

Both these books are from the collection of Sion College, London

[WILLIAM SHAKESPEARE]

Lucrece

First edition of Shakespeare's third published book, of which only nine other copies are recorded, London, 1594
London £35,000($59,500). 13.VI.77

CARLO RUINI
Dell'Anatomia et dell'Infirmita del Cavallo
First edition, with 64 full-page woodcuts of the anatomy of the
horse, Bologna, 1598
London £3,600($6,120). 1.XI.76

POPE JOHN XXI
Thesoro delos Pobres en Medicina & Cirurgia
First Spanish edition, bound with three other rare Spanish
medical works in contemporary limp goatskin, Granada, 1519
London £7,500(£12,750). 29.XI.76
From the collection of Sir Thomas Phillipps, Bt (1792–1872)

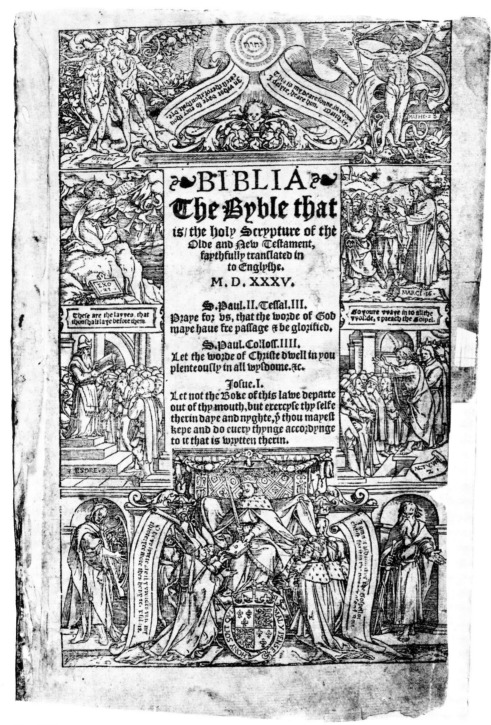

The Bible
First edition of the first complete English Bible, translated by Miles Coverdale, like all other known copies this one is imperfect, lacking 9 leaves, [Cologne, 1535]
London £30,000($51,000). 14.II.77
From the collection of P. Ashe, a descendant of the Haden family who owned it in the sixteenth century

DAVID HERRLIBERGUER
Topographie Helvetique
58 engraved plates,
Neuchatel, [*circa* 1753]
London £5,200($8,840).
15.II.77

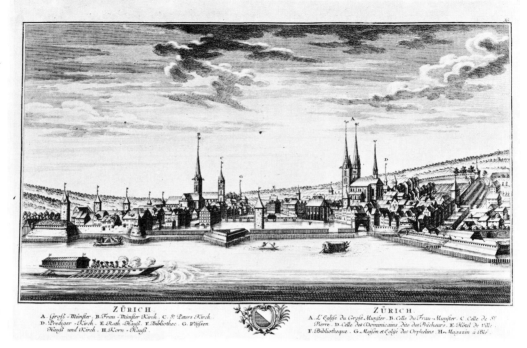

Megillat Esther (Scroll of Esther)
Hebrew manuscript on vellum, richly illuminated in gold and colours, [North Italy, early eighteenth century]
London £15,500($26,350). 13.XII.76

J. G. LOCRE
Esprit du Code Napoléon
Five volumes, first edition, contemporary French red morocco, gilt, the arms of the Emperor
Napoleon on the sides, once in the library of Talleyrand, Paris, 1805-7
London £2,000($3,400). 1.XI.76

LUDOVICO ARIOSTO
Orlando furioso
Four volumes, engraved
plates, a fine London
binding by John
Baumgarten, of
contemporary red
morocco, gilt,
Birmingham, 1773
London £2,100($3,570).
1.XI.76

JAMES HAKEWILL
A Picturesque Tour of the island of Jamaica
21 coloured aquatints, London, 1825
London £1,500($2,550). 7.XII.76

WILLIAM DANIELL and
RICHARD AYTON
*A Voyage round Great
Britain*
Eight volumes, 308 hand-
coloured aquatints,
contemporary red
morocco, gilt, London,
1814-25
New York $13,000
(£7,647). 24.V.77
From the Pierpont Morgan
Library

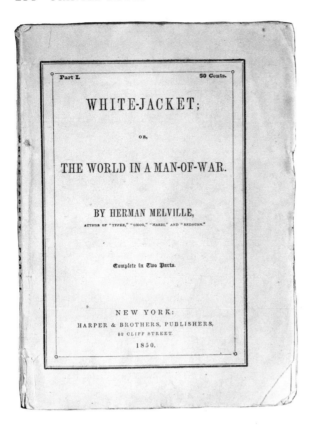

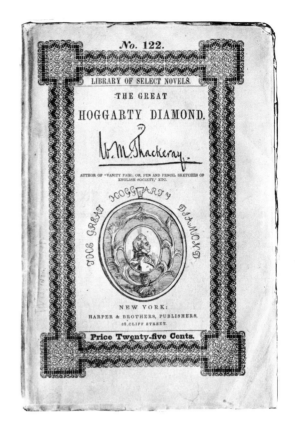

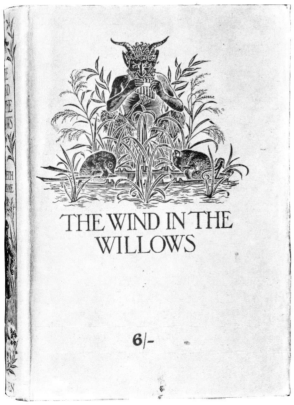

WILLIAM MAKEPEACE THACKERAY
The Great Hoggarty Diamond
First issue of the first edition, New York, [1848]
New York $8,000(£4,705). 6.X.76

Above left
HERMAN MELVILLE
White-Jacket; or, the World in a Man-of-War
First issue of the first American edition, two
volumes, New York, 1850
New York $7,500(£4,411). 6.X.76

Left
KENNETH GRAHAME
The Wind in the Willows
First edition, with the rare dust jacket,
London, 1908
New York $3,500(£2,058). 6.X.77

All three books illustrated on this page are from
the collection of Katherine de B. Parsons, a library
of Victorian and later fiction notable for its fine
condition

HERMAN MELVILLE
The Whale
Three volumes, first edition, a unique
presentation copy from the author to Henry
Hubbard, a fellow shipmate on the *Achushnet*,
London, 1851
New York $53,000(£31,176). 26.I.77
From the collection of the late Henry
Hubbard Middlecoff
Now in the University of Chicago Library

The novel is better known as *Moby Dick*,
which was the author's title. The alternative
was suggested by George Bentley, the
publisher of the English edition, which
preceded the American. Henry Hubbard and
Melville were among the twenty-six men
who sailed from New Bedford,
Massachusetts, aboard the *Achushnet* in
January 1841. Melville used a number of
real life details for his novel and Hubbard
makes interesting manuscript notations
which relate the people and events aboard
the *Achushnet* to episodes in Melville's tale

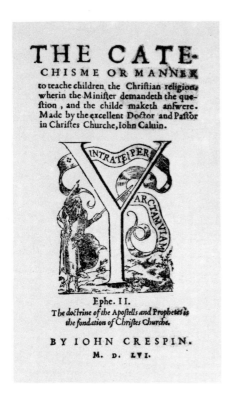

Left

JOHN CALVIN
*The Catechisme, or Manner
to Teach Children the
Christian Religion*
First edition in English, 1556
London £260. 2.VII.74

Right
*The Mothers Blessing, being
several Godly Admonitions
given by a Mother, to her
Children upon her Deathbed*
circa 1660
London £170. 22.X.76

*War with the Devil, or the
Young Man's Conflict with
the Powers of Darkness*
1678
London £198. 17.X.75

Collecting historical children's books

Justin G. Schiller

Although children's book-collecting is frequently considered a recent innovation, its roots extend deep into the nineteenth century through contemporary interest in the illustrations of Thomas Bewick and George Cruikshank. By 1880 Charles Welsh and Andrew W. Tuer were among book historians who cultivated an awareness of early juvenile literature, and though few in number their scholarship encouraged the production of several facsimiles. These reprints even attempted to simulate the decorative floral covers or hand-coloured pictures which typically characterised books for children a century earlier, and their primitive mode of illustration re-vitalised a facet of graphic art as seen in the bold woodcut images of Joseph Crawhall or in some of the private press books of Kelmscott and the Birmingham School. In effect, a subculture gradually developed as collectors quietly accumulated lib-raries of old children's books; some of them chronicled these efforts,[1] but most simply waited for the time when such nursery relics would be legitimately accepted as worthy of collection. It took longer than might have been expected.

Even today there are some who still dismiss the entire field of juvenile literature as trivia, arguing that by definition these books are inconsequential and without any significant literary importance. The medieval concept that children are immature adults and must be discounted until fully grown is still evident, and the cultural struggle in getting childhood recognised as a prominent stage in development is sometimes disregarded. The preachings of John Bunyan and James Janeway threat-ened continual damnation if the child did not repent from its own childishness, and it was a long time before childhood became accepted as a major learning experience. There were many obstacles to combat in this progress, and each step illuminates our understanding of what we now take for granted as a tradition or heritage.

During the past four years Sotheby Parke Bernet of London has serialised in six sections 'a highly important collection of children's books'. This may have seemed like part of their regular juvenile sales (begun in 1967), but rather it comprised part of the finest library of historical children's literature ever assembled. Depending chiefly

---

[1] Welsh, Charles, *A Bookseller of the Last Century being some account of the life of John Newbery and of the books he published* (London, 1885); Field, (Mrs.) E. M., *The Child and his Book* (London, 1891); Tuer, Andrew W., *History of the Horn-Book* (London, 1896); Halsey, Rosalie V., *Forgotten Books of the American Nursery* (Boston, 1911); Stone, Wilbur Macey, *The Divine and Moral Songs of Isaac Watts* (New York, 1918).

on the country of origin, other portions have come up for auction in the United States, Germany and France, and still more may yet be offered in Britain; together these catalogues read like an international history of children's book publishing, from the sixteenth century down to the first decade of our present one. Many rare editions of all varieties have been included, with original manuscripts and significant material not otherwise recorded. Each sale seems to produce more treasures, and as a whole the emergence of these books has solved some bibliographical puzzles – including several we did not anticipate – the evidence being in books hitherto unknown. The methods employed in assembling this library, and a brief history of those involved in putting it together, may account for the reason it is so comprehensive.

The actual beginnings were probably early in this century, perhaps even incorporating a few smaller (now anonymous) collections. The architect during this first period was F. R. Bussell, a Lloyd's underwriter who lived in the heart of the Kent countryside. Not much is known of him except that he methodically brought together all sorts of juvenile items: children's stories and verse, instruction and educational aids, illustrated books, mechanical and movable books and paper toys, jigsaw puzzles, board-games and peep-shows. Details of his original collection are known from a separate Sotheby catalogue of January 1945 when his estate consigned the library for auction. The brief descriptions and heavy grouping indicate the lack of interest in the subject at this time. Through the energies of Percy H. Muir and the finances of the Hearst Magazine syndicate, the entire collection was purchased *en bloc* and its treasures exhibited during May 1946 at the National Book League in Albemarle Street. At first the collection was considered as the basis for a modern publishing project, but nothing further developed and the library was stored away; in 1949 a selection of the books was exhibited in parts of America as 'The Good Housekeeping Collection'.

About this time Edgar S. Oppenheimer, a German textile manufacturer then living in New York, had tired of collecting press books and fine bindings. He wanted to begin a new field of bibliophily which would prove more challenging, and with the guidance of the antiquarian bookseller Walter Schatzki he decided to collect historical juveniles in all languages. Schatzki managed to purchase the Bussell Collection from Hearst, and it served as the foundation of Oppenheimer's eventual library. Duplicate copies of the same title were always purchased if there were any notable differences – coloured or uncoloured illustrations, type of binding, variant imprint, or even translation into other languages. In 1954 a notable portion of these books were lent for an exhibition of children's literature at the Pierpont Morgan Library, anticipated by a smaller display of juveniles the previous year at the Grolier Club. Mr Oppenheimer died unexpectedly in 1958, and his collection remained with the family intact until it was purchased by the present consignor. What had until then been accessible to very few now became available to modern scholars and collectors through the auction rooms of Europe.

The books do not carry any ownership marks to identify them as once belonging to Oppenheimer, except (perhaps) their generally uniformly-styled protective slipcases. Some do contain bookplates or signatures of early owners including Edward Arnold (of Dorking), Jean Hersholt, Walter Schatzki, Wilbur Macey Stone, Andrew W. Tuer, and Carolyn Wells. Those included in the original 1946 NBL exhibition contain the catalogue reference number circled in pencil inside the front cover. And the presence of familiar trade markings and prices of two decades earlier attest to the vast quantity of books purchased from Schatzki, Elkin Mathews Ltd, Maxwell Hunley, and Seven Gables Bookshop. Today, many of these volumes have been re-distributed between the more prominent private and institutional collections, all of them benefiting from the far-sighted efforts of a few pioneer collectors and dealers who preserved even fragmentary remains of what we now know to be unique and virtually unobtainable editions.

The earliest work printed in English in this collection is quite typical of the very first books prepared for youth: John Calvin's *Catechisme, or Manner to Teach Children the Christian Religion* (Geneva, 1556). Following the teachings of Paul and Augustine, Calvin argued that all Creation was now depraved and impregnated with Satan. 'In Adam's fall, we sinned all.' But God, out of His mercy, had elected some to be saved. The Calvinist (and the Puritan) genuinely desired spiritual salvation for himself and others, and hoped that through prayers and deeds he might prove himself worthy of being chosen. Thus, in being able to justify the urgent need for good lessons, religion managed to place extra emphasis on the production of books aimed at the edification of children.

For nearly two centuries there was little change; religion had become more of a threat than a comfort, and the child was guided with instruction during every waking moment to sustain its youthful piety. Other early works included in these sales suggest the Calvinistic sternness which permeated the times: *The Mothers Blessing being several Godly Admonitions given by a Mother to her Children upon her Deathbed* (circa 1660), *A Looking Glass for Children being a Narrative of God's Gracious Dealings* (1673), *War With The Devil or the Young Man's Conflict with the Powers of Darkness* (1678). There were even abridged versions of the Bible, including some miniature editions, which the child was to carry and read at idle moments. Few of these books contain illustrations, and when they were included they usually personified the torments to which sinning could lead; in no way could they be considered entertaining. In fact, the very experience of enjoying oneself was contradictory to the Church since happiness was achieved as a reward only *after* a pious existence on earth.

Some Thoughts Concerning Education (1693) by John Locke began to undermine traditional pedagogy, although puritanical influences continued in varying degrees for another 175 years. Gradually, a popularity for English fiction produced many transitional books which were not specifically written for children but had ultimately become adopted by them. The fables of Reynard the Fox and Aesop, were now printed with simplified texts, large woodcut illustrations, and in a size comfortable for small hands to hold; fairy tales intended for adult amusement at the French court provided the right balance of fantasy with realism to perpetuate the stories of Cinderella, Red Riding Hood, and the White Cat; while abridged versions of *Robinson Crusoe* and *Gulliver's Travels* retained only the adventurous spirit of the original without its digressions and sermonising.

About 1740 didacticism gave way to milder forms of instruction with a series of miniature guide-books for children telling them of the wonders to be seen around London and the City of Westminster. And in 1744 John Newbery began cultivating his own brand of 'plum-cake philosophy' to a ready and waiting audience. Many of his books were decorated with amusing woodcuts or copper engravings, and they were often bound in brightly-coloured paper boards to attract the child's eye. His texts never lingered uncomfortably on a moralising tone, and often one can find

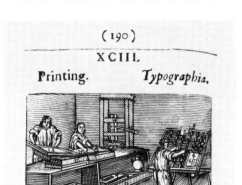

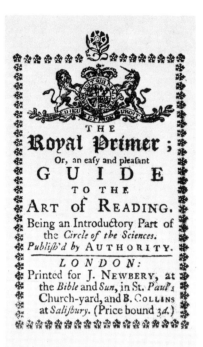

A Guide for the Child and Youth
1723
London £176. 16.X.75

Right
The Royal Primer, or an Easy
and Pleasant Guide to the Art
of Reading
Second edition, John Newbery,
1751-52
London £410. 22.IV.77

J. A. COMENIUS
Orbis Sensualium Pictus. Visible World
1659
London £120. 21.X.74

The Renowned History, or the Life and Death of
Guy Earl of Warwick
circa 1710
London £140. 21.IV.77

The History of Little Goody Two-shoes
Second edition, John Newbery, 1766
London £1,250. 16.X.75

ingredients between the same covers to satisfy both the parent and the young owner: first a poem giving thanks for Christian parentage, and then a story like that of Giles Gingerbread who (quite literally) lived upon learning – since each day his father gave him a fresh gingerbread cake with the alphabet stamped on it, and Giles thoroughly devoured every letter.

Newbery wrote or commissioned more than a hundred titles himself, and following his death in 1767 his heirs continued to publish under the family name; in all, by 1802, they had produced about 400 different juvenile works totalling some 2,400 separate editions. But despite this large number, many of these printings are known only by advertisements while others survive in only one or two copies. The Oppenheimer Collection has proved a cornucopia for Newbery imprints: the unique first printings of Tommy Tagg's *Collection of Pretty Poems* (1756), *Food for the Mind or a New Riddle Book* (also 1756) 'by John-the-Giant-Killer', and *The Prettiest Book for Children being the History of the Enchanted Castle . . . governed by the giant Instruction* (1772) with its title-leaf on a stub; the rare (and valuable) 1766 second printing of the *History of Little Goody Two-Shoes*, sometimes attributed to Oliver Goldsmith, and the first printing of Christopher Smart's *Hymns for the Amusement of Children* (1771); the *Lilliputian Magazine* (1783) engraved with signed woodcuts by Thomas Bewick; and even a pirated edition of Newbery's first juvenile (1744), *A Little Pretty Pocket Book* (London: John Marshall, *circa* 1775) of which the two earliest Newbery versions located (1760, 1763) are both incomplete.

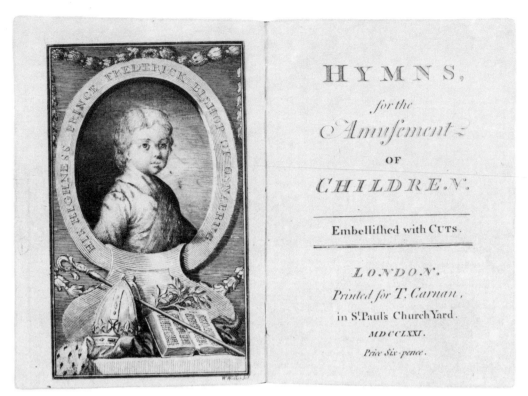

CHRISTOPHER SMART
*Hymns for the
Amusement of Children*
First edition, 1771
London £1,750.
22.IV.77

Concurrent with Newbery, other writers attempted to produce books for children. Sarah Fielding, sister of the novelist Henry and herself a recognised literary talent, wrote *The Governess; or, Little Female Academy* (1749) 'calculated for the entertainment and instruction of young ladies'. It is basically a collection of stories told to or by the pupils of Mrs Teachum's school, linked together by a common framework. Where Bussell had only a fifth printing (1768) in his collection, Oppenheimer added a first edition and also an updated version modelled sixty years later by Charles and Mary Lamb (*Mrs Leicester's School*). The engraver George Bickham is represented by two enchanting illustrated juveniles, both *circa* 1740 and influenced by Callot: *Youth's Pastime* and *First Principles of Geometry Explained*. Also included are first editions of Thomas Day's *History of Sandford and Merton* (1783–89) and *History of Little Jack* (1788), the latter containing twenty-two fine woodcuts by John Bewick. And the writings of Dorothy and Mary Ann Kilner are equally well-represented: *The Adventures of a Pincushion, Life and Perambulations of a Mouse, Memoirs of a Peg-Top* (all *circa* 1785-90).

By the end of the century there were very few firms which did not include some type of children's book series in their annual production. About this time a concerted effort began to educate the poor and lower middle classes, and best suited to the capacities of these new readers were short stories and verse inexpensively produced like pamphlets with paper wrapper bindings. These are called chapbooks, which existed in different forms much earlier but actually came into mass popularity at the start of the nineteenth century. The word 'chapbook' itself is probably a corruption

The Rational Exhibition for Children
First edition, 1800
London £195. 22.X.76

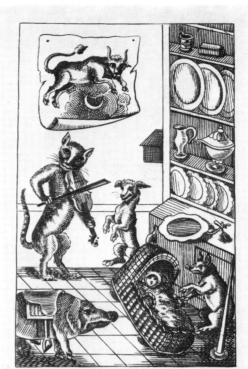

Mother Goose's Melody, or Sonnets for the Cradle
1803
London £195. 22.X.76

*The Rational
Primer*, 1804
London £130.
21.IV.77

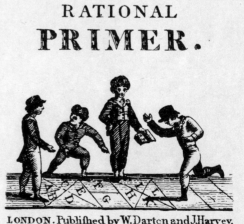

of the term 'cheap book' which would get hawked around the streets by itinerant tradesmen, 'strolling stationers' as they were called, selling their merchandise out of wheelbarrows or pushcarts in competition with the more elegant and expensive bookshops. By their very nature these books were meant to be ephemeral, and the large number of previously unrecorded editions found in the Oppenheimer sales is quite remarkable.

Combined with the educational reforms of Pestalozzi and their later refinements by Froebel, the future of books for the amusement of children was guaranteed. Rhymed levities like the *Comic Adventures of Old Mother Hubbard and her Dog* (1805), *The Butterfly's Ball and the Grasshopper's Feast* (1807) by William Roscoe, and 'Humpty Dumpty' (in *Gammer Gurton's Garland*, 1810) appeared in quick succession and were frequently reprinted; a contemporary advertisement states that 40,000 copies of Roscoe's poem (with its companion, *The Peacock at Home*) sold within the first twelve months. Charles Lamb, William Godwin, and Thomas Love Peacock each contributed versified texts while poetry by Wordsworth and Robert Bloomfield was simply extracted from already published works. The folk stories collected in German by the Grimm brothers were newly illustrated by George Cruikshank (1823–26), and by 1835 Hans Andersen had printed in Denmark his first collection of children's tales. In the next decade Charles Dickens wrote *A Christmas Carol* (1843) and Edward Lear published his wonderful nonsense limericks (1846). In 1865 Lewis Carroll's stories of Alice, the White Rabbit, and the Cheshire Cat began to entertain a new generation of children, just as their children enjoyed the picture toybooks of Walter Crane, Kate Greenaway, and Randolph Caldecott. And by the next generation Beatrix Potter began telling her *Tale of Peter Rabbit* (1901), *The Tailor of Gloucester* (1902), along with such favourite characters as Jemima Puddle-Duck and Tom Kitten.

This is essentially an outline history of English children's books up till 1910, but it is also a survey of part of the Bussell-Oppenheimer Collection. In most instances the books themselves have been remarkable for conditon, carefully restored by experts when necessary at a time when the restoration and protective casings probably cost more than it did to purchase them. This is no longer true. During the past four years these books and drawings brought relatively healthy prices, although they must still be under-valued as we read over the price lists and yearn to buy them again at the prices realised only a few years ago. When they may come back on the market again is unpredictable; the important items will undoubtedly remain with the major collections that acquired them. But even the identity of these successful buyers is difficult to know since institutions frequently used dealers to represent them – sometimes even different dealers at the same sale to protect their anonymity. Unfamiliar names on these sale reports like Ashton, Armour, Dix, Coleman and Jerrold further conceal the identity of the actual purchasers. Who would have thought collecting children's books required such intrigue and mystery? Clearly we are not dealing with trivia any more!

SARAH CATHERINE MARTIN
*The Comic Adventures of Old Mother Hubbard
and her Dog*
First edition, 1805—6
London £360. 19.II.73

Harlequin's ABC
circa 1850
London £71.50. 16.X.73

The Royal Nursery
circa 1850—60
London £130($221). 22.X.76

jadys bien apparut en l'armée de Sennacherib. Doncques, s'il te plaist à ceste heure me estre en ayde, comme en toy seul est ma totale confiance et espoir, je te fais veu que par toutes contrées, tant de ce pays de Utopie que d'ailleurs, où je auray puissance et auctorité, je feray prescher ton sainct Evangile, purement, simplement et entierement, si que les abus d'un tas de papelars et

161

FRANÇOIS RABELAIS
Les Horribles et Espovantables Faictz et Prouesses du très renommé Pantagruel
One of 35 special copies with an extra suite of the plates, 180 coloured woodcuts by André Derain, Paris, 1943
London £4,600($7,820). 8.X.76

GEORGES LEPAPE
Les Choses de Paul Poiret
Limited to 1,000 copies, 12 coloured plates by the
author, Paris, 1911
London £330($561). 18.III.77

ARTHUR RACKHAM
Don Quixote and Sancho Panza
Ink and watercolour on paper, signed and dated *'04*
London £1,300($2,210). 12.XI.76

CACATUA OPHTHALMICA, *Sclater.*

JOHN GOULD *The Birds of New Guinea*
Five volumes, 320 hand-coloured plates, a fine set in contemporary red morocco, gilt,
London, 1875-88
New York $26,000(£15,294). 24.V.77

Photographs

ROBERT HOWLETT
Portrait of Isambard Kingdom Brunel standing before the launching chains of 'The Leviathan' ('The Great Eastern')
Albumen print, mounted on card with printed publisher's credit *London Stereoscopic and Photographic Company 54 Cheapside & 110 Regent Street, London*, with the subject's facsimile signature, issued 1863-64, printed from the negative of 1857, 11in by 8⅜in (27.8cm by 21.4cm)
London £5,200($8,840). 1.VII.77

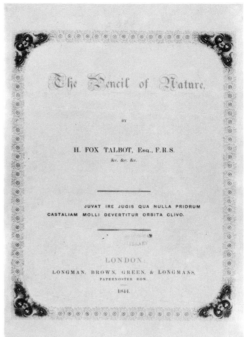

Far Left
LEWIS CARROLL
Alice Liddell as a beggar-girl
Albumen print, *circa* 1859, 6⅜in by 4¼in (16.2cm by 10.9cm)
London £5,000($8,500). 1.VII.77

Left
WILLIAM HENRY FOX TALBOT
The Pencil of Nature
Complete with twenty-four Talbotype plates with accompanying letterpress, bound soon after April 1846 from the six parts issued between 1844 and 1846
London £18,000 ($30,600). 1.VII.77

CHARLES SHEELER
Still life
Warm toned silver print backed with photographic paper, 1938, 7⅝in by 9⅝in (19.4cm by 24.4cm)
New York $8,750 (£5,147). 20.V.77

Works of Art

A white alabaster group
of the Adoration,
probably Middle Rhine,
circa 1440, height
11½in (29.2cm)
London £9,500($16,150).
14.VII.77

A South German ivory group of Hercules killing the Hydra, *circa* 1650, on an ebony base with a central band of ivory carved with a continuous scene of the rape of the Sabines, *circa* 1700, overall height 22in (56cm) Mentmore £20,000($34,000). 23.V.77

An Italian ivory figure, probably of Cosimo de Medici (1519-74), sixteenth century, height 11¾in (30cm) Mentmore £30,000($51,000). 23.V.77

The long neck, rather protruding eyes and position of the head recall the bust of Cosimo de Medici by Cellini of 1545, although the above example shows him at an older age. The armour which he wears is typical of a parade armour of the mid sixteenth century in the classical manner, but is not that in the Bargello, Florence, of 1546, which is said to have belonged to Cosimo

A Trier volcanic stone group of the Virgin and
Child, *circa* 1370, height 34¼in (87cm)
London £10,000($17,000). 9.XII.76

A South German limewood group of the Virgin
and Child, probably Franconian, *circa* 1520,
height 57in (145cm)
London £8,500($14,450). 9.XII.76

A drawing of the bronze in the oratory at Strawberry Hill in 1784

A bronze figure of an angel, eighteenth century, height 34in (86cm)
London £30,000($51,000). 14.VII.77

Although the style of this figure suggests an earlier date, no trace of this piece can be found further back than the *Description of the Villa of Mr Horace Walpole at Strawberry Hill near Twickenham*, printed at Strawberry Hill in 1784, where its position is described as follows: 'Entering by the great North Gate, the first object that presents itself is a small oratory enclosed with iron rails; in front, an altar, on which stands a saint in bronze.' The bronze is shown in the frontispiece of this book and in a drawing by Carter of the *View of the Oratory looking West* (see above), in Richard Bull's extra-illustrated edition of the same date, reproduced here by kind permission of the Lewis Walpole Library, Farmington, Connecticut

An English ivory portrait bust of Mr Francis Sambrooke by David Le Marchand, dated *1704*, signed on the reverse *Le Marchand fac. 1704* and inscribed *Mr Fran. Sambrooke Aetat. Suae 42*, height $7\frac{1}{2}$in (20cm) London £40,000($68,000). 14.VII.77

David Le Marchand (1674-1726), a Huguenot refugee, is chiefly known for his ivory portrait reliefs but he appears to have executed two other dated busts in the round at this early date – one of Louis XIV dated 1700 and another of Lord Somers dated 1706

An Italian bronze figure
of Neptune from the
workshop of Pietro da
Barga, sixteenth century,
height 29in (73.5cm)
Mentmore
£21,000($35,700).18.V.77

A Roman marble relief, probably early sixteenth century, height 20in (51cm)
Florence L19,000,000(£12,666:$21,533). 21.X.76
Formerly in the Barberini Collection

This relief is one of a group of eight sculptures, originally from Palazzo Barberini in Rome, which were sold together in Florence. (The two sarcophagi included in the group were bought by the Italian Government to be replaced in Palazzo Barberini.) The other pieces were all antique Roman from the first to the fourth centuries AD, and indeed the present sculpture was for years considered to be of classical origin. An engraving of it was published in 1693 (P. S. Bartoli and G. Bellori, *Admiranda Romanorum Antiquitatum oc veteris sculpturae vestigia* (Rome, 1693), plate 73). However both the iconography and the origin remain obscure and whilst it has been suggested that it is either an Early Christian piece or a classical relief recarved in the sixteenth century, it seems more likely that it dates from the early sixteenth century

An Italian bronze mortar decorated with various aquatic subjects including Neptune and his
sea-horses, probably Venetian, second half of the sixteenth century, height 19⅝in (50cm)
London £13,500($22,950). 14.VII.77

Fig 1   A *grisaille* oblong panel with gilding by Léonard Limosin, signed *L.L.* and dated *1541*,
9½in by 14½in (24cm by 37cm)
£9,000($15,300). 20.V.77.
The source is an engraving by Jean Mignon; other works of his were used at Limoges by
M. D. Pape, Pierre Reymond and Pierre Courteys

Fig 2   A *grisaille* roundel of Julia, daughter of Julius Caesar,
by Jean II Pénicaud, *signed I.P., circa* 1540–45,
diameter 10in (25.5cm)
£1,350($2,295). 20.V.77.
Plaques of this kind were probably intended for panelling.

Fig 3   A polychrome oblong portrait plaque of
Martin Luther by Léonard Limosin, signed *L.L.*,
dated *1539*, 4⅞in by 4in (12.5cm by 10cm)
£5,000($8,500). 20.V.77.

The Mentmore Limoges enamels

Roger Pinkham

The Mentmore collection of enamels must have been one of the last, if not the very last of the great private collections to be sold. The Bernal, the Duke of Hamilton, the Duke of Marlborough, the Spitzer, the Magniac, and numerous smaller collections have all gone under the hammer and their catalogues now make up the corpus of knowledge on which the study of this subject has been based. In the same way the Mentmore sale of Baron Mayer Amschel de Rothschild's Collection should extend knowledge. Despite the fact that a privately-printed catalogue of the Mentmore works of art has existed since 1883 it has been known only to a few, even among scholars.

The Mentmore collection was a limited one in number and scope when compared to the Spitzer or the Magniac. It was formed specifically around the Renaissance masters who were active from about 1530 to the 1570s; the artists Léonard Limosin, Pierre Reymond, Jean de Court, M. D. Pape and Pierre Courteys forming its backbone. The early period of painted enamelling at Limoges, from *circa* 1475 to 1530, was not represented at Mentmore, and the number of later seventeenth-century enamels was few.

Before discussing the pieces in detail it is necessary to explain the techniques of enamelling as they were practised at Limoges, which was, and in fact is still, the leading centre of the craft. Until probably the middle of the fifteenth century the customary method was *champlevé* enamelling – the coloured enamels were bedded into the surface of the various copper articles made usually for Christian ritual. It is hard to decide whether painted enamels were first made in Italy or France, since they are also known to have been produced at Venice and one or two other Italian centres in the fifteenth century, but with regard to those made at Limoges the technique was fairly well developed by the 1470s when the 'Monvaerni' Master was active. His work is the first of this kind to have come down to us. With the newer technique the enamel colours were painted on a prepared copper surface following a design previously traced. The subsequent firing was fairly quick. The colours of these enamels still had the directness and simplicity of the medieval period, the tones being limited to blues, greens, purple and flesh tones, and there was additional enhancement with the lavish use of gilding and 'jewels' of translucent enamel in relief, the latter aptly placed to increase the sense of depth.

Almost overnight the greater versatility of the painted technique gave the artisan maker of enamels the same freedom as the illuminator and easel-painter. But as

Fig 4 A *grisaille* tazza and cover of *The Story of Adam and Eve* painted with flesh tones by Jean Court *dit*
Vigier, signed *I.C.D.V., circa* 1560, diameter 6¾in (17cm)
£7,000($11,900). 20.V.77
Vigier was one of the subtlest painters of the *grisaille* method. Here he used engravings by Lucas van
Leyden. Other engravings used at Limoges include the ones for *Les Preux* and *The Follies of Man*

enamellers were not usually inventive, they established the practice, which became
standard, of copying or basing their subjects on contemporary engravings which
were then likely to be German, or sometimes Flemish.

The late Gothic period, which lasted in France until about 1510, saw intense activity
at Limoges, and the rise of several important workshops including that of the
anonymous Master of the Orléans triptych, the Louis XII triptych, and that of Nardon
Pénicaud. Most of the products made were plaques with religious themes. Already by
the late fifteenth century the architectural frameworks of the Italian Renaissance,
introduced by Fouquet and Bourdichon in their paintings and miniatures, respectively, were emulated in enamels, thus making inevitable a gradual progression
towards a complete Renaissance iconography. Other influences included engravings
by Dürer and various Italian prints. Of greatest importance was François I's energetic
drive to transform his court into a cultural Mecca in the Italian style. In a short time
the influence of the French-based Italian artists Rosso and Primaticcio, who both
worked on the palace of Fontainebleau, was to be decisive.

By 1530 most of the Limoges ateliers were inclining towards *grisaille* painting

Fig 5   A *grisaille* dish of *The Defeat of Amalek* by Pierre Reymond, dated *1561*,
width 20in (51cm)
£3,500($5,950). 20.V.77
The source is probably by a French engraver who based his ideas on earlier engravings by
Marco Dente or Agostino Veneziano. The subject is popular in *grisaille* and other artists who
used it include the Master KIP, Pierre Reymond, M. D. Pape and Jean de Court

rather than to polychrome, and this trend continued. One of the finest practitioners of
this new technique of painting grey to white tones on a black ground was Jean II
Pénicaud (active 1530-49) (Fig 2), a grandson of Nardon Pénicaud who founded the
important family workshop of the Pénicaud. In the Mentmore collection there were
also enamels by those other superb *grisaille* workers, M. D. Pape (active 1550–75) and
Jean Court *dit* Vigier (active 1555-65) (Fig 4).

The Pénicaud workshop trained a number of distinguished enamellers. The greatest of these was Léonard Limosin (active 1532-75) who brought credit to the trade and
to himself subsequent to his entrée to the French court, probably in 1535. A little after
this date it is likely that he began his career as one of the earliest portraitists in enamel.
About 130 portraits executed in the ambience of the court remain, and at their best
they show his ability to portray the character of his sitters and a mastery of various
methods of painting, many of which were probably his own innovations (Fig 3).
Limosin was also brilliant as a *grisaille* painter (Fig 1) and the source he used in this
example of his work was a Mignon engraving based on a drawing by Luca Penni. This
points to the fact that by the 1540s (this enamel is dated 1541), French engravers had

Fig 6   One of a pair of *grisaille* tazzas and covers painted with flesh tones by Pierre Reymond, signed *P.R.*, *circa* 1560, diameter 7¼in (18.5cm) £6,800($11,560). 20.V.77

The main scenes are from the life of Moses illustrated in Salomon's *Bible* of 1554; the underside subjects are adapted from various *Triumphs* by J. A. du Cerceau, one of the most inventive of the Fontainebleau designers. The juxtaposition of solemn religious and pagan themes is quite common in the workshops after the middle of the century

begun to revive in their own idioms the works of Rosso, Primaticcio and other Italian artists who had worked in France. This circle of French engravers had become important as part of the School of Fontainebleau, and as their work was prolific much of it is to be found being used in the Limoges workshops by about 1540. Limosin's workshop made much decorative tableware but perhaps not so much as the workshop of Pierre Reymond (active 1534-84). Much of Reymond's early and middle work is in *grisaille* (Fig 6) while many of his later pieces, done in the '60s and '70s, were executed in polychrome which was then returning to favour. His engraved sources were not only French (Fig 5) but also German and Italian. Perhaps no other Limoges artist was as successful at adapting the bitty and pernickety style of the Fontainebleau School to the complex forms of tableware. Slightly less adroit than Reymond but with a strong sense of drama are the enamels of Pierre Courteys (active 1544-81) who, with Jean de Court, represented at Mentmore the latter part of the

Fig 7   A set of four polychrome plaques of the *Months* (April, August, September, December with their constellations) by Pierre Courteys, signed *P.C.*, *circa* 1570, height 14⅛in (36cm) £40,000($68,000). 20.V.77

The source is the set of engravings by Etienne Delaune first published in 1568 and very popular in the Reymond workshop

sixteenth century when polychrome and a delight in complicated patterns came to the fore. Courteys' portraits are rare and only seven signed ones, all of men, have been recorded: two were in the Mentmore collection; two are in the Walters Art Gallery, Baltimore; one is in the Glasgow Art Gallery; one appeared in the Séligmann Society sale in Paris, 9-12 March 1914, lot 73; and the seventh, described in the catalogue as of 'Henry VIII' (presumably of England), was sold at Christie's sale of 22 February, 1867, lot 62. Courteys' engraved sources include the work of Bernard Salomon; these he often used. Salomon's *Bible* illustrations published at Lyons in 1554, and subsequently, were extremely popular in all the Limoges ateliers. Another engraver, equally popular, was Etienne Delaune. The sumptuously-coloured plaques illustrated here (Fig 7), date from about 1570 and typify Courteys' style at its grandest, as well as displaying the complexity of the enamelling craft at this date, for here are used coloured, *grisaille*, and translucent enamels in each scene.

Fig 8   A polychrome oval dish of *Jacob's Dream* after Bernard Salomon, from the workshops of Jean I Limosin or perhaps Suzanne de Court, *circa* 1580–1600, width $10\frac{5}{8}$in (27.5cm) £8,000($13,600). 20.V.77

In addition to his engravings for *The Bible*, Salomon also illustrated Ovid's *Metamorphosis* (1559) and Aesop's *Fables* (1570), both published by de Tournes at Lyons

Fig 9   A polychrome salt of the *Muses* in translucent enamels by Jean I Limosin, signed *I.L.*, late sixteenth century, height $3\frac{1}{2}$in (9cm) £2,600($4,420) 20.V.77

The sources are probably the engravings published by Virgil Solis, *circa* 1565

Fig 10   A polychrome oblong plaque of Louis XIV, represented as Phoebus Apollo, by Jacques I Laudin, signed *Laudin Emailleur a Limoges I.L., circa* late seventeenth century, 7½in by 9½in (19cm by 24cm) £7,200($12,240). 20.V.77

The later pieces in the Mentmore collection illustrate the trend in the last years of the sixteenth century towards the making of smaller objects with delicate patterns in gold. Jean I Limosin, a descendant of Léonard, exemplifies work of this kind (Figs 8 and 9), as do Jean de Court (active 1555-85) and Suzanne de Court, one of the only two women enamellers recorded at Limoges.

Overall, the enamels of the seventeenth century differ greatly from those of their immediate predecessors; they are plainer in colour, their range of forms is more limited, and there is a prevailing seriousness of mood. Mentmore enamels of this period were not large in number but included some by Jacques I Laudin (active 1626-95) (Fig 10). The work of Laudin, the most important artist of that name in a family atelier which had only one serious rival in the Nouailher family, recalls the most versatile *grisaille* painting of the sixteenth century, but with the difference that Laudin is inspired by such baroque artists as Goltzius. In consequence, Laudin's style is full-bodied, robust, yet at the same time subtle, and he can be said to have been the last enameller at Limoges among his contemporaries, who was seriously interested in extending the enameller's craft.

A silver and enamel casket with scenes from the story of Hercules, attributed to Pierre Reymond, Limoges, mid sixteenth century, length $7\frac{7}{8}$in (20cm)
New York $18,000(£10,588). 26.XI.76

A Milanese rock crystal ewer from the Saracchi Workshop, mid sixteenth century, height 9½in (24.2cm) Mentmore £28,000($47,600). 23.V.77

Kunstkabinet objects of this kind are typical of the taste of Baron Mayer Amschel de Rothschild and formed a major part of the collection at Mentmore. The following pages 251, 252, 253 and 265 illustrate the wide variety of such objects in the collection.

For further discussion and illustration of the Rothschild taste in works of art at Mentmore see the article by Sir Francis Watson, pp 15-17

Two from a set of twelve Limoges painted enamel plates by Joseph Limosin, signed *I.L.*, *circa* 1625, diameter 6⅞in (17cm)
London £26,000($44,200). 9.XII.76

The plates depict scenes from *Genesis* after Bernard Salomon. Above (from left to right) are Chapter 7, *The Flood* and Chapter 13, *Abraham and Lot separating their herds and going into Canaan and Jordan*

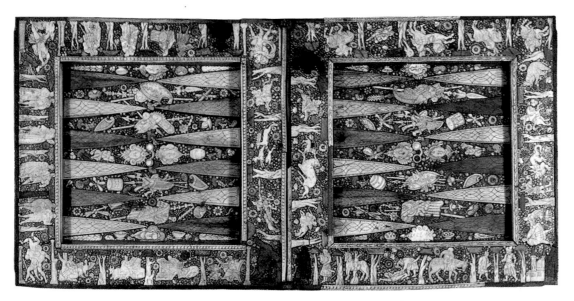

A South German white and green stained horn games box, mid sixteenth century, 15½in (39.3cm) square
London £10,000($17,000). 9.XII.76

The inside is decorated with various mythological, religious and hunting scenes after contemporary engravings

An Augsburg ebony house altar and table cabinet with silver mounts, the metalwork attributed to
the goldsmith Matthias Walbaum, *circa* 1600, height 30in (76cm)
Mentmore £11,000($18,700). 20.V.77

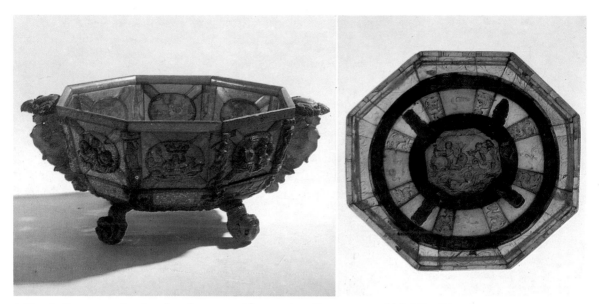

A North German amber bowl and cover, mid seventeenth century, width 12in (31cm)
Mentmore £24,000($40,800). 23.V.77

A Dresden carved ivory figure of a knife grinder, his grinding wheel of coloured glass, gilt-bronze
brilliants and gemstones, on a gilt-bronze base set with brilliants and rubies, first half of the
eighteenth century, height 5in (12.7cm)
Mentmore £15,500($26,350). 23.V.77

A South German iron and gilt-bronze casket, probably Augsburg, late sixteenth century, height 6¾in (17cm)
Mentmore £19,000($32,300).
20.V.77

Below

An agate portrait bust of Queen Elizabeth I, late sixteenth century, height 3½in (9cm)
Mentmore £25,000($42,500).
23.V.77

The nearest comparable piece to this bust is the large cameo of Omphale wearing the lion skin, also in jasper, in the Ambrosiana, Milan. They may both be the work of the Milanese hardstone carver Ottavia Miseroni, who was appointed to the Imperial Court Workshop in Prague in 1589

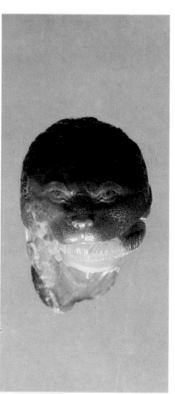

A boxwood model for the upper part of a silver sword or dagger sheath, probably after
a design by Virgil Solis of Nuremberg (1514-62) and intended for the Elector Moritz of
Saxony or another member of the ruling House of Wettin, Nuremberg, *circa* 1540,
height 6¾in (16.9cm)
London £4,300($7,310). 7.IV.77

Goldsmiths' models carved in wood are of extreme rarity and were only made in the
case of important commissions, whereas bronze patterns for sheath mounts have
survived in number

A bronze figure of
St George by Sir Alfred
Gilbert, MVO, RA, 1893-94,
height 19in (48.5cm)
London £5,000($8,500).
11.V.77

The figure of St George is
one of the central themes to
the Clarence Memorial at
Windsor, commissioned by
the Prince and Princess of
Wales in 1892. A similar
model was made in
aluminium. The Windsor
Chapel is Gothic and
Gilbert wished to retain
this feeling but without
imitating its style

An English bronze group of *Custer's Last Stand* by Walter Winans, signed and dated *1891*, stamped with the Crystal Palace Exhibition mark, height 17½in (44.5cm)
London £5,900($10,030). 16.III.77

Walter Winans was an English painter and sculptor, who was born in Russia in 1852 and travelled extensively. He worked throughout the United States and died in 1920

An American marble group entitled *The Sleeping Faun* by Harriet Hosmer, signed *H. Hosmer, fascit Roma*, circa 1864, height 50in (127cm)
London £12,000($20,400). 16.III.77

Harriet Hosmer worked in America, Italy and England. She arrived in Rome in 1852 studying under John Gibson in studios once occupied by Canova

The Korsun Mother of God, Moscow, mid sixteenth century, 12in by 10in (30cm by 25cm)
London £5,600($9,520). 20.VI.77

The Iverskaya Mother of God, the oklad
embellished with silver-gilt and enamel,
maker's mark *I.T.* unidentified, Moscow,
1899-1908, 12¼in by 10¾in (31.5cm by 27cm)
London £4,000($6,800). 20.VI.77

St Dimitri of Thesaloniki, Greek mainland,
sixteenth century, 18in by 12½in
(46.5cm by 32cm)
London £2,600($4,420). 20.VI.77

The Deisis, Greek,
sixteenth century,
14½in by 18¼in
(36.5cm by 46cm)
London £5,200($8,840).
20.VI.77

A silver-gilt and shaded enamel jewel box, the lid painted *en plein* with a scene representing the *Three epic heroes* of ancient 'Rus', after Victor Vasnetsov, Moscow, *circa* 1910, length 8in (20.3cm) New York $15,000(£8,823). 25.V.77

The original oil painting by Victor Vasnetsov (1848–1927), from which this scene is taken, is in the Tretyakov Gallery, Moscow. During his lifetime Vasnetsov enjoyed a great reputation as a painter who popularised old Russian cultural themes, greatly influencing the Slavic Revival movement at the turn of the century. He also designed the Tretyakov Gallery, and uniforms for the army. The pseudo-Byzantine frescoes he devised for the Vladimir Cathedral in Kiev (inaugurated in 1896) were much admired. Diaghilev devoted the first volume of his periodical *World of Art* (1898) entirely to his work

A circular gold and enamel box, maker's mark of *Jean-Francois Xavier Bouddé, St Petersburg, circa* 1782, diameter 3in (7.5cm)
London £1,300($2,210). 20.VI.77

Bouddé was a master goldsmith and jeweller of a foreign trade corporation in St Petersburg from 1769 and alderman 1779-85. This box was made to commemorate the erection of Falconet's monument to Peter the Great (the gold inscription is the date of the inauguration)

A Fabergé gold charka mounted with a cabochon sapphire and rubies, workmaster Michael Perchin, St Petersburg, last quarter of the nineteenth century, width 3½in (9cm)
London £3,400($5,780). 20.VI.77

A Fabergé silver and shaded enamel salver, Moscow, *circa* 1900, diameter 6⅜in (16.2cm)
New York $3,500(£2,058). 10.XII.76

A Fabergé silver-gilt polychrome *cloisonné* enamel beaker, maker's mark of Feodor Ruckert, Moscow, 1899-1908, height 6¼in (15.5cm)
London £4,400($7,480). 20.VI.77
From the collection of R. G. Heseltine

A Fabergé silver and translucent enamel repeating clock, workmaster Michael Perchin,
St Petersburg, *circa* 1900, height 7in (17.8cm)
New York $14,500(£8,529). 10.XII.76

A silver and *champlevé* polychrome enamel vodka carafe, inscribed in Russian *To drink is no hindrance, but youth's diversion*, maker's mark of Khlebnikov, Moscow, 1874, height 9in (23cm)
London £3,000($5,100). 20.VI.77

One of a pair of Nicholas I Imperial porcelain vases, painted with scenes of the chase signed by the miniature painter N. Kornilov, one dated *1835*, the other *1836*, mark and period of Nicholas I, height 53in (135cm)
London £14,000($23,800). 20.VI.77

These vases were presented by the Emperor Nicholas I Pavlovitch to the Austrian Ambassador Count Carl Louis de Fiquelmont upon his departure from St Petersburg. The original paintings by Philips Wouwerman, on which Kornilov's miniatures are based, were acquired at the sale of the Duc de Choiseul by Catherine II for the Imperial Hermitage

A steel and gold snuff box, inscribed *Kolbe à St. Petersburg, circa* 1765-75, width 3⅜in (8.6cm)
Zurich SF66,000
(£15,348:$26,091). 19.XI.76

A mother-of-pearl and gold sewing case, possibly German, *circa* 1740-50, width 4¾in (12cm)
London £4,800($8,160).
30.V.77

Three Neapolitan tortoiseshell piqué objects,
circa 1725:
Above   An inkstand, width 10¼in (26cm)
London £5,000($8,500). 30.V.77
From the collection of Henry Nyburg
Right   A counter box, width 7¼in (18.5cm)
Monte Carlo Fr54,000(£6,429:$10,929). 4.V.77
Below   A dish, width 12¾in (32.5cm)
Mentmore £5,500($9,350). 23.V.77

Above left A Swiss gold and enamel snuff box, late eighteenth century, width 3¼in (8.3cm) $6,000(£3,529)

Above right A Swiss gold, enamel and hardstone snuff box set with diamonds, late nineteenth century, width 3¼in (8.2cm) $11,000(£6,471)

Centre above A Swiss gold and enamel snuff box, *circa* 1780, width 2⅝in (6.7cm) $5,250(£3,088)

Centre below A gold and mother-of-pearl *carnet de bal*, Paris, 1768-74, height 3½in (8.9cm) $1,300(£765)

Below left A gold and enamel *carnet de bal* set with jewels, probably Swiss, early nineteenth century, height 3¼in (8.2cm) $2,500(£1,470)

Below right A gold and enamel *carnet de bal*, probably Swiss, late eighteenth or early nineteenth century, height 3⅝in (8.5cm) $3,000(£1,765)

The objects on this page are from the collection of the Metropolitan Museum of Art and were sold in New York on 27 October 1976

Above left A documentary Birmingham/London snuff box, inscribed *Mary Complin June 10th 1765, circa 1765*, width 2½in (6.5cm) £580($986)
Above right A Birmingham/Wednesbury snuff box, the lid painted with a portrait of Frederick the Great above an inscription *Fre:Great K.Prussia, circa* 1756-70, width 2¾in (7cm) £310($527)
Below left A Bilston snuff box, *circa* 1765, width 2½in (6.5cm) £480($816)
Below right A 'Honeysuckle group' portrait snuff box, the lid painted with a portrait, apparently of the Duke of Cumberland, *circa* 1760, width 2¾in (7cm) £680($1,156)

These objects are from the collection of the late Sir William Mullens, DSO, TD, DL and were sold in London on 22 February 1977

An oval French gold and hardstone snuff box, the miniature signed *J. J. De Gau.. (lt), circa* 1789, maker's mark *A?* probably for Adrien-Jean-Maximilien Vachette, width 2⅝in (6.7cm)
London £4,500($7,650). 13.XII.76

A gold and enamel snuff box, maker's mark of Adrien-Jean-Maximilien Vachette, *2e titre*, 1795-97, *titre* and *garantie*, 1819-38, width 3⅛in (8cm) London £5,000($8,500). 13.XII.76

A Swiss export gold, enamel and diamond sucrier, *circa* 1840, height 5in (12.5cm)
London £10,000($17,000). 30.V.77
Formerly in the collection of Prince Kémal El Dine Hussein

A Swiss gold and enamel musical automaton spy glass with watch, the watch signed *Puyroche*, *circa* 1800, height 3in (7.6cm)
New York $50,000(£29,411). 27.X.76

A four-colour gold and diamond presentation snuff box, probably Swiss, early nineteenth century, width 3¼in (8.2cm)
London £4,400 ($7,480). 30.V.77

This box is said to have belonged to Tzar Alexander I and to have been on view at the Hermitage Museum, Leningrad

A pair of Viennese enamel and silver vases, maker's mark of Hermann Böhm, *circa* 1875, height 16½in (42cm)
London £8,000($13,600). 9.VI.77

Fig 1
JEAN BAPTISTE ISABEY, Prince Napoleon Louis, aged five years, signed and dated *1810*,
height 8½in (21.5cm)
London £24,000($40,800). 28.III.77
Now in the Museum of the Chancery of the Netherlands Orders of Knighthood, The Hague

Portrait miniatures from the Holzscheiter Collection

Jane Strutt

Ernst Holzscheiter, a Swiss businessman, formed his collection some fifty years ago and when his miniatures were offered at auction this year they represented one of the largest and most important collections of miniatures to appear on the market since the Pierpont Morgan sale in 1935. The sale's success was the culmination of a developing interest in continental miniatures which had recently been stimulated by various sales in Europe, notably that of the Felix Panhard Collection in Paris, December 1975.

The importance of the collection was indicated by the meticulous notes that Holzscheiter made about each of the miniatures which revealed, through their documentation, the exacting criteria which influenced his selection. The collection was moreover significant for its fascinating array of identified sitters, always a rewarding aspect for any collector of portrait miniatures. The portraits ranged from the charmingly demure and intimate study by Jean Etienne Liotard of his niece, Mlle Lavergne, whom he is thought to have painted in 1781 during a visit to Lyons, to the miniature by Daffinger of the mysterious Countess Pereras and the more formal portrait of Alexander I of Russia as Grand Duke by Augustin Ritt.

The most memorable miniature in the collection was the superb portrait by Isabey of the five-year old Prince Napoleon Louis, second son of Louis Bonaparte, King of Holland and Hortense de Beauharnais, shown standing in the doorway of the Galerie François I of the Château de Fontainebleau (Fig 1). This miniature realised the highest price ever paid for a continental miniature and was purchased, most fittingly, by a Dutch museum. The prince, whose younger brother afterwards became Napoleon III, was to die in Italy at the age of twenty-seven in the Romagna rising against the Pope. The artist, Jean Baptiste Isabey, like England's Samuel Cooper, survived the political turmoil of his time and his aristocratic clientele prior to the Revolution of 1789 was easily replaced by France's new rulers. Just as Cooper, in earlier years, painted both Oliver Cromwell and Charles II, Isabey progressed from Marie-Antoinette's commission to paint the children of the Comte d'Artois to his appointment as drawing master to Eugène and Hortense de Beauharnais, Josephine Bonaparte's children by her first marriage.

Another miniaturist to turn the reverses of fortune in French history to his own advantage was Jean Baptiste Augustin, who, having first achieved success as a miniaturist in Paris in 1781, was subsequently nominated by Napoleon I as official painter to the Imperial Court and later became painter in ordinary to the cabinet of Louis XVIII. The Holzscheiter Collection included Augustin's portrait of Charles Ferdinand d'Artois, duc de Berry (Fig 7), the ill-fated second son of Charles X who met

Left
Fig 2
RICHARD GIBSON, a lady, and the reverse J BOSSE, a gentleman, signed and dated *1667*, 2⅜in (6cm)
£1,200($2,040)

Right
Fig 3
JOHN HOSKINS, a gentleman aged thirty-two, signed and inscribed with the age of the sitter, *circa* 1625, 1⅜in (3.5cm)
£3,000($5,100)

his death at the hand of an assassin, Louvel, on 13 February 1820. The miniature was in a presentation frame and had been given, in his memory, by the Duke's widow to the Bishop of Chartres.

Portrait miniatures of children have a perennial appeal and the Holzscheiter Collection was not lacking in examples (Figs 4 and 5). The identities of the boy and the girl by Daniel Saint are not known but their innocence and refreshing charm are admirably portrayed by this former pupil of Isabey, who, like his master, enjoyed royal patronage.

Although it is unquestionably for its continental miniatures that this collection will be remembered, it also contained a number of important examples of English miniatures from the seventeenth to the nineteenth centuries. The majority of the more interesting examples were to be found however amongst the earlier works. It has been said of John Hoskins that 'the whole effect of his portraits is simple and dignified',[1] a statement which is substantiated by Hoskins' miniature of an unknown man, aged thirty-two (Fig 3). The miniature is particularly interesting as an early example of Hoskins' work, his earliest known portrait dating from about 1620. It is painted against the blue background characteristic of many of his works prior to 1632.

Cornelius Jonson's oil miniature of Sir Dudley Carleton, later Viscount Dorchester (1573–1632), was perhaps the most significant work in the English section since the artist's work appears rarely at auction (Fig 6). That it should be of a known sitter increases its importance. Carleton himself is remembered not so much in his capacity as diplomat and ambassador as for his suspected complicity in the Gunpowder Plot of 1606. Like Jonson, Richard Gibson, 'the Dwarf', is an artist whose work appears infrequently in the saleroom. He was employed as a page by Charles I. His miniature of a widow (Fig 2) was doubly interesting because the reverse contained a good plumbago portrait of a gentleman, possibly the sitter's husband, by a previously unknown artist, J. Bosse.

It is impossible to discuss here all the works in a collection of this magnitude, but that the sale offered a rare opportunity to collectors and museums alike to acquire works of unique quality and provenance cannot be doubted.

[1] D. Foskett, *Dictionary of British Miniature Painters* (1972), vol I, p 340.

Fig 4
DANIEL SAINT, a young boy, signed, $2\frac{3}{8}$in (6cm)
£1,900($3,230)

Fig 5
DANIEL SAINT, a young girl, signed, $3\frac{7}{8}$in (10cm)
£2,600($4,420)

Fig 6
CORNELIUS JONSON THE ELDER, Sir Dudley Carleton,
later Viscount Dorchester, on copper, $3\frac{3}{4}$in (9.5cm)
£2,600($4,420)

Fig 7
JEAN BAPTISTE AUGUSTIN, Charles Ferdinand
D'Artois, duc de Berry, inscribed *Donné à Mgr
l'Evêque de Chartres, Par S.A.R. Madame la Dsse de
Berry*, $3\frac{3}{8}$in (8.7cm)
£5,800($9,860)

The miniatures illustrated on these two pages were sold in London on 28 March 1977

CONTINENTAL SCHOOL (early
seventeenth century), a young
child holding a parrot, 2in (5.2cm)
£8,200($13,940)

Right
NICHOLAS HILLIARD, a lady aged 31,
dated *1576*, diameter 1½in (3.8cm)
£7,000($11,900)

NICHOLAS HILLIARD, a nobleman, aged 33, signed
with monogram *NH* and dated *1572*
£64,000($108,800)
This is one of eight recorded signed miniatures
by Hilliard

PETER CROSS, Robert Kerr, 4th Earl and 1st
Marquess of Lothian, signed with initials and
dated *1667*, and repeated on the reverse, 2⅞in (7.5cm)
£5,000($8,500)

JOHN HOSKINS, Lady Anne Fanshawe, signed
and dated *1657*, 2½in (6.5cm)
£8,000($13,600)

The miniatures on this page are from the collection of the late Greta S. Heckett and were sold in London on
11 July 1977

ROSALBA CARRIERA, a woman as
Cleopatra, executed at Venice, *circa* 1720,
3¾in (9.5cm)
Fr36,000(£4,285:$7,284)

Right
JEAN PETITOT, *La Grande Mademoiselle*
Anne-Marie-Louise d'Orléans,
Duchess of Montpensier, *circa* 1680,
1¾in (4.4cm)
Fr26,000(£3,095:$5,261)

HEINRICH FRIEDRICH FÜGER, the
young Archduchess Marie
Clémentine of Austria, 3¼in (8.3cm)
Fr65,000(£7,738:$13,154)

CORNELIUS HOYER, a young artist seated on a
couch, signed, diameter 2½in (6.5cm)
Fr18,000(£2,142:$3,642).

BERNHARD, CHEVALIER DE GUERARD, reputedly
Comte Nicholas Esterhazy and his young wife,
la Marquise de Roisin, *circa* 1799,
diameter 3½in (9cm)
Fr30,000(£3,571:$6,071)

The miniatures on this page are from the collection of the late Greta S. Heckett and were sold in Monte Carlo on
4 May 1977

PETER BOY THE ELDER, an Imperial enamel miniature on gold of Augustus II, King of Poland and Elector of Saxony, inscribed on the reverse *AUGUSTUS. II./REX POLONIARUM/ELECTOR SAXONIAE/coronatus d:15 sept:/Anno 1697, circa* 1720, 4¾in (12cm)
London £11,000($18,700). 13.XII.76

Silver and Pewter

One of a pair of Charles II candlesticks, maker's mark of Jacob Bodendick, London, 1667,
height 9¼in (23.5cm) London £33,000($56,100). 2.VI.77
From the collection of The Most Hon the Marquess of Lansdowne, PC

A German parcel-gilt two-handled covered bowl, probably by Niklaus (Claus) Schmidt, Lubeck, *circa* 1680, diameter 8¾in (21.6cm) £10,000($17,000)

A pair of Dutch standing salts, maker's mark of Thomas Bogaert, Utrecht, 1624, height 7¼in (18.5cm) £22,000($37,400) From the collection of His Grace The Duke of Hamilton and Brandon

Thomas Bogaert was born in Utrecht, probably in 1598. He was apprenticed in 1611, perhaps to Adam van Vianen, and became a master in 1622. His work was strongly influenced by Adam van Vianen, illustrated in this instance by his use of the lobate ornament, and the figures modelled in the round

These salts were formerly in the collection of William Beckford

The objects illustrated on this page were sold in London on 2 June 1977

A South German wood casket, fitted with a silver-gilt and polychrome enamel toilet set including five pieces by Tob. Baur, Augsburg, *circa* 1710, width of the casket 17½in (44.5cm) £10,000($17,000)

A pair of Louis XIV silver-gilt table candlesticks, maker's mark of Pierre Masse, Paris, 1664, height 6¾in (17.4cm) £30,000($51,000)

The objects illustrated on this page were sold at Mentmore on 19 May 1977

A Dutch ewer and companion basin, maker's mark on both pieces of Christian van Vianen, Utrecht, 1632, height of the ewer 9½in (24.3cm), width of the basin 20½in (52cm)
London £125,000($212,500). 2.VI.77

Christian van Vianen was Court Goldsmith to Charles I of England and arrived in the country early in 1630, being granted a pension of £39 per annum in April of that year. He subsequently returned to Utrecht, where he made this ewer and basin, but was back in England by 1633 and remained there until about 1643

The arms are those of Augustus Frederick, Duke of Sussex, superimposed on the arms of the original Dutch owner. These pieces probably came to England in the early nineteenth century and were acquired by the Duke of Sussex (1773-1843), son of George III and a keen collector of silver. They probably comprised lot 78 in the sale of the Duke's collection (Christie's, 22 June 1843) where they fetched £85

A German silver-gilt ewer and
sideboard dish, maker's mark *D.R.*,
conjoined for Peter or Salomon von der
Rennen, Danzig, *circa* 1650, height of
ewer 13in (33cm), width of dish
25¼in (64cm)
New York $32,000(£18,823). 26.X.76

Fig 1   A portrait of Paul Revere II (1735-1818) by John Singleton Copley, painted *circa* 1768-70. Museum of Fine Arts, Boston, gift of Joseph W., William B. and Edward H. R. Revere

Among the numerous portraits by Copley of prominent Bostonians, this one is most unusual as the artist has depicted his sitter dressed in craftsman's attire with his tools close by and a teapot in hand awaiting the burin

Paul Revere, Boston's versatile goldsmith

Wendy Cooper

New England's most widely known colonial patriot is, undoubtedly, Paul Revere. The famous ride that he took on the evening of 18 April, 1775 to warn the towns-people between Boston and Concord of the movement of the British troops, has immortalised him in the hearts and minds of generations of school children and adults. Henry Wordsworth Longfellow further strengthened the creation of this American folk hero in 1860 when he popularised him in verse in *Tales of a Wayside Inn*. Yet the men and women of Boston who knew Revere during his lifetime must surely have had a different perspective of the man. Not only was his craftsmanship the finest and his clientele the most notable, but his civic accomplishments were numerous and well-known and his benevolent service to the public unqualified.

Revere began his mature life as a highly talented artisan, but by the end of his career he had become one of Boston's foremost businessmen and entrepreneurs. His lifetime spanned not only the birth of a new nation and a significant change in style and fashion, but more importantly he witnessed a society dependent upon a hand-crafted technology change dramatically with the advance of technology and mechan-isation. Throughout this era of great change Revere was in the forefront, not only as a prominent and conscientious citizen adding to the Revolutionary fervour with his incendiary print-making, but also with his own distinct shift in artistic style after the Revolution and his important work in the iron-founding and copper-rolling businesses.

Today Revere is of prime importance to silver collectors and scholars since such a great volume of his work survives to document the changing tastes and fashions of one of colonial America's most prosperous and *élite* societies. Furthermore much of his work is enumerated in his Daybooks, which document work from the early 1760s to the 1790s. These records are a rare survival, for they are among only a handful of accounts of the work of an eighteenth-century goldsmith still extant. However, they do not record everything that Revere wrought: for example, his best-known commis-sion, the famed Liberty Bowl of 1768, is not recorded in these books. Though they detail specifically Revere's clients, what he was making for them, and how much he charged, they do not, unfortunately, tell us anything about the makeup of his shop, the number of apprentices he had, and who they were.

Born in Boston in 1735, Paul Revere's destiny was probably pretty well determined for him at an early age since his father, Paul Revere I, was a master goldsmith who

Fig 2   A silver standing cup, Paul Revere,
Boston, 1758, marked ·*REVERE* on rim,
height 10in (25.5cm)
Old South Church, Boston

could train his son to follow in his craft. Paul Revere II was a first generation
American. His father, Apollos Rivoire, was a French Huguenot, born in Riaucaud,
France, who came to New England around 1716 and very shortly became apprenticed
to Boston's leading goldsmith, John Coney. When Coney died in 1722, the young
Rivoire became an independent goldsmith. In 1729 he married Deborah Hitchbourne,
and it was probably at this time that he anglicised his name, and has since been known
as Paul Revere I. The second child (and first son) born to Deborah and Paul Revere was
Paul, the patriot. He was apprenticed to his father, but the elder Paul died in 1754
before his son had completed the specified seven year apprenticeship. However, Paul
was probably quite competent by that time and he carried on in his father's shop,
helping his mother as she managed the family business. In 1756 he was commissioned
as a second-lieutenant in the infantry and left Boston for a short time to fight in the
French and Indian wars. By the end of that year Revere was back in Boston working as
a master goldsmith, and in 1757 he married Sara Orne, the first of his two wives, each
of whom bore him eight children.

Fig 3   A silver sugar bowl and creampot, Paul Revere, Boston, 1761, both marked ·*REVERE* and script *PR* on bottom, and cover of bowl marked at base of finial with script *PR*, both engraved with Chandler coat of arms and crest; height of sugar bowl 6½in (16.5cm), height of creampot 4⅜in (11cm)
Museum of Fine Arts, Boston, Pauline Revere Thayer Collection

Although Revere's Daybooks do not begin to record his work until 1761, his earliest dated piece of silver known today is a standing communion cup (Fig 2) made in 1758 as a gift to the South Church in Boston, from the Reverend Thomas Prince. In his will, dated 2 October 1758, Prince left money for the church to purchase 'a Piece of Plate of the Form and Height of that last presented to ye sd Church'.[1] Apparently the last piece of silver that had been presented to the Church was a French chalice made in 1692 by the Parisian goldsmith Adrian Daveau (active 1656–94), and given by Mr Anthony Brackett.

By the early 1760s Revere had mastered the fine craft of goldsmithing, and several of his early works firmly attest to his competence. A superbly wrought covered sugar bowl and a matching creampot with overall *repoussé* decoration and heraldic engraving are foremost examples of what this twenty-six year old goldsmith was capable of achieving (Fig 3). These two pieces were commissioned by the little-known goldsmith Benjamin Greene as wedding presents to his sister-in-law, Lucretia Chandler, in 1761. Both of these pieces of silver are recorded in the Daybooks; however, Revere did not charge Greene for the 'sugar dish' until 11 March 1762. Upon Lucretia Chandler's marriage, Revere also made for her a handsome circular salver with a moulded edge and applied scroll and shell motifs, the epitome of rococo expression. In the centre of this salver Revere engraved the Chandler coat of arms in an elaborate cartouche surmounted by the family crest. Curiously, this salver does not appear in Revere's Daybooks although there are entries for other salvers in the books. Revere made an almost identical salver for Sarah Tyng in the same year, and correspondingly engraved it with the Tyng arms.[2] Perhaps the most interesting salvers made by any

[1] E. Alfred Jones, *The Old Silver of American Churches*, (Letchworth, 1913), p 50, pls XXI and XXIII.
[2] Kathryn C. Buhler, *American Silver 1655–1825*, (Boston: Museum of Fine Arts, 1972), vol II, no 343, pp 392–93.

Fig 4   A silver tankard, Paul Revere, Boston, *circa* 1770, marked with maker's name in full on body and base, height 8½in (21.5cm)
New York $45,000. 27.IV.76
Formerly in the collection of the late J. P. Morgan

colonial goldsmith are the pair Revere fashioned in 1762, and sold to his fellow goldsmith-engraver, Nathaniel Hurd. Hurd then apparently engraved them with the Franklin family coat of arms, marked them on the upper side with his own mark, (Revere had marked them on the bottom) and then sold them to his own client. These salvers are just one of several instances of Revere's fellow goldsmiths buying silver pieces from him and then re-marketing them. Among the other goldsmiths recorded in Revere's accounts are John Coburn, Nathaniel Austin, Samuel Minott, Jonathan Trott and Joseph Coolidge, Jr.

Drinking vessels were popular items, principally tankards and canns, and Revere made a large number of these, varying greatly in size and weight. Occasionally they were made in pairs, and in 1772 Revere recorded making a set of six that were sold to Jonathan Trott.[3] The largest tankard that Revere is recorded as having made was for Captain Joseph Goodwin in 1769.[4] Its total weight was 44 oz, 10 dwt. The Goodwin tankard is distinguished not only by its unusually heavy weight, but also by a plain domed top, double-scroll handle and finely engraved arms in cartouche flanked at the bottom with scrolls bearing the name of the owner and the whole surmounted with his crest. Another fine tankard (Fig 4), probably fashioned by Revere about the same

[3] Martha Gandy Fales, *American Silver in The Henry Francis DuPont Winterthur Museum,* (Winterthur 1958), no 117.
[4] Museum of Fine Arts, Boston, *Paul Revere's Boston: 1735–1818,* (Boston, 1972), no 13, pp 24–25.

Fig 5   A silver teapot and
creampot, Paul Revere,
Boston, 1783, both
marked ·*REVERE* and
inscribed *MRH* for Moses
and Rachel Hayes, height
of teapot 6½in (16.5cm),
height of creampot
5¼in (13.5cm)
Private collection

time as the Goodwin example, is of slightly lesser weight, but has an equally fine
engraved coat of arms in cartouche. The arms on this tankard are presently unidentified, and it does not appear to be recorded in the Daybooks. The S-scroll handle
terminating in a cast grotesque mask and the wrythen finial crowning the top make
this a notable example of Revere's finest workmanship.

Revere's production prior to the Revolution was not only outstanding in quality, it
was also extremely varied. He cleaned and repaired silver for his customers, as well as
repairing china, cleaning false teeth, and selling dentifrice. His copperplate engraving
was extensive, both for Boston's most popular printers, Edes and Gill, and for
individuals who wanted their arms engraved upon bookplates, and for various
associations that desired notices and certificates. In September 1764 Revere charged
Andrew Oliver £4 'To Making a Sugar Dish out of an Ostrich Egg', and in November
1772, John Welsh bought 'a Silver Squirrel Chain' from him for 10 shillings. Revere
appears to have worked steadily up until April of 1775, although much of the
recorded work during the last few months was for engraving copperplates for *The
Royal American Magazine*, and a few other miscellaneous sales and jobs.

Revere's involvement in Boston's Revolutionary activity between 1775 and 1779 is
well-known, including his commission as a major and later as a lieutenant-colonel of
the artillery. For several years he was in command of Castle William, a fortress in
Boston harbour, and in 1779 he led the artillery forces in the ill-fated Penobscot
Expedition. His Daybooks indicate that by 1781 he had resumed his goldsmithing
activities, and the next year he was making silver in the newly fashionable neo-classical
style. This is exemplified by the round, drum-form teapot that he made in 1782 for
his cousin Thomas Hichborn, weighing 17oz, with gadrooned decoration. The next year
Revere made an almost identical pot for Michael Moses Hayes, but this time he made it
even more fashionable with the addition of applied, beaded decoration, distinctly
neo-classical in taste (Fig 5). At the same time that Revere made the teapot for Hayes,
he also fashioned an inverted, pyriform creampot with a double scroll handle and
matching beaded, decoration on the foot. Both of these pieces he engraved with the
cypher *MRH* for Moses and Rachel Hayes. Hayes was a steady client of Revere's as
well as a friend and fellow Mason. He was also Boston's most prominent Jew and was
married to Rachel Myers, sister of the well-known New York goldsmith, Myer Myers.

Fig 7   A silver teapot and sugar dish, Paul Revere, Boston, 1791, unmarked, each inscribed on bottom *HR* for Hannah Rowe, height of teapot 6¾in (17cm), height of sugar dish (including handle) 7⅛in (18cm)
New York $30,000. 25.I.74

Although Revere neglected to place his mark on either of these pieces he did record them in his Daybook on February 1791. The sugar dish appears to be a unique form in his repertoire of neo-classical silver. Also in 1791, Revere billed Hannah Rowe for 'a Silver Tea Urn' weighing 111oz, the total cost of which was £84 12s 4d, including the cost of the ivory key which controlled the flow through the spigot

Fig 6   A silver teapot and stand, Paul Revere, Boston, 1786, both marked *REVERE* on base and
inscribed *PW* in oval medallion on front of pot and *LW to PW* on top of tray, overall height
6in (15cm)
New York $37,000(£21,765). 19.XI.76

This teapot and stand was made for Miss Peggy White (the beautiful young woman shown in the
miniature accompanying it) upon her marriage to Bailey Bartlett of Haverhill, Massachusetts,
21 November 1786. While apparently unrecorded by Revere in his Daybooks, it was purchased
as a gift by Leonard White, the brother of the bride

Sometime in the later 1780s or '90s Revere made a set of four butter boats for Hayes
(Fig 8), and while these are not recorded in the Daybooks, they correspond with other
Hayes silver in the application of the beaded decoration. Among the other purchases
that Hayes made from Revere were 'knee Buckles', 'a pr of Spectagal Frames', '6 large
Silver spoons', 'Pr Gold knee buckles', 'Pr Women's shoe buckles paste pattern', 'A
pr large silver Hooks & Eyes', 'a Silver Sword hilt', 'a new Scabboard', and finally
'4 Silver goblets' with engraved cyphers.

By 1785 Revere was making elliptical shaped teapots using sheet silver seamed on
the side instead of raising the bodies as he had done with his drumform pots of just a
few years before. These oval pots were the latest fashion and varied from a simple,
plain elliptical form, such as the one made for John Warren in 1785, to the moulded
oval form (Fig 6), and also the very popular fluted form (Fig 7) that was used for urn-
shaped sugar bowls, creampots, a rare sugar dish, as well as monumental tea and

coffee urns. Occasionally the oval teapots were accompanied by small conforming trays or stands. By the 1790s it was much more customary for a client to order a whole service of matching silver, and Revere had two such clients in 1792 and 1793 who desired these full services. The largest service that he made was for John Templeman in 1792,[5] and while this did not include a large tea urn, it did include an unusual tea caddy and a tea-shell used to remove the tea from the caddy. In 1793 Burrell Carnes of Lancaster, Massachusetts, ordered a large fluted and engraved coffee urn as well as a fluted teapot and stand, a fluted sugar urn, and a scalloped tureen ladle.[6]

While Revere is known to have made at least five scalloped-edge salvers before the Revolution, there is only one known piece of this type that he produced after the war. Among a number of articles requested by the Derby family of Salem is a magnificent salver made in 1797 for Elias Hasket Derby (Fig 9). This piece is listed in Revere's Daybooks as weighing 41 oz, 11 dwt, and in a small Cash Book among the Revere Papers[7] there are some sketches for the engraved decoration with the notation 'waiter'. This superb piece is certainly among the most beautiful and significant creations of Revere's later years.

Revere's post-Revolutionary interests were more varied than ever, and by 1788 he was involved in an iron-foundry business with his son Joseph Warren Revere. The primary output in this venture was the production of at least 395 bells, the first of which was cast in 1792. By 1800 Revere had purchased property in Canton, Massachusetts, and established copper-rolling mills — the first commercially successful production of this commodity in the country. Copper from his mills was eventually used for the dome of Boston's new State House designed by Charles Bulfinch and the bottom of the frigate *Constitution*.

Presumably by 1810 Revere had finished his active goldsmithing, since he was then seventy-four and resided mostly in Canton Dale, as he called his country property. The latest known dated piece of silver by Revere is a pitcher made in 1806 and presented to Samuel Gilbert.[8] Its form was derived from the popular Liverpool earthenware pitchers from England. In 1813 Gilbert Stuart's painting depicts Revere as a distinguished, ageing entrepreneur who had obviously led a very full and successful life. No longer was he the youthful, talented goldsmith of the Copley picture (Fig 1), but rather an enterprising businessman who had distinguished himself in the service of his country, as an active Bostonian, an outstanding Mason, and a benevolent neighbour. When Revere passed away in May of 1818, *The Boston Intelligencer* noted that his death was 'an irreparable loss', especially to the 'extensive circle of his own connections', and furthermore declared that:

'Every person, whose whole life, when considered in regard to the public, or to its private transactions has been spent in active exertions, in useful pursuits, in the performance of acts of disinterested benevolence or general utility, or in the exercise of the best affectations of the heart and most practical qualities of understanding, has an undoubted title to posthumous panegyric.'

[5] *Colonial Silversmiths, Masters and Apprentices* (Boston: Museum of Fine Arts, 1956), p 77, fig 64.
[6] Buhler, *American Silver*, no 343, pp 392–93.
[7] The Revere family papers are now in the possession of The Massachusetts Historical Society.
[8] This pitcher is owned by the Paul Revere Insurance Company. Revere is known to have made at least eleven pitchers in this form.

Fig 8   A pair of silver butter boats (from a set of four), Paul Revere, Boston, *circa* 1790, marked *REVERE* in rectangle and *·REVERE* on each bottom, and inscribed *Hays* on each front, length of each 8in (20cm)
Sold in New York in 1973 for $36,500.
Private collection

Fig 9   A silver salver, Paul Revere, Boston, 1797, marked *REVERE* in rectangle, inscribed *EHD* on face, length 17in (43cm)
Yale University Art Gallery, the Mabel Brady Garvan Collection

A pair of George III silver-gilt three light candelabra, maker's mark of John Scofield, London, 1791-92, height 21in (53.4cm)
$20,000(£11,764)

A George III silver-gilt two-handled cup and cover, maker's mark of Robert Sharp, London, 1792, height 20½in (52cm)
$3,000(£1,764)
The arms are those of H. S. H. Christian Frederick, Margrave of Brandenburg Anspach and Bayreuth, who married Elizabeth, daughter of Augustus, 4th Earl of Berkeley, on 13 October 1791

The pieces illustrated on these two pages are from the collection of the Dick family and were sold in New York on 16 December 1976. The Dick family silver was acquired in England and Ireland over three generations, between about 1765-1850. Quintin Dick I, one of the founders of the Bank of Ireland, was responsible for the early acquisitions, including the Thomas Gilpin Cup (p 295) made in 1750. His grandsons Hugh and Quintin Dick II, were responsible for adding the bulk of the collection between the Regency period and the mid nineteenth century. The brothers died unmarried and the collection went to relations whose descendants eventually settled in Canada

A George II silver-gilt sideboard dish, maker's mark of Paul Crespin, London, 1727, diameter 28in (71cm)
$28,000(£16,470).

The arms are those of Richard, Marquess of Buckingham, KG, Earl Temple of Stowe, who later
became Duke of Buckingham and Chandos

One from a set of four mid eighteenth-century table candlesticks, two depicting Daphne (one illustrated) and two depicting Apollo, apparently unmarked, attributed to George Michael Moser, RA, height 14¾in (37.5cm) London £13,500($22,950). 2.VI.77
From the collection of Mrs E. M. P. Capell

A drawing for a candlestick by Moser (illustrated above right) is in the Victoria and Albert Museum and forms the subject of an article by Shirley Bury and Desmond Fitz-Gerald in the Museum Year Book, 1969. This Daphne candlestick is an almost identical representation of Moser's drawing and it seems very likely that the manufacture of these candlesticks was supervised by Moser and possible that he also did the chasing. Although Moser was principally an enameller and gold chaser, the lack of any silversmith's mark or hallmark on the candlesticks adds weight to this attribution. In an obituary written by Sir Joshua Reynolds (1783), Moser is described as the first gold chaser in the Kingdom, possessed of a universal knowledge of all branches of painting and sculpture, 'in every sense the father of the present race of artists'

A George II two-handled cup and cover, maker's mark of Thomas Gilpin, London, 1750, height 18in (45.7cm)
New York $12,500(£7,352). 16.XII.76
From the collection of the Dick family

The monogram and crest are those of Quintin Dick

Opposite above
A George III oval wine cistern, maker's mark of Daniel Smith and Robert Sharp, London, 1773, width 34in (86.4cm) London £27,000($45,900). 10.III.77

The arms are those of Primrose quartering Cressy for Neil, 3rd Earl of Rosebery who was born in 1729

Opposite below
An electroplated electrotype of an English wine cistern, maker's mark of Elkington & Co, Birmingham, after 1881, the silver original of 1734 is in Leningrad, height 37in (94cm) New York $18,000(£10,588). 22.IX.76

Elkington & Co visited Russia in 1881, after signing an agreement with the Tsesarevich Nicholas, to make casts for a range of electrotype copies

The Brighton Cup, Brighton Races, 1871. A parcel-gilt and partially frosted trophy-vase and cover, maker's mark of Frederick Elkington of Elkington & Co, Birmingham, 1870, height 33in (84.2cm) Mentmore £9,000($15,300). 23.V.77

This cup is inscribed on one side: *Won by/Favonius* and decorated on the other with a scene in relief depicting an incident in the early history of Brighton (AD 1276), in which the Earl de Warenne, 7th Lord of the Manor of Brighton and Lewes, was called before the justices to show cause why his lands should not be confiscated to the Crown. Drawing an old rusty sword, he declared: *By this instrument doe I holde my landes and by the same I entende to defende them*

A sauceboat and
stand, maker's mark of
Martelé, The Gorham Co,
Providence, R.I., *circa*
1900, length of stand
9$\frac{3}{8}$in (24cm)
New York $1,100(£647).
19.XI.76

A silver-gilt inkstand,
maker's mark of Robert
Garard II of R. & S.
Garrard, London, 1845,
length 10$\frac{1}{2}$in (26.7cm)
Mentmore £1,500
($2,550). 23.V.77

A presentation ewer 'in the florid style of Louis XIV', maker's mark of Robert Garrard II of R. & S. Garrard, London, 1835, height 30in (76.4cm) London £12,000($20,400). 13.I.77
From the collection of His Grace The Duke of Beaufort, KG, PC, GCVO

This ewer was shown at the Great Exhibition, 1851, from which catalogue the above description is quoted

A centrepiece and mirror plateau, maker's mark of Robert Garrard II of R. & S. Garrard, London, 1842, diameter 33in (84cm)
London £32,000($54,400). 28.VII.77
From the collection of the Worshipful Company of Grocers

The Brighton Cup, Brighton Races, 1869. A centrepiece of frosted silver and bronze, from designs and models by Raphael Monti, maker's mark of C. F. Hancocks & Co., London, 1869, height 23¾in (59.7cm) Mentmore £13,000($22,100). 23.V.77

One inscription reads: *Won by/Baron M. Rothschild's/'Restitution'/4 Yrs. Old*. The subject is the assembling of the British warriors and their Druids on the rocks of Pevensey Bay to resist the landing of Caesar and his legions

One of a pair of broad-rimmed dishes by James Taudin, dated *1680*, diameter 14½in (36.9cm) London £1,200($2,040). 13.VI.77 From the collection of K. W. Bradshaw

A pair of Queen Anne relief-cast porringers by John Quick of London, *circa* 1710-15, diameter 7¼in (18.4cm) London £3,000($5,100). 16.III.77

A late William and Mary double-handled posset pot, maker's mark *IL* stamped three times, *circa* 1695, height 5¾in (14.5cm) London £2,400($4,080). 13.VI.77 From the collection of K. W. Bradshaw

An American domed-top tankard by William Will, Philadelphia, *circa* 1764-98, height 7½in (19cm) New York $7,750(£4,558). 27.I.77

Arms, Armour and Militaria

Detail

A Dutch East India Company bronze cannon, the breech inscribed *De Vereenichde Oost-Indische Comp^e*, the finial re-inforce with the weight 5320 (in Amsterdam pounds) and signed *Henricus Mevrs Me Fecit 1604*, length $152\frac{1}{4}$in (385.7cm)
London £9,000($15,300). 19.IV.77
Sold on behalf of and by arrangement with the legal owner, the State of The Netherlands

The inscription on the breech of this cannon shows that it was cast by the Dutch founder Master Henricus Meurs in 1604 for the Dutch East India Company which had been founded in 1602. It was recovered by the Belgian underwater explorer Robert Stenuit from the wreck of the Dutch East Indiaman *Witte Leeuw* which was sunk off the island of St Helena in 1613. A dozen iron and three bronze cannon were counted on the sea-bed but only the latter were retrieved. They are in remarkably good condition and of particular interest being the earliest guns of the East India Company extant. In addition to the finely moulded decorative mouldings the cannon bears an excellent representation of an early seventeenth-century three masted ship under full sail, surmounted by the initial of the Amsterdam Chamber of the Company

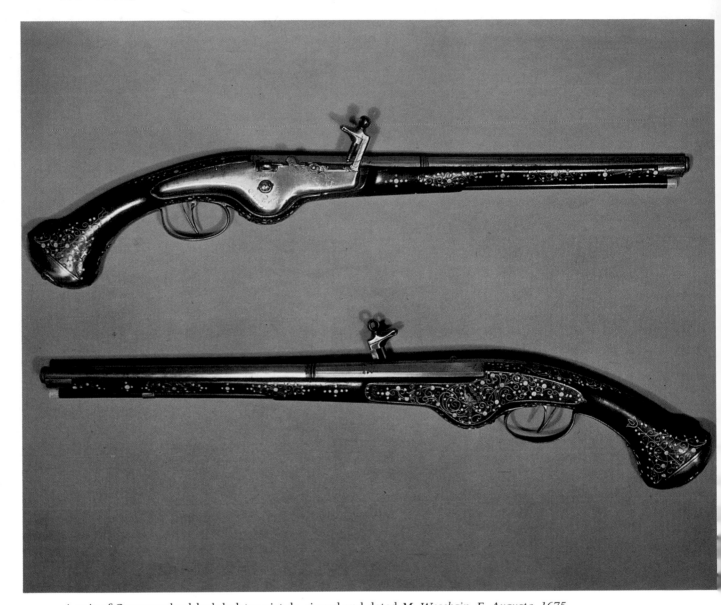

A pair of German wheel-lock holster pistols, signed and dated *M. Weschgin. F. Augusta, 1675*, stamped *G.V.T.H.*, length 22⅝in (57.5cm)
London £9,800($16,660). 12.X.76

Augusta is the Latin name for Augsburg. Melchior Wetschgin is believed to have worked at Augsburg, *circa* 1675

The gold sword of honour presented by the Continental Congress in 1779 to General Marie Jean Joseph Lafayette, Paris, overall length 38½in (97.8cm) New York $145,000(£85,294). 20.XI.76

On 24 August 1779 Benjamin Franklin wrote to Lafayette, stating that 'The Congress, sensible of your merit towards the United States, but unable adequately to reward it, determined to present you with a sword, as a mark of their grateful acknowledgements. They directed it to be ornamented with suitable devices . . .'. Shown in this illustration, in the oval medallion on the pommel, is a Frenchman treading on a lion, symbolising Lafayette's victory over the British forces. Also evident are Lafayette's arms on the ovoid terminal and trophies of war on the handle. The guard is inscribed *FROM THE AMERICAN CONGRESS TO THE MARQUIS DE LA FAYETTE 1779.*

The leather sheath is mounted in gold with a relief on one side only, showing the seated figure of Victory from which hangs a banner bearing the arms of France.

During the 'Terror' in Paris, Lafayette hid the sword underground, with the result that the blade corroded. It was replaced by the steel blade from the sword presented to him by the Garde National de Paris in 1791. This blade was forged with iron bolts of the Bastille and is inscribed *Réveil de la Liberte* [*sic*] recalling the heroic part that Lafayette had played during the first period of the French Revolution.

The union of this blade and hilt, each with its own associations, gives the sword a double historical significance

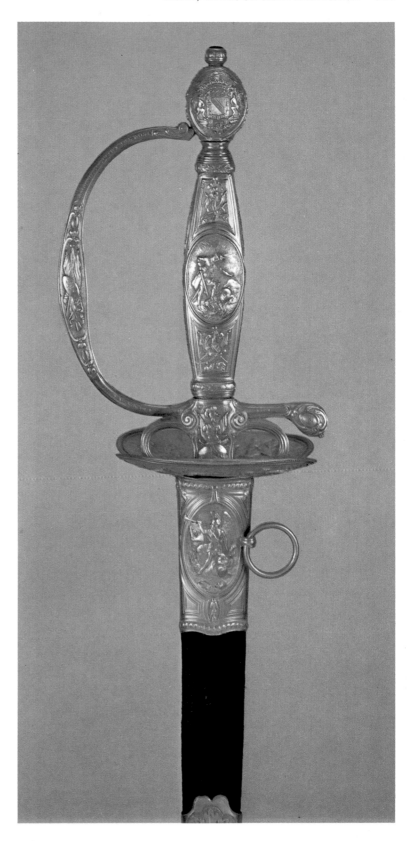

An engraved Henry rifle, serial number *8845*, initials on the top of the frame *G.C.U.*, overall length 43½in (110.5cm)
Los Angeles $17,000(£10,000). 27.III.77

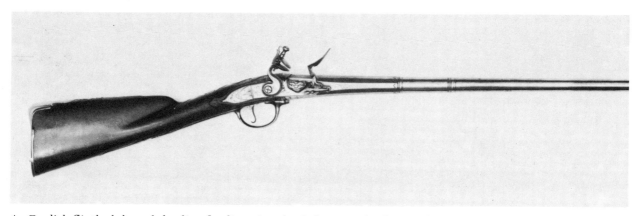

An English flintlock breech-loading fowling piece by Robert Rowland, signed, struck with London
and Foreigners mark of the Gunmakers' Company and inscribed *Mr John Tournay, near London
Bridge or Near Kingston in Surrey, 1718*, length 54in (137.2cm)
London £5,400($9,180). 15.II.77

A pair of D.B. 12-bore semi-self-opening single-trigger
round-action sidelock ejector sporting guns by Boss &
Co, serial numbers *7915/7916*, length 44¾in (113.7cm)
Gleneagles £6,500($11,050). 23.VIII.76
From the collection of Captain W. Butler-Bowdon

A pair of D.B. 12-bore self-opening sidelock ejector
sporting guns by J. Purdey & Sons, serial numbers
28063/28064, length 45⅛in (114.6cm)
London £11,000($18,700). 14.XII.76

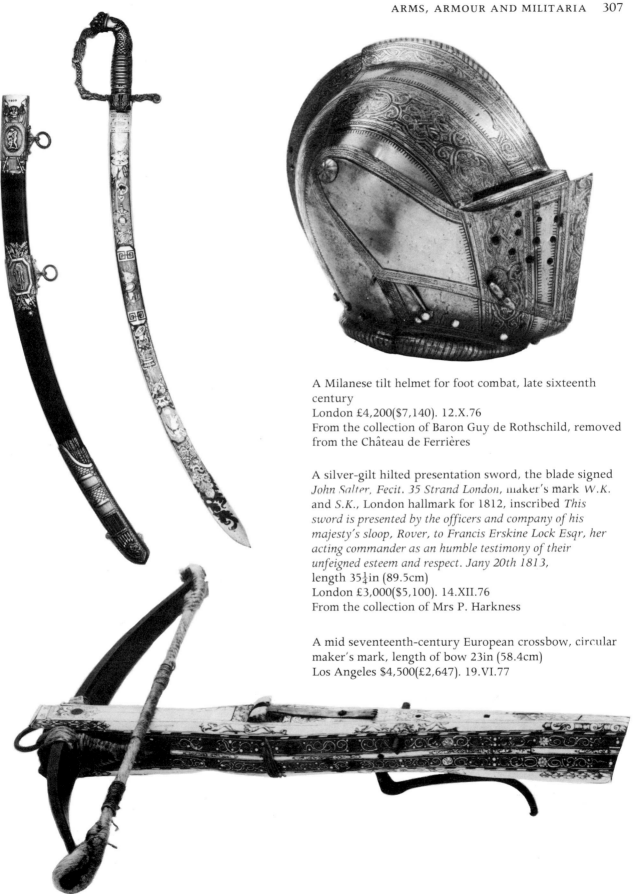

A Milanese tilt helmet for foot combat, late sixteenth century
London £4,200($7,140). 12.X.76
From the collection of Baron Guy de Rothschild, removed from the Château de Ferrières

A silver-gilt hilted presentation sword, the blade signed *John Salter, Fecit. 35 Strand London*, maker's mark *W.K.* and *S.K.*, London hallmark for 1812, inscribed *This sword is presented by the officers and company of his majesty's sloop, Rover, to Francis Erskine Lock Esqr, her acting commander as an humble testimony of their unfeigned esteem and respect. Jany 20th 1813*, length 35¼in (89.5cm)
London £3,000($5,100). 14.XII.76
From the collection of Mrs P. Harkness

A mid seventeenth-century European crossbow, circular maker's mark, length of bow 23in (58.4cm)
Los Angeles $4,500(£2,647). 19.VI.77

A jacket which belonged to Napoleon Bonaparte, part of the uniform of the Chasseurs à Cheval worn by the Emperor at the battle of Waterloo, 1815
Monte Carlo Fr190,000 (£22,619:$38,452). 4.XII.76
Formerly in the collection of Marshal Blücher von Wahlstatt

This jacket was captured on the night of the battle from Napoleon's coach, an elaborate vehicle made by Symonds of Brussels for the Russian campaign. It contained many of the Emperor's personal belongings, some of which are also in the Wellington Collection, for example, his silver-gilt travelling canteen. Together these will form a special group in the projected Wellington Museum at Stratfield Saye

An Emperor's jacket

The Duke of Wellington

For those attending the Monte Carlo sale of December 1976, the military tunic worn by Napoleon Bonaparte and captured from his coach as he fled from the scene of his last battle on the field of Waterloo, 18 June 1815, symbolised not only a great and complex character in European history, but also his catastrophic fall from world power in a single day. The record price indicated, to some extent, the emotional response which Napoleon's name can still invoke in the Western world. After the sale, the jacket was presented to the Wellington Museum Trust by the Wellington Collection and it will be one of the most important exhibits in the proposed Wellington Museum for which the Trust, a registered charity, has been set up to generate funds. It is at present displayed in the house at Stratfield Saye.

The coat belongs to the undress uniform of the Chasseurs à Cheval of the Imperial Guard of which unit Napoleon was Colonel. Three similar jackets are known. Napoleon is buried in one; the second is at the Musée de l'Armée, Paris, and the third in the Musée de Sens. The one at Stratfield Saye had been in the collection of the Blücher family since it was presented to Marshal Blücher, Commander of the Prussian Army at Waterloo, together with other items taken from Napoleon's coach.

The uniform of the Chasseurs à Cheval was habitually worn by the Emperor except on ceremonial occasions, and was the one which symbolised for the army his dual personality, Emperor of the French and Citizen Soldier. To emphasise still further the comradely image, he usually wore the insignia of a non-commissioned officer – hence the well known nickname 'Little Corporal', a term not of derision but affection when used by his men.

The history of this uniform begins in Italy in 1796, when Napoleon took over the guides he found at Albenga and from these men formed his own 'Company of Guides of the Commander-in-Chief', the forerunners of the Chasseurs à Cheval of the Imperial Guard. Bonaparte's Guides soon created an illustrious reputation for bravery and devotion. They traditionally wore green, which was also Napoleon's favourite colour. During the campaign in the Po Valley he relied very heavily on this unit and in return, Napoleon concerned himself with every detail of their welfare. It was from this period that Napoleon adopted their uniform. When he was appointed General Commander of the Eastern Army in 1798 he sent for his Guides and they fought brilliantly in Egypt and Syria. The unit was reunited in Paris in 1802 and on 6 August they were officially incorporated in the Imperial Guard, joining the second squadron, the Chasseurs à Cheval.

On the disastrous day at Waterloo, wearing his Chasseurs uniform, he watched their last heroic action as part of the Imperial Guard from the rise of La Belle Alliance. Up to that moment, during eight hours of battle, he had maintained his usual serenity but, shortly after 6 o'clock, as he watched the British attack through his spy glass, he suddenly became 'as pale as death'. The Old Guard were not only receiving a frontal attack, but Blücher's canons were firing into their flank. They began to break. 'All is lost for the present', said Napoleon, and rode off the field.

His movements after this are obscure. Some authorities state that he rode directly to Charleroi, but the account given by a Prussian officer, Major von Keller, in command of a contingent of troops pursuing the enemy, seems authentic. He reported that the Prussians arrived at the town of Genappe, not far from Waterloo, at 11 o'clock on the night of 18 June. The town was barricaded and held by the French, who maintained a constant barrage of artillery and musket fire. However, the place was taken by storm and near the entrance to the village von Keller met Napoleon's travelling carriage, drawn by six horses with the coachman and postillion ready mounted. Confident that he was about to capture Bonaparte, he ordered the coachman to stop but he did not obey and was immediately killed, together with the two leading coach horses. Von Keller then forced open one of the doors of the carriage but in the interval Napoleon had escaped by the opposite door, leaving in such haste that he dropped his hat, sword and cloak and these were afterwards picked up in the road.

Von Keller claimed the carriage as his booty. He later brought it to England and sold it to the British Government. A full description of its contents on arrival was printed for William Bullock of the London Museum in 1816, together with a detailed account of the capture and the following letter from Prince Blücher to his wife, written immediately after the battle. This letter throws an interesting light on how he acquired the jacket.

My dear wife, you will remember what I promised you, and I have kept my word. The enemy's superiority of numbers obliged me to give way on the 17th; but on the 18th, in conjunction with my friend Wellington, I put an end at once to Buonaparte's dancing. His army is completely routed, and the whole of his artillery, baggage, caissons, and equipages, are in my hands; the insignia of all the various orders he had worn, are just brought to me, having been found in his carriage, in a casket. I had two horses killed under me yesterday. It will soon be all over with Buonaparte. Blücher.

Further evidence regarding the jacket exists in a letter from Horace Churchill who served with Wellington at Waterloo. Writing to his father from Le Cateau on 24 June 1815, he says. 'I rode over yesterday with Lord Wellington to see Blücher. We saw Bonaparte's carriage – his hat, cloak, coat and all his orders taken in it. His hat fits me exactly! Would I had such a head under it!'

It is interesting to note that after all its vicissitudes, the jacket worn by Napoleon and recovered from his coach after Waterloo should at last have found a resting place beside the jackets of his famous adversary, the 1st Duke of Wellington. Clothes seem to take on the character of those who wear them and when preparing Napoleon's jacket for display, after padding out that rounded, fleshy back and thickset chest, for a moment the man himself seemed to stand there, small, stocky, slightly bowed – the 'Little Corporal', Emperor of the French – Napoleon.

Antiquities, Nepalese and Primitive Art

A Benin bronze head of a queen mother,
eighteenth century AD, height 17¼in (43.7cm)
New York $60,000(£35,294). 11.II.77
From the collection of Mary McFadden

Fig 1   A Teotihuacán pale greenstone mask, Teotihuacán III-IV, Classic, *circa* 250-750, height 7⅜in (18.5cm)
London £59,000($100,300). 9.V.77

The Pinto Collection of Primitive Art

J. B. Donne

Since the Second World War, and particularly since the early 1960s, the appreciation of primitive art and the consequent competition for master-pieces among the world's great collectors as well as museums have been so great that it would appear unlikely that any one person could still put together a fine collection from scratch. Yet this has been the achievement of Mr and Mrs Morris J. Pinto, an American couple who have lived in France since 1954. Already ardent collectors in other fields, they turned their attention to primitive art only ten or twelve years ago. Some of the results were to be seen at the sale of part of the collection on 9 May 1977, which broke several auction records and made a total of £360,000 ($612,000).

Though the Pintos' preference was clearly for African art, they also collected Oceanic, American Indian and Pre-Columbian pieces. Indeed it was a Pre-Columbian stone mask from Teotihuacán (Fig 1) which made both the highest price of the sale at £59,000 ($100,300), and the highest ever paid for an example of Pre-Columbian art at auction. The mask itself is relatively small – just under life-size, bearing in mind that the carver restricted himself to showing the face only, terminating at the hair-line. The material used is a pale greenstone. The carving is simple, sensitive, and in the case of the curling lips of the half-open mouth, sensual. The almond-shaped eyes are recessed and may well have originally contained an inlay of iron pyrites, just as the small, wing-like ears are pierced for holding ear-rings in another material, presumably gold. The purpose of such masks is not known, but, although hollowed out behind and having attachment holes at the sides of the face, they could not have been intended to be worn by living people, and it has been suggested that they were originally tied to burial bundles to represent the features of the dead.

The African portion ranged through most of the famous art-producing tribes of West and Central Africa, but was remarkable for the high quality and even rarity of many of the pieces. For example, there was an unusual ivory double-figure from the Lega of eastern Congo/Kinshasa resembling a pair of Siamese twins joined at the back of their heads (Fig 2). According to Dr Biebuyck, such figures are known as Mr Many-Heads and represent the wisdom and impartiality of the elders. Two fine *tankagle* face-masks from the northern Dan of the Liberia/Ivory Coast border fetched £11,000 ($18,700) and £16,500 ($28,050) (Fig 3), the second having previously been in the sale of the Helena Rubinstein Collection in 1966 when it fetched a mere $1,650. Such masks are among the largest the Dan produce, and despite the many variations in their

Fig 2   A Lega carved ivory double statuette, eastern Congo, height 5½in (14cm) London £5,000($8,500). 9.V.77

features they have in common not only this large size but also the slit eyes and the representation of Dan ideals of beauty, which so often approach European canons. They are regarded as 'friendly' masks for they act and sing in public performances of pantomimes.

The art of the Senufo of Mali and the Ivory Coast is well and widely known for they continue to produce an enormous quantity of masks and figure carvings, but outstanding examples of their work are correspondingly rare. However, a strange and most impressive carving of a standing male figure fetched £8,800 ($14,960) despite the fact that the arms were missing. Although 25⅝in high it may well have originally been mounted on a staff, but whatever its purpose its superbly prognathous face and jaw – exaggerated even by Senufo standards – revealed it as a most powerful piece of sculpture.

A Senufo *deble* or rhythm pounder achieved an auction record for a piece of African woodcarving (Fig 5). This tall female figure is a remarkable example of the possibilities of so-called pole sculpture. Working from a single cylindrical piece of

Fig 3   A Dan carved wood dance mask, northern Ivory Coast, height 10¼in (26cm)
London £16,500($28,050). 9.V.77
Formerly in the Helena Rubinstein Collection

Fig 4   A Benin ceremonial agate headdress and coral fly-whisk, height of headdress 17in (43cm),
length of fly-whisk 45½in (116cm)
London £17,000($28,900). 9.V.77

Fig 5   A Senufo wood rhythm pounder (*deble*),
height 41in (104cm)
London £32,000($54,400). 9.V.77

wood the carver takes advantage of its length to give the figure an exaggerated height in contrast with the narrowness of the body itself, which is limited by the diameter of the block of wood. Here the carver's skill is shown by the manner in which he succeeds in freeing the arms from the body, especially at the level of the elbows, returning them to the trunk again at the point where the hands rest on the thighs. The upright breasts also protrude to the full width of the wood and thus represent realistically the Senufo ideal of beauty in the young nubile girl. In contrast the profile of the face is cut away vertically and left almost completely flat. The rhythm pounders are carried in certain dances and used to beat the ground, not only to add a further rhythm to the drums but also in order to call up the spirits of the ancestors from below the earth. On other occasions they are borne on the heads of women to celebrate and increase female fertility.

A very rare and spectacular Benin item, formerly in the Pitt-Rivers Collection at Farnham, consisted of a bead headdress and a corresponding ceremonial fly-whisk (Fig 4). The British Museum has a similar pair which was purchased in 1898, following the Benin Punitive Expedition of the previous year, but though it shows perhaps more use it does not appear to be of such fine workmanship. The cap, consisting of a network of red beads imported from Europe (and variously described as agate or coral) is in a form often seen on Benin bronze heads of Obas, and was therefore probably a royal crown. The fly-whisk, also made of red beads, the handle containing a wooden armature, includes four 'flaps', two of which are decorated with what appear to be crocodiles, Benin emblems of physical power. This whisk, which has also been referred to as a whip, is clearly too delicate to have withstood physical use and must have served as a wand of office.

A group of Kota reliquary figures from Gabon was much appreciated (Fig 6). These objects were first brought to the attention of Europeans by the great explorer of Italian origin but in French employ, Savorgnan de Brazza, who, in an article in *Le Tour du Monde* in 1887, illustrated several placed in their baskets of ancestral bones in a Kota shrine, but it is only in recent years that scholars have begun to resolve the considerable differences of style among the various Kota sub-groups. In all cases the figures are made up of a wooden armature representing the head and a highly schematised body, the whole covered with brass or copper of European origin. The two shown here, with copper strips covering most of the face, are from the northern Mahongwe and are known as *bwete*. The third, covered with sheet copper throughout and with the body shaped like a hollow diamond, is from the southern Obambo but with features borrowed from the Shamaye of central Gabon, and is known locally as *m'bulu*. The ancestor cult with which these objects were associated was suppressed by missionaries in the 1920s and the figures themselves were destroyed, or cast into the swamps, or hidden and their whereabouts subsequently forgotten. These old examples can be counted among the finest items in the Pinto Collection.

But with the dispersal of so many splendid pieces, the Collection will not completely lose its identity. From now on, in many books and catalogues devoted to primitive art we can expect to read the words 'ex-Pinto Collection' again and again in the captions to the photographs and in lists of provenances.

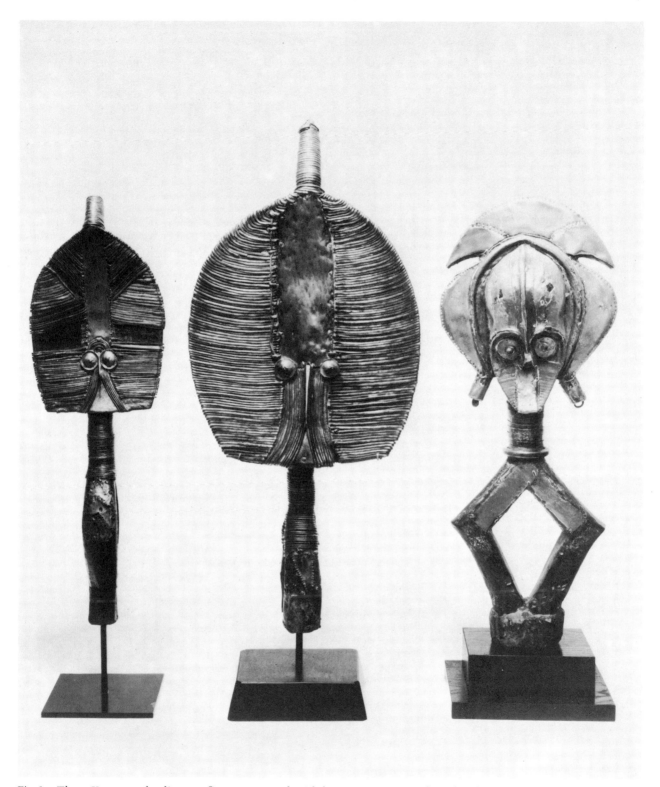

Fig 6   Three Kota wood reliquary figures covered with brass or copper, Gabon, heights from left to right 19¾in (50.2cm), 23⅜in (59.5cm), 21in (53.4cm)
London £9,800($16,600), £22,000($37,400), £19,000($32,300). 9.V.77

A Roman lead-glazed pottery cup, Asia Minor, *circa* first century BC, diameter 6⅞in (17.5cm)
New York $9,500(£5,588). 21.V.77
From the collection of the late Fahim Kouchakji

A Roman bronze figure of a pantheress, first/second century AD, length 6⅝in (16.7cm)
New York $25,000(£14,705). 21.V.77
From the collection of the late Greta S. Heckett

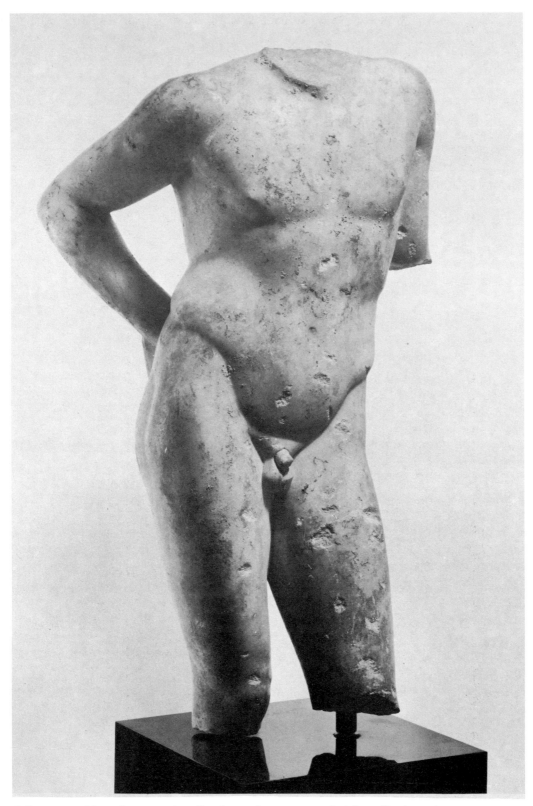

A Roman marble male torso, *circa* first/second century AD, height 26¾in (68cm)
London £11,000($18,700). 4.IV.77

An Egyptian quartzite figure of an official, late twelfth/thirteenth Dynasty, *circa* 1880-1650 BC, height 9⅝in (24.4cm)
New York $16,500(£9,705). 11.XII.76

An Egyptian wood figure of a man, first half of the twelfth Dynasty, *circa* 1991-1878 BC, height 14½in (36.8cm)
New York $18,000(£10,588). 21.V.77

A monumental bronze
figure of Horus,
Ptolemaic/early Roman
period, *circa* 305-1 BC,
height 26½in (67.3cm)
New York $20,000(£11,764).
11.XII.76
From the collection of the
late Michel Abemayor

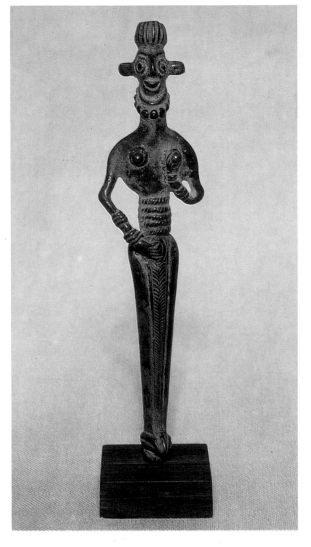

An Egyptian bronze figure of a cat, twenty-second/thirtieth Dynasty, 946-342 BC, height 4⅞in (12.5cm)
New York $17,500(£10,294). 21.V.77
From the collection of the late Greta S. Heckett

A Luristan bronze tubular finial in the form of a stylised goddess, late eighth/early seventh century BC, height 7¼in (18.5cm)
London £12,000($20,400). 4.IV.77

Two Luristan bronze cheekpieces from horses' bits, eighth/seventh century BC, height 6⅝in (16.9cm)
London £8,000($13,600). 4.IV.77

A Huetar stone crouching male figure,
circa 800-1500 AD, height 11in (27.9cm)
New York $3,750(£2,205). 11.II.77
From the collection of Dr F. R. Boyd

A Zapotec greyware pottery
urn of a seated god, Monte
Alban III A-B, *circa* 500-700 AD,
height 19½in (49.5cm)
New York $8,000(£4,705).
11.II.77
From the collection of
Jay C. Leff

An Egyptian stucco mask, first century BC/first century AD, height 12in (30.5cm)
London £12,000($20,400). 4.IV.77

A bronze royal or divine head, probably twenty-second Dynasty, period of Sheshonk I/Osorkon II, 946-861 BC, height 3¾in (9.5cm) New York $44,000 (£25,882). 21.V.77 From the collection of the late Greta S. Heckett

An Egyptian amethyst and gold vase, late pre-dynastic period, Gerzean, *circa* 3500-3000 BC, height 3in (7.65cm) New York $32,000 (£18,823). 11.XII.76 From the collection of Grace Giffen Medlicott

An Egyptian wood mummy mask, twenty-sixth Dynasty, height 13¼in (33.8cm)
London £9,000($15,300). 11.VII.77
From the collection of Sir Ralph Richardson

A Nepalese gilt-bronze figure of the Bodhisattva Vasudhara, seated in *lalitasana* on a double-waisted lotus throne, fifteenth/sixteenth century AD, height 8⅜in (21.2cm)
London £6,800($11,560). 9.V.77

Islamic Works of Art

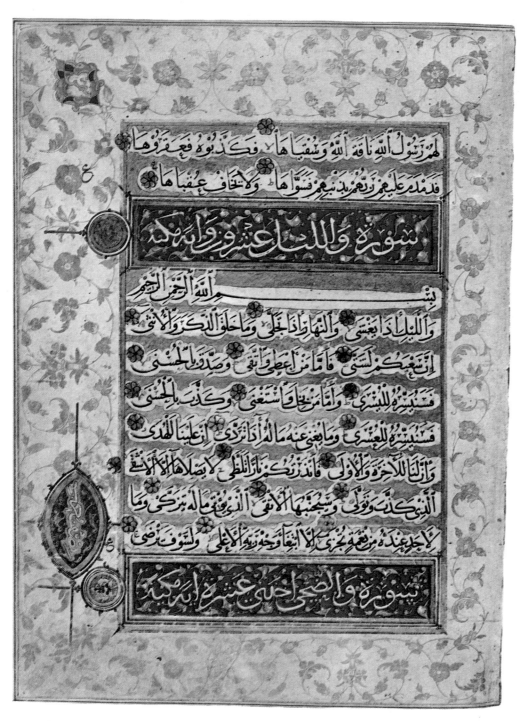

A Qur'an copied by the scribe Yaqut Al-Musta'simi, Baghdad, dated 681 AH/1282 AD,
14⅛in by 9½in (36cm by 24.1cm)
London £62,000($105,400). 20.VII.77
From the collection of V. Hillel

Left
A Mesopotamian tin-glazed pottery bowl, with a short horizontal frieze of Kufic inscription, ninth century AD, diameter 6in (15.2cm) £1,500($2,550)

Right
A Mesopotamian tin-glazed pottery bowl, ninth century AD, diameter 6⅜in (16.3cm) £1,700($2,890)

A Nishapur lead-glazed pottery bowl, with a frieze of Kufic inscription reading *Generosity is (one) of the qualities of the blessed – Peace and blessing*, ninth/tenth century AD, diameter 13¾in (35cm) £9,800($16,660)

The bowls illustrated on this page are from the collection of the late Peter Harris and were sold in London on 11 July 1977

An Isnik blue-and-white pottery dish, early sixteenth century, diameter $15\frac{3}{8}$in (39cm)
New York $23,000(£13,529). 21.V.77
From the collection of Mr and Mrs Arend Drost

A seventeenth-century Kuba dragon carpet, 13ft 9in by 6ft 6in
(419cm by 198cm)
New York $30,000(£17,647). 5.II.77
From the collection of Paulette Goddard Remarque

An early seventeenth-century Kashan *Polonaise* kelim rug, 7ft 1in by 4ft 11in
(216cm by 150cm)
London £58,000($98,600). 18.XI.76
From the collection of Baron Giorgio Franchetti

A Meshed carpet probably woven by Amoghli, 13ft by 10ft (396cm by 305cm)
New York $44,000(£25,882). 4.II.77

A Herez silk carpet, *circa* 1840, 12ft 6in by 9ft (381cm by 274cm)
New York $200,000(£117,647). 4.II.77

A raised silk Kashan prayer rug, *circa* 1920, 7ft by 4ft 2in
(213cm by 127cm)
London £10,000($17,000). 24.VI.77

A silk Kashan prayer rug, *circa* 1900, 6ft 9in by 4ft 3in
(206cm by 129cm)
London £8,000($13,600). 6.V.77

A Nain carpet, signed *Ahmad Imad Sayyid* in a cartouche at one end, *circa* 1950, 13ft 10in by 9ft 3in (422cm by 282cm) London £14,000($23,800). 10.XII.76

A Fereghan rug, *circa* 1840, 6ft 4in by 4ft 3in (193cm by 129cm) London £8,500($14,450). 6.V.77

A Karatchoph Kazak rug, *circa* 1840, 7ft 5in by 5ft 1in
(226cm by 155cm)
London £4,000($6,800). 11.II.77

A Verné kelim rug, *circa* 1880, 6ft 6in by 5ft (198cm by 152cm)
London £4,800($8,160). 11.II.77

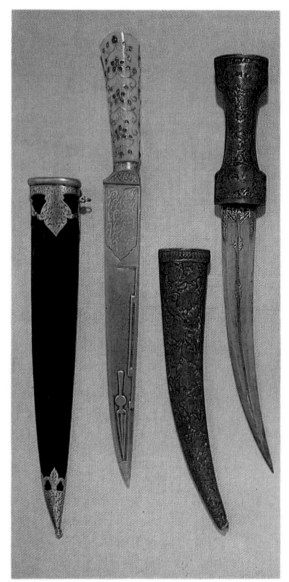

Above from left to right
A Persian kard, eighteenth century, length
17¼in (44cm), the scabbard nineteenth century
London £1,900($3,230). 22.XI.76
An Indian jambiya, dated *1151* (1738), length
15in (38cm)
London £850($1,445). 22.XI.76
From the collection of Mrs W. D. Casey

Left
A Persian jambiya with Qajar enamel
decoration, early nineteenth century, length
16¾in (42.5cm)
London £10,000($17,000). 22.XI.76

Four Qajar gold Qalian bowls:
Above Signed *Ahmad ibn Najaf Ali* and dated *1288H* (1871 AD), height $2\frac{5}{8}$in (6.7cm) £22,000($37,400)
Left Mid nineteenth century, height $2\frac{1}{2}$in (6.3cm) £20,000($34,000)
Right Late nineteenth century, height $2\frac{1}{8}$in (5.4cm) £15,000($25,500)
Below Late nineteenth century, height $2\frac{3}{4}$in (7cm) £19,000($32,300)

These bowls were sold in London on 22 November 1976

A Qajar lacquer mirror case by Muhammad Isma'il, dated 1274 (1857),
11¾in by 7⅝in (30cm by 19.2cm)
London £22,000($37,400). 23.XI.76

Chinese Ceramics and Works of Art

A detail from a Buddhist temple wall painting, *circa* AD 1300, 156in by 61in (369.5cm by 155cm)
New York $72,000(£42,353). 23.X.76
From the collection of the Cranbrook Academy of Art

A gilt-bronze figure of a striding lion, T'ang Dynasty, height 6⅛in (15.6cm)
New York $100,000(£58,823). 23.X.76

A ritual bronze covered vessel, Shang Dynasty, height 9¼in (23.5cm)
New York $180,000(£105,882). 23.X.76

A cinnabar lacquer cupstand, incised six character mark of Yung Lo inside the footrim, and of the period, fifteenth century, diameter 6⅝in (16.8cm) London £15,000($25,500). 14.XII.76

A documentary Ming three-colour lacquer dish, signed *Wang Ming* and dated 1489, period of Hung Chih, diameter 7½in (19cm) London £31,000 ($52,700). 14.XII.76

A silver raft cup by Chu Pi-shan, signed and dated 1345, Yüan Dynasty, length 8¼in (21cm)
London £26,000($44,200). 14.XII.76

This piece is one of three silver raft cups dated 1345 from the Imperial Collection in Peking. It belonged to the Yüan-ming-yüan Palace outside Peking and was lost during the Boxer Rebellion in 1860. It was later purchased by General Sir Robert Riddulph in 1861. Chu Pi-shan, also called Hua-yü, a native of Wei-t'ang in Chai-hsing, Chekiang Province, was a silversmith living between 1300 and 1362. His most productive years were 1328-68 when he made numerous crab-cups and shrimp-cups, but most famous are his raft cups which were made in two types, one with the figure seated inside the raft as in this example and the other with the figure seated on the log reading a book. The figure here is believed to depict Chang Ch'ien, the famous Han explorer at the time of the Emperor Han Wu-ti, who travelled across Asia as far as Ferghana in the second century BC. In later legend he is said to have sought the source of the Yellow River which was fabled to flow from the Milky Way

A pair of jadeite table screens, incised four character marks *ch'ien lung yü chih* but nineteenth century, height 17¼in (43.9cm)
Hong Kong HK$1,400,000(£175,000:$297,500). 2.XII.76

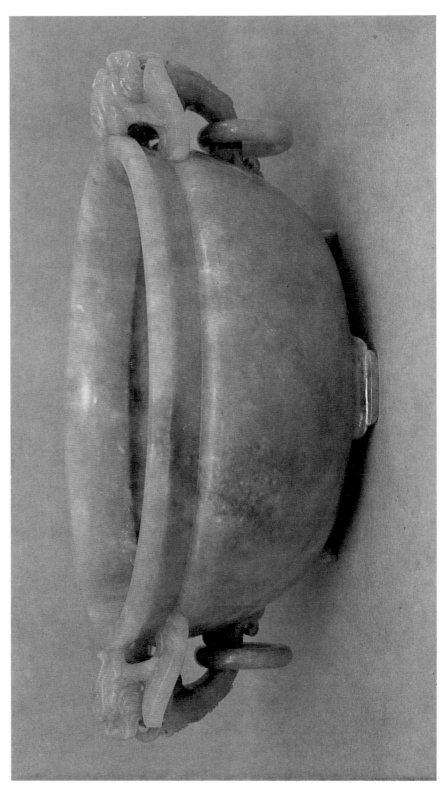

A jadeite double-handled bowl, period of Ch'ien Lung, width 11in (27.9cm)
Hong Kong HK$220,000(£27,500:$46,750). 2.XII.76

Fig 1   A Honan ribbed black-glazed jar, Northern Sung Dynasty, height 11in (28cm)
London £62,000($105,400). 29.III.77

The Malcolm Collection of Chinese ceramics and works of art

John Ayers

It is not difficult to account for the high prices paid for Chinese works of art today. In the last fifteen years this has become possibly the most international of all collectors' markets, New York vying with Tokyo, Stockholm, Melbourne or Hong Kong to secure the outstanding items which are nowadays so expertly described and illustrated in every proper auction room catalogue. Competition is therefore brisker than ever for what must be a shrinking, and no doubt irreplenishable supply. Yet somehow, and despite all prophecies of decline, the sheer volume of good material turned over is still undiminished, and the number of worthwhile sales in a good year seems even to increase.

To regular sale-goers all this presents a heartening and entertaining spectacle and enthusiasm probably matches that seen at the famous sales of the '30s to '50s. But while record prices provide a periodic fizz of excitement the underlying interest naturally enough runs deeper. Founded on discoveries which are still quite recent, our knowledge of Chinese art can be likened to a giant jigsaw from which more of the key elements than usual are missing. Thus all fresh material is eagerly scanned for its value as evidence, and each sale becomes part of a continuing process by which previously unknown or half-forgotten pieces come under review.

Collectors who approach matters in this enquiring spirit may therefore find the search doubly rewarding. While fashion brings periodic changes in preference from one dynasty or art form to another, the sheer range and consistent quality of this material easily upholds its popularity, and it has attracted a growing, and increasingly world-wide audience. Amidst all this, nevertheless, it is noticeable that the English collector bids far less often than in former days and with reduced panache; and it can be concluded that the generation which stamped its collecting seal so firmly on certain aspects of Chinese art collecting – above all perhaps that of ceramics – is now of the past. At the same time the collector will realise, probably with regret, that the once-bottomless well of pre-War British collections has all but run dry. It is all the more fortunate that a compensating flow of material from other parts of the world has now sprung up to redress the balance in the saleroom.

The Malcolm Collection, comprising 165 lots, which was sold on 29 March 1977 for a total of £704,370, must be viewed as one of the last to date from this great period of collecting; and it is also one which in many ways highlights significant aspects of

British collecting taste of that era. Originated by Major-General Sir Neill Malcolm, KCB, DSO, a distinguished soldier, it was continued after his death at the end of the last war by his son Captain Dugald Malcolm, CMG, CVO, TD, who contributes an illuminating and reflective introduction to the sale catalogue. Sir Neill first became directly acquainted with China as long ago as 1896, travelling there on foot while on leave from his regiment in Kashmir in the company of a fellow officer. Such an adventure must surely have left abiding impressions, but there were no doubt stronger and more sophisticated incentives that went to the making of this collection, which was hardly begun until the 1920s. By that time the material available, whether in London or in the East where he served for some years, was of a different calibre from the late porcelains, metalwork or scrolls to be picked up in Peking at the turn of the century. By the '20s the excavation of early sites in China, which had previously been taboo, went on apace, while Western scholars were hard at work evaluating the results. What is more, Chinese art had begun to be seriously noticed by Western art critics, and the merits of early Buddhist sculpture or Sung pottery, for example, had been enthusiastically acclaimed by such influential pundits as Clive Bell and Roger Fry.

These critics and philosophers of art were much preoccupied at this time with such fundamental abstractions as the relationship between form, line and colour in works of art, and they were not slow to detect in Chinese work a singular balance and harmony of these qualities. Dugald Malcolm tells us that form, line and colour were in fact the guidelines that he and his father both followed in making their choice; and in surveying the collection it is not difficult to see in it the reflection of these pre-occupations. Clean lines, boldness of form, strong linear design in decoration and subtle effects of colour are everywhere apparent. They are preferences which lead naturally to a predilection for the art of certain kinds and periods — the patinated bronzes of the archaic times of the Shang and Chou, for example, and a range mostly of glazed pottery which extends from Neolithic pieces right through to the late Sung and Yüan, in the thirteenth and fourteenth centuries; although Ming and later art are virtually absent.

Outstanding among the bronzes, which include a group of eleven ritual vessels in various shapes, is the so-called 'K'ang Hou *kuei*' (Fig 2), a most imposing two-handled bowl measuring 16½ in (41.8cm) across. One of the famous 'Ni' set, and much exhibited and published (like many objects in this collection it was seen at the immensely successful and memorable International Exhibition of Chinese Art held at Burlington House during 1935–36), this was undoubtedly the star item of the collection. The inscription inside celebrates the appointment of a noble ruler to govern the state of Wei shortly after the fall of the Shang Dynasty to that of the Chou, and in consequence the piece can be dated close to the year 1010 BC. This nobly-proportioned bronze is among the most awesome surviving artistic documents of its time. Gratifyingly, it was secured for the British Museum at the highest price of the day.

Other bronze objects of this period embodying a similar strength of design in smaller compass included three pairs of chariot lynch-pins, the bosses terminating in animal heads, unusually surmounted in one instance by a human figure (Fig 3). There were also a variety of finely-shaped metal wares of the T'ang period or from Korea, and some fine T'ang silver-gilt pieces with incised work — a box and cover (Fig 4), and a pair of scissors decorated with stags, ducks and other birds, singularly elegant, which would have graced any collection (Fig 5).

Fig 2   The 'K'ang Hou *kuei*', an early Western Chou ritual bronze food vessel, *circa* 1010 BC, width 16½in (41.8cm)
London £110,000($187,000). 29.III.77
Now in the British Museum

Inside is an inscription which reads:

'The King attacked the Shang capital,
then ordered K'ang Hou Pi to Wei.
Mu's Ssu-t'u, Ni, and Pi made for their
Father this sacrificial vessel. X' (an undeciphered clan name).

This *kuei* is one of a series known as the 'Ni' set, and was evidently made by Ni and Pi (ruling officials in Mu and K'ang) as a ritual sacrifice to their father. The inscription also refers to the appointment of Pi to govern the Wei state. It is of unusual documentary importance in its relation to events connected with the fall of the Shang Dynasty and rise of the Chou.
   The set was probably discovered at Ku-yü ts'un in Hui Hsien, Honan province in 1931

Fig 3   Three pairs of
bronze lynch-pins (one of
each illustrated), Western
Chou Dynasty, heights
$4\frac{3}{4}$in (12cm), $5\frac{3}{8}$in (13.6cm),
$4\frac{1}{4}$in (10.7cm)
London £5,500($9,350),
£6,200($10,540),
£9,200($15,640). 29.III.77

Fig 4   A silver-gilt box and
cover, T'ang Dynasty,
height $1\frac{1}{4}$in (3.2cm),
diameter 4in (10cm)
London £26,000($44,200).
29.III.77

It is in its ceramics, however, that the motivating principles of this collection are most clearly shown and vindicated. There is no parallel elsewhere in the world for the story of technological and artistic success which marks out the Chinese potters' progress, and this collection points out some of its most quintessential features. Sensitivity of form and a superior technique are both evident even in so seemingly plain a pot as the jar of the Warring States period (Fig 6), with its simple mat-impressed decoration and incipient glaze, which indicates the emergence of that uniquely Chinese invention, high-fired stoneware. A striking series of early jars from the Yüeh district of South-east China represents its slow development in that region from about the fourth century to the tenth century (Fig 7); and shows how the natural celadon-green of this type of glaze was cultivated with empiric skill to produce objects of increasingly refined style and seemingly inevitable, unforced beauty.

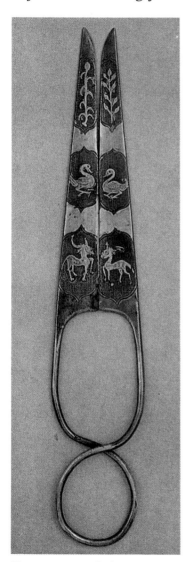

Fig 5   A pair of silver-gilt scissors, T'ang Dynasty, length 7½in (19cm) London £8,000($13,600). 29.III.77

Fig 6   A Warring States jar, sixth/fifth century BC, height 9½in (24.1cm) London £3,400($5,780). 29.III.77

Fig 7   Two carved Yüeh-yao funerary vases with covers, ninth/tenth century, heights $15\frac{3}{4}$in (40cm) and $13\frac{1}{2}$in (34.25cm)
London £11,000($18,700) and £14,000($23,800). 29.III.77

Fig 8   A carved Northern celadon basin, Northern Sung Dynasty, height 9½in (24.1cm)
London £29,000($49,300). 29.III.77

Under the Sung Dynasty this classic glazed stoneware tradition blossomed out in a varied production of unrivalled splendour, with glazes in skilfully-controlled tints, perfect flower-like forms and designs of a sparing, naturalistic kind in a notable harmony. This fortunate moment is summed up in such a piece as the Northern celadon basin (Fig 8), with its freely-carved design of peony radiating from a central medallion; although as regards glaze quality an even greater distinction is achieved by the somewhat later wares of Lung-ch'üan. A technical opposite, in a way, to these types are the various brown- or black-glazed wares, well represented in this collection, which are essentially the result of oxidising rather than 'reduced' firing conditions. The appeal of the varied types – often spotted, streaked and dappled in differing tints – is distinctive; but we can perhaps best represent the family here by the remarkable two-handled jar, of exceptional proportions (Fig 1), on which the rather matt, even and moist-looking brown-black glaze is decoratively relieved by vertical ribs of white clay judiciously applied to the body beneath. The almost Greek shape shows precisely that combination of classic proportion and unselfconsciously skilful handling that marks out the Sung potter's genius.

Even before the Sung period Chinese potters had pioneered a new course – almost unconsciously it seems – which was to engage much of their efforts in later centuries: the invention of what in the West is called porcelain. It is hard to believe that such a white, ringing and brilliantly-glazed ware did not excite wonder among the T'ang Chinese when it first appeared. A beautifully-made cup with straight, tapered sides, the stoneware body semi-translucent, shows a late stage in its evolution (Fig 11). This type of ware leads naturally on to the characteristic cream-white Ting porcelain which some prefer to all other wares of the Sung period. Of several fine examples in this collection, the most sought-after was a dish with a moulded dragon design (Fig 10).

The Malcolms must deliberately have avoided Ming porcelain with its growing tendency towards mass-produced forms, pictorial designs and strong contrasts of bright colour. They had no apparent qualms, however, about adding such an item as the Ming jade stemcup (Fig 9), now acquired by the Victoria and Albert Museum. There must be a strong case for ascribing this unique jade to the fifteenth century simply on account of its form; but at the same time there is a sense in which its fine lines, hand-worked on the cutting-wheel, and the striking natural markings of the grey-green stone hark back to the taste of an earlier era. The classic strain in Chinese art, it seems to tell us, is all but irrepressible.

Fig 9 A Ming jade stemcup, fifteenth century, height 4¼in (11cm) London £5,000($8,500). 29.III.77 Now in the Victoria and Albert Museum

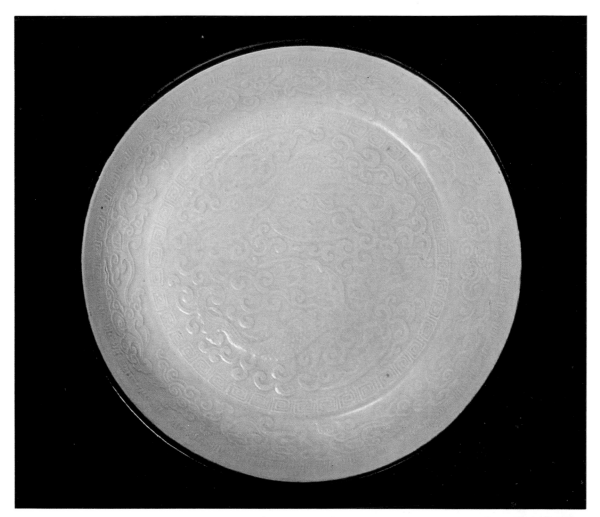

Fig 10   A moulded Ting-yao dish,
Chin Dynasty, height 6¾in (17.1cm)
London £11,000($18,700). 29.III.77

Fig 11   A winecup, T'ang Dynasty,
height 2⅝in (6.5cm)
London £2,500($4,250). 29.III.77

A glazed pottery equestrian figure, T'ang Dynasty, height 15¼in (38.7cm)
New York $32,000(£18,823). 23.X.76
From the collection of the late John H. Wilkins

A pair of green-glazed pottery flasks, Liao Dynasty, height 8¾in (22.2cm)
New York $25,000(£14,705). 2.VI.77
From the collection of Mrs Fredrick L. Ehrman

A Yüeh-yao waterpot modelled in the form of a recumbent ram, Wu Dynasty, second half of the third century AD, length 13in (33cm) London £47,000($79,900). 14.XII.76

An aubergine-ground engraved bowl, six character mark of Wan Li in underglaze blue within a double circle, and of the period, diameter 6in (15.3cm) Hong Kong HK$360,000(£45,000:$76,500). 16.V.77

An early blue and white jar, fourteenth century, diameter 12¼in (31.1cm)
New York $130,000(£76,470). 23.X.76

A blue and white *mei p'ing* (two views illustrated), early fourteenth century, height 6½in (16.5cm)
London £40,000($68,000). 5.VII.77

A blue and white stemcup, six character mark of Hsüan Tê, and of the period, early fifteenth century, height 3½in (8.9cm)
London £32,000($54,400). 5.VII.77

An early Ming blue and white moon flask, period of Yung Lo, height 10in (25.4cm)
London £115,000($195,500). 5.VII.77

A blue and white stemcup, four character mark of Hsüan Tê in a line below the lip, and of the
period, early fifteenth century, height 8¾in (22.3cm)
Hong Kong HK$1,150,000(£143,750:$244,375). 16.V.77
Previously sold in London on 2 February 1971 for £44,000

An export tea caddy and cover for the American market, 1790-1810, height 5¾in (14.5cm)
New York $700(£411). 18.XI.76

An export orange 'Fitzhugh' oval platter with American eagle decoration, 1800-1820, width 14½in (36.8cm)
New York $6,750(£3,970). 18.XI.76

One of a pair of *famille rose* sparrow-hawks on Louis XV ormolu plinths, period of Ch'ien Lung,
overall height 19¼in (49cm)
Monte Carlo Fr250,000(£29,761:$50,595). 3.V.77
From the collection of the Comtesse Alexandre de Casteja

Opposite page: Left
A lavender-blue bottle,
seal mark of Yung Chêng
in underglaze blue, and of
the period, height 10in (25.4cm)
Hong Kong HK$85,000
(£10,625:$18,063). 16.V.77

Right
A blue-flecked vase, seal
mark of Yung Chêng in
underglaze blue, and of
the period, height 10¾in (27.3cm)
Hong Kong HK$62,000
(£7,750:$13,175). 16.V.77

Far left
One of a pair of celadon
covered vases, six
character marks of Yung
Chêng within double
rings, and of the period,
height 11½in (29.2cm)
Hong Kong HK$120,000
(£15,000:$25,500).
29.XI.76

Left
An imitation Ju-glazed
vase of *hu* shape, seal
mark of Yung Chêng in
underglaze blue, and of
the period, height 10½in (26.7cm)
Hong Kong HK$52,000
(£6,500:$11,050). 29.XI.76

A pair of green glazed bowls, six character marks of Yung Chêng within double circles in
underglaze blue, and of the period, diameter 5½in (14cm)
Hong Kong HK$120,000(£15,000:$25,500). 16.V.77

A pale blue-glazed bowl, six character mark of Yung Chêng in archaic script, and of the period, diameter 13¼in (33.6cm)
Hong Kong HK$74,000(£9,250:$15,725). 16.V.77

A large Chinese taste *famille rose* vase, six character mark of Ch'ien Lung, and of the period, height 19¾in (50.2cm)
New York $70,000(£41,176). 23.X.76
From the collection of the late Victoria Dreyfus

A *tou ts'ai* vase, seal mark and period of Ch'ien Lung, height 21½in (54.6cm)
Hong Kong HK$185,000(£23,125:$39,312). 29.XI.76

A pair of *famille rose* small bowls, six character marks of K'ang Hsi, and of the period, diameter 3⅞in (9.9cm)
Hong Kong HK$305,000(£38,125:$64,812). 29.XI.76

A pair of ruby-back wine cups, six character marks of Yung Chêng, and of the period, diameter 3¼in (8.3cm)
Hong Kong HK$300,000(£37,500:$63,750). 29.XI.76

Japanese and Korean Works of Art

A Kakiemon ewer of
Middle Eastern inspired
form, mid seventeenth
century, height 11¾in (30cm)
London £13,000($22,100).
23.II.77

An Arita charger, *circa* 1660-80, diameter $21\frac{7}{8}$in (55.6cm)
New York \$2,100(£1,235).
14.VI.77

Below left
An Arita bowl and cover, late seventeenth century, diameter $16\frac{1}{2}$in (42cm)
London £1,700(\$2,890). 24.II.77

Below right
An Arita apothecary's bottle, the base with the initials *I.C.* within a wreath, late seventeenth century, height $10\frac{1}{4}$in (26cm)
London £2,800(\$4,760). 10.VI.77

An inlaid bronze vase, cover and stand, stamped *Kasai*,
late nineteenth century, height 31½in (80cm)
London £3,200($5,440). 14.X.76

A porcelain vase and cover, late nineteenth century,
height 45in (114.3cm)
London £2,050($3,485). 21.IV.77

An underglaze iron red storage jar, Kaesong, seventeenth/eighteenth century, height 11¾in (29.8cm)
New York $6,000(£3,529). 14.VI.77

A Nara gilt and dry lacquer figure of Monju, eighth century, height 30½in (77.5cm)
New York $24,000(£14,117). 14.VI.77

A gold lacquer *tansu*, Meiji period,
height 7⅜in (18.5cm)
Los Angeles $8,250(£4,825). 17.VI.77

A late Edo-Meiji silver-mounted
suzuribako and writing table, length of
table 25⅝in (61.6cm), length of *suzuribako*
10⅛in (24.3cm)
Los Angeles $8,000(£4,705). 10.III.77

The interior of the *suzuribako* is fitted
with a gold lacquered inkstone, silver
mizuire, two *gyobu* brushes,
silver-mounted prick and inkstick holder

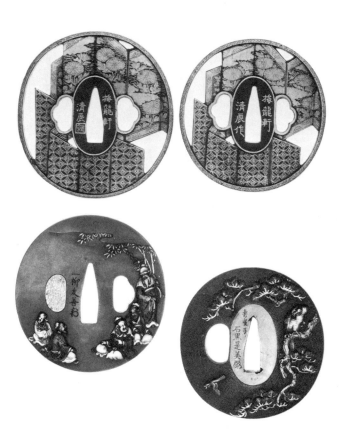

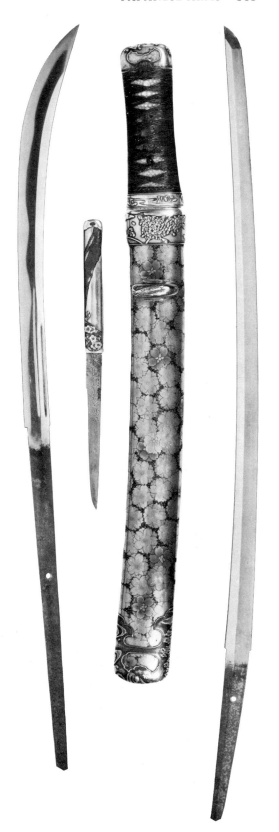

Above
A pair of *Kenjo tsuba* for a *daisho*, signed in gold *nunome*
Bairyuken Kiyotoki with seal *Rin*, diameters 3¼in (8.4cm) and
3in (7.8cm) £1,100($1,870)
Centre left
A *shakudo tsuba*, signed *Hitotsuyanagi Tomoyoshi* with
kakihan, diameter 2⅛in (7.4cm) £680($1,156)
Centre right
A *shibuichi nanako tsuba*, signed *Jukakoshi Ishiguro Koreyoshi*
with *kakihan* £2,000($3,400)

These *tsuba* were sold in London on 26 October 1976

Right
A *Naginata* blade, signed *Tadatsuna saku,* length 15⅝in (39.9cm)
London £2,000($3,400). 7.VII.77
Centre right
A *Shinshinto aikuchi* attributed to *Bizen Munetsugu* (second
generation), in silver mounts, signed *Nakagawa Issho saku,*
length 11¾in (30cm)
New York $5,250(£3,088). 14.VI.77
Far right
A *Katana* blade, length 29⅞in (75.9cm)
London £3,200($5,440). 31.V.77
From the collection of P. Bowron

OKATOMO: An ivory model of a bitch and pup, Kyoto, eighteenth century
Honolulu $9,500(£5,588). 22.I.77

SUKETADA: A wood kappa and clam, Hida, early nineteenth century
Honolulu $3,400(£2,000). 22.I.77

IKKAN: A wood model of a hare, Nagoya, early nineteenth century
London £3,900($6,630). 24.II.77

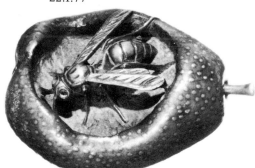

From left to right above
KANO TOMOKAZU: A wood study of a mountain cat, Gifu, early nineteenth century
London £2,850($4,845). 10.VI.77
ICHIMINSAI: A wood 'Wasp in a Pear', mid nineteenth century
London £2,900($4,930). 9.XI.76
TOYOMASA: A wood study of a kirin, Tamba, early nineteenth century
London £8,100($13,770). 24.II.77

From left to right below
An ivory figure of Kwan Yu, Kyoto, eighteenth century, unsigned
Honolulu $8,000(£4,705). 22.I.77
MASANAO: An ivory study of a kirin, Kyoto, eighteenth century
Honolulu $11,500(£6,764). 22.I.77
TOMOTADA: An ivory study of a wolf, Kyoto, eighteenth century
London £8,500($14,450). 10.VI.77

Left
A *shibayama* and gold lacquer *inro* decorated with mother of pearl, ivory and silver, signed *Nemmoto tsukuru, circa* 1900, length 4½in (11.5cm) London £2,100($3,570). 3.II.77
From the Hood Collection

Right
A *shibayama* and gold lacquer *inro* decorated with mother of pearl, signed *Nemmoto, circa* 1900, length 4¼in (10.8cm) London £2,300($3,910). 3.II.77
From the Hood Collection

A gold lacquer and ivory skull, signed *Yanikishi*, late nineteenth century, height 6½in (16.5cm) London £3,600($6,120). 3.II.77
From the Hood Collection

An ivory figure of a mask carver by Ishikawa Komei, signed *Komei, circa* 1900, height 9¼in (23.5cm) London £2,500($4,250). 3.II.77
From the collection of Sidney Larnach

HIROSHIGE *Oban yoko-e:* four from an album containing the complete set of the fifty-five colour prints comprising the first Tokaido set, all signed
London £21,000($35,700). 19.I.77

KITAO MASANOBU
A Mirror Comparing the Handwriting of New and Beautiful Courtesans of the Yoshiwara, one of seven colour prints, signed, from an illustrated book the preface dated Temmei 4, commencement of spring in the Dragon Year (1784)
London £7,000($11,900). 19.I.77

CHUBAN
A girl parachuting, colour print, an *egoyomi* for 1765
London £8,600($14,620). 24.III.77
From the collection of the late Henri Vever

The girl in this print, according to an old superstition, has launched herself from the viewing platform of Kiyomizu Temple, making the jump a test of Buddha's judgement of her prospective marriage; if the ground is reached safely, he approves; if not, there is instant death

One of a pair of gold paper six-fold screens, late eighteenth/early nineteenth century, gold silk brocade mounts, 61¼in by 136½in (155.5cm by 346.7cm) $5,750(£3,382).

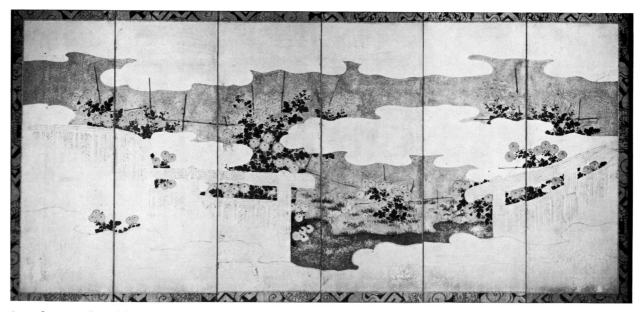

One of a pair of six-fold screens of *The seasons*, late eighteenth/early nineteenth century, gold silk brocade mounts, 61¼in by 136½in (155.5cm by 346.7cm) $6,750(£3,970).

These screens were sold in New York on 14 June 1977

Coins and Medals

A unique gold portrait medal of Queen Elizabeth I, after the miniature by Isaac Oliver, executed by
Simon de Passe (*circa* 1615)
London £22,000($37,400), 25.V.77
From the collection of the late Greta S. Heckett

Greta S. Heckett's collection of seventeenth-century English historical medals was one of the most
comprehensive to appear at public auction in recent years, and in addition to the gold medal
illustrated above, examples of most of the de Passe silver medals depicting the royal family of
James I were included in the sale.

Simon de Passe was born in Cologne (*circa* 1595) and worked in London from 1615 to 1622. Most
of his medallic portraits were copied from works by other artists, but there is continuing
controversy regarding his technique. The fineness of detail on his medals suggests hand-engraving,
but the striking resemblance between examples of the same portrait makes it more likely that a
master die was used, at least for the initial impression. Whatever his method, the finished medals
displayed an almost photographic quality which time and toning have even further improved

A rare and previously unknown gold quarter-ounce (enlarged), struck at
Port Phillip, Australia, in 1853. These Port Phillip pieces are amongst
the earliest coins of the Australian series and were issued as a result
of the acute shortage of coinage caused by the 'Gold Rush' of the
early 1850s
London £11,000($18,700), 16.II.77

A rare Roman gold bar found in Bulgaria in 1904; the countermarks at
either end show that the bar was cast by a certain Proculus,
presumably a mint official, late fourth century AD
Zurich SF60,000 (£13,953: $23,720), 10.VI.77

England, Elizabeth I, a cast bronze medal commemorating the departure of the
Earl of Leicester from Belgium after his removal from the command of the army, 1587
London £480($816), 25.V.77
From the collection of the late Greta S. Heckett

Roman, Claudius II (AD 268-70), a gold medallion of 8 aurei, struck at Milan; discovered off the coast of Corsica in the mid nineteenth century
Zurich SF80,000(£18,604; $31,627), 10.VI.77

Ancient Greek, distater of Thurium in South Italy, *circa* 412 BC, signed by the artist Phrygillos
Zurich SF13,500(£3,139;$5,337), 10.VI.77
From the collection of the late Greta S. Heckett

South Africa, President Thomas Burgers, Pattern crown, 1894, struck in gilt-bronze
Johannesburg R4,500(£3,000; $5,100), 20.IV.77

Roman, Augustus (27 BC–AD 14), denarius, struck in Rome
London, £1,500($2,550), 1.XII.76
From the collection of Eton College

Italy, cast bronze medal of Taddeo di Guidacci Manfredi, Count of Faenza, by Gianfrancesco Enzola, fifteenth century
London £310($529), 27.IV.77

England, James I, Second Coinage, an extremely rare half-angel, mint mark crescent (1617–18), struck at the Tower mint and probably unique
London £2,600($4,420), 30.III.77

An important group of insignia of the Most Noble Order of the Garter and the Most Illustrious Order of St Patrick made for Charles, Second Earl Talbot, KG (1844), Lord Lieutenant of Ireland (1817-22).

Above left
Great George (*collar badge*) of the Garter
London £10,000($17,000), 22.VI.77

Above right
Lesser George (*sash badge*) of the Garter
London £10,000($17,000), 26.I.77

Left
Grand Master's badge of the Order of St Patrick
London £10,000($17,000), 26.I.77

European Ceramics

An early Meissen turtle box and cover, probably modelled by Georg Fritzsche, the interior with a large crossed swords mark in underglaze blue, *circa* 1725, length 7⅝in (20cm)
New York $18,000(£10,588). 23.XI.76

A Sèvres miniature cup and saucer, *circa* 1760
Mentmore £5,800($9,860). 24.V.77
This type of chinoiserie decoration appears to have been copied directly from Chinese porcelain or
famille rose enamels

A Sèvres *écuelle*, cover and stand, marked with interlaced *L*s in blue and other incised marks,
circa 1760, width 9in (22.7cm)
Mentmore £17,000($28,900). 24.V.77

A Vincennes pot-pourri vase and cover, 1750-55, height 18½in (47cm)
Mentmore £19,000($32,300). 24.V.77

This shape, which is called 'vase pot poury Pompadour' in the factory sales records, was evidently very popular. It was produced from 1752 in four sizes, of which this is the largest. A contemporary drawing for the model, probably designed by Duplessis, is preserved in the archives at Sèvres

A pair of Sèvres vases and covers, vase Bâchelier, marked with interlaced *L*s, date letter *O*, 1767, height 32in (81.3cm)
Mentmore £6,000($10,200). 24.V.77

A Sèvres blue-ground vase and cover, marked with interlaced *L*s, date letter *P*, 1768, painter's mark
for Xhrouet in blue enamel and incised marks, height 17in (43.2cm)
New York $24,000(£14,117). 23.IV.77
From the collection of Dr Annella Brown

A Meissen snuffbox, *circa* 1740-50, width
2⅞in (7.3cm)
London £750($1,275). 26.IV.77

A Meissen snuffbox, *circa* 1730-35, width 3in (7.5cm)
London £3,000($5,100). 26.IV.77

A Meissen gold-mounted snuffbox, painted in the
manner of Christian Friedrich Herold, *circa* 1740,
width 3½in (8.8cm)
New York $10,000(£5,882). 23.XI.76
From the collection of Mrs Woolworth Donahue

A commemorative Berlin snuffbox, inscribed *Vive Paul
Petrowitzch grand Prince de Russie*, *circa* 1775, width
4⅛in (10.5cm)
London £1,900($3,230). 26.IV.77
This snuffbox was probably made to commemorate the
Crown Prince of Russia's marriage in 1775 to Sophia
Dorothea of Württemberg

A Meissen purple ground tea and coffee service, crossed swords mark in underglaze blue, gilder's mark *31*, workman's incised marks, impressed numerals on tea caddy, *circa* 1735
London £16,000($27,200). 19.X.76

The difference in the style of painting on the various pieces suggest that two and possibly three painters were employed on decorating this service. One of them was probably Christian Friedrich Herold, while some pieces are clearly related to the style of painting associated with Bonaventura Gottlieb Hauer

A Frankenthal cup and saucer, crowned *CT* mark in underglaze blue, incised marks, *71* on cup and *72* in underglaze blue, 1771-72
London £1,050($1,785). 19.X.76

One panel from part of an important documentary medieval tile floor, each tile 6in (15.2cm) square
London £12,880($21,896). 9.XI.76

This floor was probably removed from Hailes Abbey, near Winchcombe, Gloucestershire, but was
first recorded in the Manor House at Southam de la Bere nearby. Each tile has a design inlaid in
cream slip and covered with lead glaze. The above panel includes examples with the monogram and
rebus for Abbot Anthony Melton (1508-27). The centre of the floor consists of nine similar designs
which were surrounded by a double border of various motifs including *fleur-de-lys*, Tudor rose and
a double-headed eagle.

The floor was purchased jointly by the Department of the Environment and the British Museum
and will be displayed at Hailes Abbey and the British Museum

A 'tailor' toby jug of Whieldon type, *circa* 1750, height 6¼in (15.9cm)
London £2,000($3,400). 10.V.77

This toby belongs to a group known as 'Rodney's sailors' and includes various subjects
which in the main appear to depict musicians

One of two Chelsea figures representing 'Smelling' (illustrated) and 'Tasting' from a set of the Senses, modelled by Joseph Willems, red anchor mark, *circa* 1758, heights 11¼in (28.5cm) and 11½in (29.2cm)
London £2,500($4,250). 9.XI.76

One of a pair of Lowestoft musician figures, *circa* 1780-90, height 7in (17.8cm) London £1,350($2,295). 5.X.76

A Chelsea figure of a masquerader, gold anchor mark, *circa* 1760, height 7¾in (19.7cm) London £1,200($2,040). 26.VII.77

This figure is one of a series probably made to commemorate a masquerade given in the Ranelagh Gardens to celebrate the birthday of George, Prince of Wales, on 24 May 1759

A Derby 'named view' part tea and coffee service, each piece painted probably by
Thomas 'Jockey' Hill, marked in blue enamel, *circa* 1795
London £4,100($6,970). 10.V.77
From the collection of R. Spencer C. Copeland

A Derby green-ground
cabaret, each piece
painted with 'named'
shipping scenes by
George Robertson, fully
marked in blue enamel,
impressed and incised
numerals, *circa* 1800
London £3,400($5,780).
5.X.76

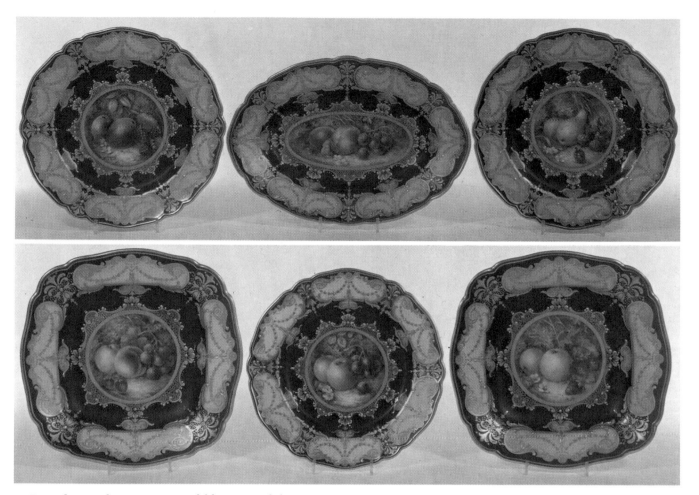

Part of a Royal Worcester royal-blue-ground dessert service, each piece painted by R. Sebright, the majority signed, printed crowned circle, painted pattern number *W8860*, date codes for 1912 and 1913, diameter of a plate 8¾in (22.3cm)
London £2,000($3,400). 17.III.77

A Berlin plaque painted by C. Meinelt, signed with monogram, after Rubens, impressed *KPM* and sceptre, second half of the nineteenth century, 16¼in by 21¾in (41.3cm by 55cm)
London £6,500($11,050). 10.III.77

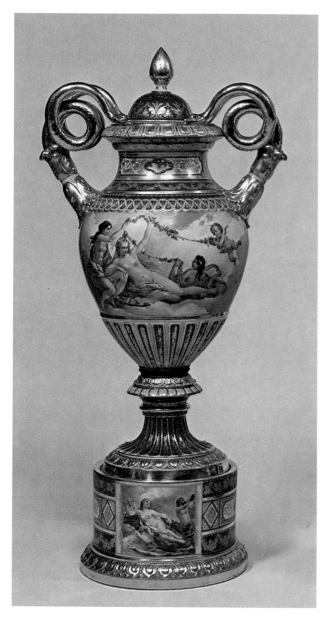

One of a pair of monumental Dresden urns, stands and covers, *Dresden* and *W* in underglaze blue, second half of the nineteenth century, height 43½in (111cm) New York $17,000(£10,000). 5.II.77

One of a pair of 'Vienna' *bleu-de-roi* ground vases, covers and stands, each ovoid body painted by H. Stadler, signed, painted shield in blue, late nineteenth century, height 29in (99.1cm) London £8,000($13,600). 10.III.77

From left to right
A Royal Doulton Chang vase by C. Noke and H. Nixon, *circa* 1930,
height 7½in (19cm) £450($765).
A Royal Doulton Flambé vase, *circa* 1935, height 6in (15.3cm) £110($187).
A Royal Doulton Chang vase by C. Noke and H. Nixon, *circa* 1930,
height 7¼in (18.5cm) £270($459).
These vases were sold on London on 31 March 1977

A De Morgan amphora, early Fulham period, *circa* 1890, height 16¾in (42.6cm) London £720($1,224). 31.III.77

De Morgan's effective career as a designer and organiser of a pottery spans the years from 1872, when a glaze experiment set fire to his rooms in Fitzroy Square and he moved to Chelsea, until 1905, and his retirement from the Sands End, Fulham factory.

Although deriving inspiration from a great variety of Eastern, European and classical sources, his designs are immediately recognisable with their simple, flat patterning and vividness of colour. The comparison with the work of William Morris is often made, but De Morgan's whimsical humour and capacity for invention is unique. Although he enjoyed greater success as a novelist during the latter part of his life, today he is best known and admired for his distinctive and unusual pottery

Furniture, Textiles and Decorations

A Louis XV singing bird and orange tree musical automaton by Richard of Paris, signed *Richard Rue des prouvaires à Paris* and dated *1757*, height 2ft 3½in (70cm) Mentmore £90,000($153,000). 18.V.77

The movement inside the parquetry tub is basically original and in good working order. The first of the oranges on the ground beneath the tree is the stop/start lever with facility for continuous playing; the second is for changing the tune or repeating; the third and fourth control the base and treble pipes of the organ so they can be played individually or in unison

Richard Rue des prouvaires Paris 1757

Detail

Opposite
A William and Mary black-japanned double-domed cabinet on silver gilt-wood stand, late seventeenth century, height 6ft 2in (188cm)
New York $11,500(£6,764). 15.I.77
From the collection of the late Edward Kaschak

A Queen Anne red-japanned and parcel-gilt pier mirror, early eighteenth century, height 5ft 3in (160cm)
New York $9,500(£5,588). 15.I.77

A George I gilt gesso bureau cabinet in the manner of James Moore, height 8ft 9in (257cm)
London £16,000($27,200). 3.VI.77

A Queen Anne walnut double-domed bureau cabinet, height 7ft 8in (234cm)
London £13,500($22,950). 3.VI.77

One of a pair of George II
parcel-gilt and painted
console tables, mid
eighteenth century,
height 2ft 9in (84cm)
New York $22,000 (£12,941).
9.X.76
From the collection of
Marietta Peabody Tree
and the late Ronald Tree

An early George III
kingwood marquetry
commode, height 2ft 9in (84cm)
London £13,000($22,100). 5.XI.76

Two from a set of six
George II black painted
chairs, mid eighteenth
century
New York $15,500 (£9,117).
9.X.76
From the collection of
Marietta Peabody Tree and
the late Ronald Tree

Below
A pair of George II walnut
library armchairs, mid
eighteenth century
New York $8,250 (£4,852).
6.XI.76

A pair of Queen Anne shell-carved cherrywood side chairs, Philadelphia, 1740-50
New York $140,000(£82,352). 29.I.77
From the collection of the late Mary Blackwell Moore

A Chippendale carved mahogany *bombé* chest of drawers with original rococo fire-gilt brasses,
Boston, 1765-80, height 2ft 7¾in (85.7cm)
New York $135,000(£79,411). 29.I.77

A Genoese *bombé* commode,
mid eighteenth century,
height 3ft 11⅝in (121cm)
Florence L13,500,000
(£9,000:$15,300). 2.VI.77

One of a pair of Milanese
marquetry commodes, *circa*
1790, height 3ft 6in (107cm)
Mentmore £15,500 ($26,350).
20.V.77

One of a pair of Piedmontese gilt-wood side tables in the manner of Giuseppe Maria Bonzanigo, *circa* 1780, width 3ft 8in (122cm)
Mentmore £16,000($27,200). 20.V.77

One of a pair of carved Italian gilt-wood side tables, *circa* 1700, width 5ft 10in (178cm)
Mentmore £23,500($39,950). 20.V.77

Two from a set of seventeen Italian gilt-wood armchairs, covered in Roman silk embroidery, the needlework *circa* 1720, the chairs *circa* 1850
Mentmore £37,000($62,900). 20.V.77

Opposite
One of a pair of Venetian gilt-wood throne chairs in the manner of Andrea Brustolon, *circa* 1700
Mentmore £7,500($12,750). 20.V.77

These chairs stood in the Great Hall at Mentmore. For a view of them in their original setting see p 12

A South German marquetry and parcel-gilt walnut and oak armoire, *circa* 1745, height 8ft 5in (257cm) Mentmore £44,000($74,800). 20.V.77

An Antwerp tortoiseshell and rosewood *bonheur du jour*, inlaid with pewter, copper, brass and mother of pearl, with chinoiserie scenes within arabesque borders, *circa* 1705, height 3ft 11in (119cm) Mentmore £13,000($22,100). 20.V.77

The decoration is based on engravings from *Gesandtschaft der Ost Indischen Gesellschaft* by Johann Neuhof, Amsterdam, 1669 and *Asia*, by Johann Christian Bernn, 1681. After the flight of the last Ming Emperor in 1644, the Dutch Government decided to send an embassy to Peking and Johann Neuhof was sent as steward to the ambassadors. On his return he published an account of his travels in China with accompanying engravings taken from his drawings. This led to the first widespread flowering of chinoiserie in Europe

An ormolu-mounted mahogany and satinwood commode, *circa* 1800, possibly Russian,
height 3ft 1in (94cm)
Mentmore £21,000($35,700). 20.V.77

A Russian ormolu-mounted white marble and mahogany cabinet, *circa* 1790, height 5ft (152cm) Mentmore £15,000($25,500). 20.V.77

The top of this cabinet has a *jardinière* above a pair of doors; the Empress Marie-Feodorovna was extremely fond of flowers and plants and many pieces of furniture made for her, including even chairs, incorporated *jardinières*, and it is possible that this cabinet was made for her

One of a pair of Venetian globes by P. Vincenzo Maria Coronelli, one celestial the
other (illustrated) terrestial, 1688, diameter 3ft 7¾in (110cm)
Florence L46,000,000(£30,666:$52,133). 21.X.76

A late Louis XVI gilt-bronze and *tôle peinte* chandelier, based on the design of the
Montgolfier air balloon, height 3ft 7¾in (110cm)
Monte Carlo Fr180,000(£21,428:$36,427). 3.V.77
From the collection of Comtesse Alexandre de Casteja

A Brussels Renaissance tapestry depicting *The rest on the Flight into Egypt*, early sixteenth century,
7ft 2in by 5ft 5in (220cm by 165cm)
London £52,000($88,400). 1.VII.77

One from a complete set of twelve Gobelins tapestries of the Zodiac months, this one depicting
Pisces (February), by Dominique de la Croix, including two by Michel Souet and Jean
de la Fraye, probably after Lucas van Leyden and known as *Les Mois Lucas, circa* 1700, each
approximately 11ft 6in by 10ft 6in (350cm by 320cm)
Mentmore £85,000($145,350). 20.V.77

The first set, woven at the Gobelins factory, was commissioned by Colbert from the Brussels set of
Lucas Months belonging to the Crown and is recorded in 1683: 'Une tenture, fabrique des Gobelins,
representant les Douze Mois, copie de celle des Douze Mois de la Couronne'. The original royal set
was subsequently burnt in 1797 for its content of gold and silver thread

These tapestries hung in the Great Hall at Mentmore. For a view of them in their original setting
see p 12

A Louis XIV ormolu-mounted boulle commode inlaid with *Bérainesque* designs, in brass, scarlet tortoiseshell and pewter, *circa* 1700, width 3ft 11in (119cm)
Mentmore £20,000($34,000). 19.V.77

Opposite above
A Louis XIV boulle *bureau mazarin*, inlaid with *Bérainesque* designs in scarlet tortoiseshell and brass, *circa* 1690, width 4ft (122cm)
Mentmore £17,000($28,900). 19.V.77

Opposite below
An early Louis XV ormolu-mounted kingwood parquetry commode, stamped *F.C., circa* 1730, width 4ft 9in (145cm)
Mentmore £18,000($30,600). 19.V.77

Opposite above
A Louis XV ormolu-mounted kingwood serpentine commode, stamped *Hansen JME*, circa 1750,
height 3ft (91cm)
Mentmore £65,000($110,500). 18.V.77
The stamp is that of Hubert Hansen, received Master in 1747

A Louis XV ormolu-mounted tulipwood and *bois satiné bureau plat*, signed *B.V.R.B.*, mid eighteenth century,
height 2ft 4¾in (73cm)
New York $55,000(£32,353). 7.V.77
From the collection of Mr and Mrs Alfonso Landa
The signature is that of Bernard Van Risemburgh II, received Master *circa* 1730

A Louis XV/XVI ormolu-mounted marquetry *table à écrire*, signed *C. Topino*, late eighteenth century,
height 2ft 4½in (72.5cm)
New York $23,000(£13,529). 23.IV.77
From the collection of Dr Annella Brown

The signature is that of Charles Topino, received Master in 1773

A Louis XV/XVI ormolu-mounted tulipwood parquetry *table à écrire*, signed *R.V.L.C.*, late eighteenth century,
height 2ft 3¾in (70.5cm)
New York $26,000(£15,294). 23.IV.77
From the collection of Dr Annella Brown

The initials on this table are those of Roger Van Der Cruse *dit* Lacroix, received Master in 1755

One of a pair of Louis XV carved gilt-wood console tables, probably designed by Contant d'Ivry and possibly made by N. Q. Foliot, *circa* 1755, height 3ft (91cm)
Mentmore £28,500($48,450). 18.V.77

Pierre Contant (1698-1777), known as Contant d'Ivry, was *premier architecte* to the Duc d'Orléans and an important exponent of the neo-classical style in France in the mid eighteenth century. Nicolas-Quinibert Foliot (1706-76), became the *Menuisier de la Couronne* in 1749 providing over seven hundred pieces for the royal châteaux

One of a set of five Louis XVI mahogany and gilt-wood bookcases,
height 8ft 8in (269cm)
Monte Carlo Fr650,000(£77,380:$131,547). 3.V.77

A Louis XVI black-japanned *secrétaire à abbatant*, stamped *J. H. Reisener*, height 4ft 9in (150cm)
Monte Carlo Fr1,050,000(£125,000:$212,500). 3.V.77
From the collection of Madame Bethsabée de Rothschild

This desk is believed to have been made for Marie-Antoinette's apartments at Versailles

One of a pair of ormolu-mounted lacquer and ebony side cabinets, in the style of Martin Carlin, *circa* 1870, width 6ft (183cm) Mentmore £32,000($54,400). 18.V.77

A Meissen and ebony cabinet, the drawers painted with scenes after David Teniers the Younger, the doors with harbour scenes after J. B. Weenix and with two portrait panels after N. Largillierre, with crossed swords and impressed marks, the back with a red wax seal stamped *st. Dresden, circa* 1870, height 6ft 1in (185.5cm)
London £15,500($26,350). 16.III.77

Opposite below
A ormolu-mounted kingwood *bureau plat*, the drawer stamped *Linke, circa* 1900, width 5ft 10¼in (150cm)
London £11,000($18,700). 6.VII.77

An ormolu-mounted bluejohn clock, signed *A. R. Simons à Paris*, early nineteenth century, height 2ft 3½in (70cm)
London £9,000($15,300). 16.III.77

One of a pair of French bronze and gilt-bronze candelabra of women in classical dress each holding ten-light ormolu candelabra, signed *E. Guillemin* and *F. Barbedienne, circa* 1880, overall height 8ft 9in (267cm)
London £29,000($49,300). 3.XI.76

Detail

One of a pair of ormolu-mounted Berlin porcelain vases and covers, the mounts signed *Bormann; Sgr. P* and sceptre in underglaze blue, incised *S, circa* 1890, height 3ft 5in (104.2cm)
London £22,000(£37,400). 3.XI.76

Hermann Seger (1839-93) was primarily a chemical technologist. After leaving the Berlin Royal Academy he travelled extensively in Belgium, England, Hungary and Germany, returning to Berlin in 1869 where he continued his research. In 1878 he took over the running of the Konigliche Berlin Manufactory's research institute. Here in collaboration with A. Heinecke he developed new ceramic techniques including flambé, celadon and crystal glazes for testing kiln temperatures. The result of this research was seen in an exhibition of vases covered by the new glazes held by the Manufactory in 1884. Although offered the directorship of the company, he turned it down in order to be able to continue his research and studies, but in 1882, in acknowledgement of his work the sceptre and Sgr. P. mark was placed on pieces on which his glazes were employed

An Augsburg ormolu-mounted *table mécanique*, the door to the central cupboard set with a finely-wrought silver-gilt plaque depicting *The Triumph of Ceres and Bacchus* attributed to Johann Andreas Thelot (1654-1734), *circa* 1830 but partially using a mid eighteenth-century cabinet, width 4ft 6in (137cm)
Mentmore £26,000($44,200). 20.V.77

This table was formerly in the collection of the Duke of Buckingham and Chandos, and acquired for Baron Mayer de Rothschild at the sale in 1848. In his annotated catalogue Henry Rumsey Forster, who wrote a commentary on the sale, notes: 'Of all the exquisite cabinets distributed throughout the mansion, this was decidedly the most superb. . . . This superb piece of furniture was purchased for Baron Meyer Rothschild for 235 guineas after having excited an active competition.'

The central cupboard encloses drawers and six push buttons operating the spring releases to the remaining drawers

Musical Instruments

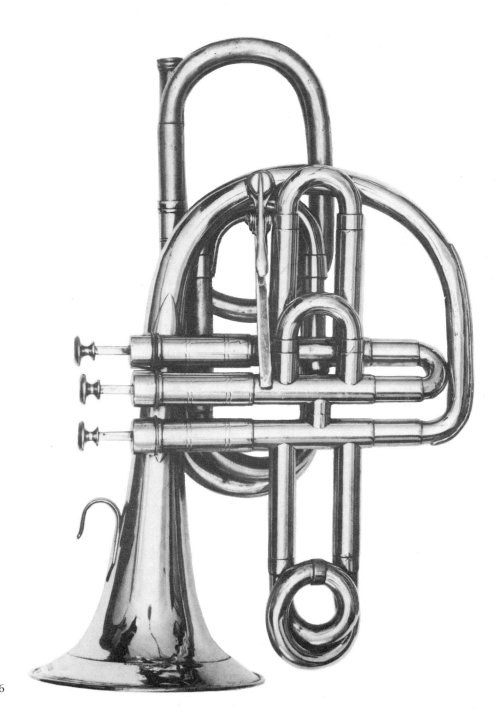

A cornopean by Thomas
Key, engraved *Key, Charing
Cross, London*
mid nineteenth century
London £280($476). 25.XI.76

A French 'Vernis-Martin' decorated grand pianoforte by Erard, stamped *B. Martin, circa* 1865, overall length 8ft 6in (260cm)
Mentmore £15,000($25,500). 18.V.76

Hannah Rothschild's diary for Friday 14 June 1867 notes: 'The Vernis-Martin piano arrived. It is quite magnificent and is placed for the present in the Hall between the fireplace and the hall of the passage leading to the library where the other piano used to stand.'

A double virginals by Hans Ruckers the Younger, Antwerp, 1623, inscribed *Joannes Ruckers me fecit*, length of parent instrument 5ft 7¼in (171cm), length of octave instrument 2ft 8¼in (82cm) New York $65,000(£38,235). 29.X.76

This instrument is one of the six double virginals by the Ruckers family known to have survived, four of these being by Hans the Younger, and the other two by his father Hans the Elder

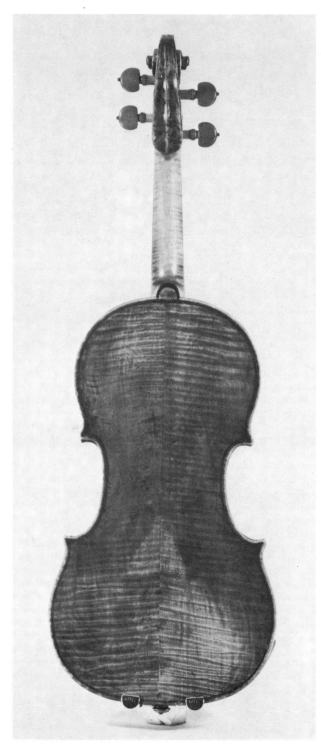 

A violin by Giuseppe Guarneri Filius Andrea, Cremona, 1703, labelled *Joseph Guarnerius filius Andrea fecit Cremona sub titulo S. Teresie 1703,* length of back $13\frac{15}{16}$in (35.4cm) London £23,000($39,100). 12.V.77

A violin by Pietro Guarneri of Venice, 1726, labelled *Petrus Guarnerius Cremonensis filiis Josef fecit Venetiis Anno 1726,* length of back $14\frac{1}{16}$in (35.7cm) London £21,000($35,700). 12.V.77

The Guarneri family of violin makers

Charles Beare

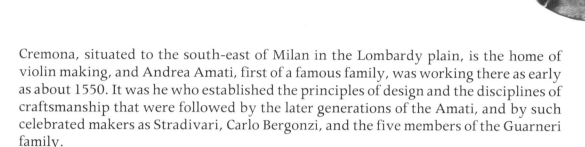

Cremona, situated to the south-east of Milan in the Lombardy plain, is the home of violin making, and Andrea Amati, first of a famous family, was working there as early as about 1550. It was he who established the principles of design and the disciplines of craftsmanship that were followed by the later generations of the Amati, and by such celebrated makers as Stradivari, Carlo Bergonzi, and the five members of the Guarneri family.

The greatest of them all was Antonio Stradivari (1644-1737), a pupil of Nicolo Amati, the grandson of Andrea. Nicolo is usually regarded as the best craftsman of the Amati, and apart from Stradivari he had several other pupils of note including Andrea Guarneri, who lived in his house from 1641 to 1646 and again from 1650 to 1654 (the house remained virtually unaltered until three years ago, when it was converted into flats).

Andrea Guarneri (*circa* 1626-98) was undoubtedly a maker of the first rank, and if he is usually regarded as less significant than his two sons and two grandsons, this is due more to the period when he worked than to any lack of natural ability. In particular many of his violins were made on what is today regarded as too small a pattern. Tonally, although it is dangerous to generalise, most players would agree that a fine Andrea has the quality of an Amati, but with more penetration. His violas and cellos are scarce but splendid instruments, and indeed most of his work illustrates that blend of good design and slightly rough finish that is often referred to as the 'Guarneri character'.

Of Andrea's seven children Pietro Guarneri I (1655-1720) was the elder of the two sons who became violin makers. He is known as 'Peter of Mantua', as he moved to that city about 1680 after several years in his father's workshop. In Mantua he not only made violins, but also took an appointment as a court musician. His work is full of personality and is neater and sharper than that of any of his relatives, the varnish of his instruments is also of unsurpassable quality. The violinist Joseph Szigeti's concert instrument was of this make, and in general his work is regarded as superior to that of his father and younger brother.

The first Giuseppe Guarneri (1666-*circa* 1739), was Andrea's younger son and is thus known as 'Joseph Filius Andrea'. From about 1685 onwards his was the dominant hand in the instruments signed by Andrea, and indeed he became his father's successor as the Casa Guarneri in Cremona's Piazza San Domenico. The artistic advantage of being almost a neighbour of Stradivari may have been cancelled out in

Joseph's eyes by the material disadvantage, for by 1700 Stradivari reigned supreme, his fame having spread all over Europe. Working hastily and sometimes with inexpensive woods, Joseph met the orders of less-wealthy clients. In the quality of his varnish he was at times Stradivari's equal, but although he could be found to be inferior in other respects his instruments nevertheless rank among the most sought-after makes. After 1715 he was evidently aided by his two sons, the second Pietro and the second Giuseppe, and by 1730 his activity was limited to the carving of scrolls, at which he was always adept.

Pietro Guarneri II (1695-1762), son of Joseph, is known as 'Peter of Venice' to distinguish him from his uncle of the same name. After a thorough training in the family workshop he left Cremona about 1718 and went to settle in Venice at what must have been a most interesting time in the city's musical history. He had outstanding contemporaries there in Domenico Montagnana and Santo Serafin, and his work is in a sense a blend of Cremonese and Venetian traditions. Probably the least productive member of the family, Pietro is today at least as highly regarded as his father and uncle.

The final member of the family, Giuseppe Guarneri del Gesu (1698-1744), is in point of tone often regarded as the most successful maker of violins of all time, and certainly the source of more romance, legend, mystery, trickery and downright forgery than any other. The example in Sotheby's sale of 12 May was entirely characteristic of him and in every way a magnificent instrument, well able to satisfy the most demanding violinist and at the same time excellently preserved. In all, about 150 of his violins have survived.

Del Gesu is often portrayed as a crude, erratic maker, and part of the dubious tradition also has it that he was given to fits of drunkenness and finished up in jail. All of this is surely far from the truth, and a fantasy in which most of the nineteenth-century imitators could indulge to the point of vulgarity. Until the last two or three years of the master's working life his story is actually one of application and of continual improvement, of a highly intelligent person and expert craftsman evolving and blending theories in quest of tonal and visual ideals. The 'ex-Adam' Guarneri is from the beginning of the late period, made in 1738, the year after Stradivari's death. A decade earlier del Gesu had set out to reconcile the best of Cremonese tonal achievement with certain characteristics of the Brescian violins made over a century before by Gasparo da Salo and Maggini, a rather darker tonal shade combined with stronger response to forceful bowing. Stradivari had attempted something similar with his 'Long Pattern' of the 1690s, violins remarkable more for their richness of tone than for power of response. With Guarneri del Gesu, however, success was complete, as acknowledged in the past by Paganini, and today by the preference for his violins shown by such artists as (among others) Grumiaux (1744), Heifetz (1742), Kogan (1729), Ricci (1734), Stern (1737 and 1740), Szeryng (1743) and Zukerman (1739).

It is as well to remember that violins, whatever their value as works of art, are primarily for the performance of music. On the other hand, there will be no end to the scarcity factor unless or until modern makers are able to assimilate the knowledge painstakingly gained by five or six successive generations of Cremonese masters, and to reproduce the tonal quality, response and volume that musicians prefer. With such world-wide interest in classical music one can only hope that this may in due course come to pass.

The 'ex-Adam', a violin by Giuseppe Guarneri del Gesu, Cremona, 1738, bearing its original label
Joseph Guarnerius fecit Cremone Anno 1738 I.H.S., length of back $13\frac{7}{8}$in (35.3cm)
London £90,000($153,000). 12.V.77

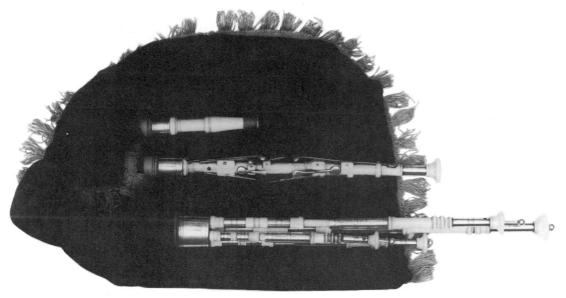

A set of Northumbrian small pipes by Robert Reid, North Shields, stamped *Reid* on each of the stocks, the bellows by Jack Armstrong, *circa* 1830
London £1,600($2,720). 12. V.77
From the collection of Jack Armstrong

Jack Armstrong was until recently Piper to His Grace the Duke of Northumberland

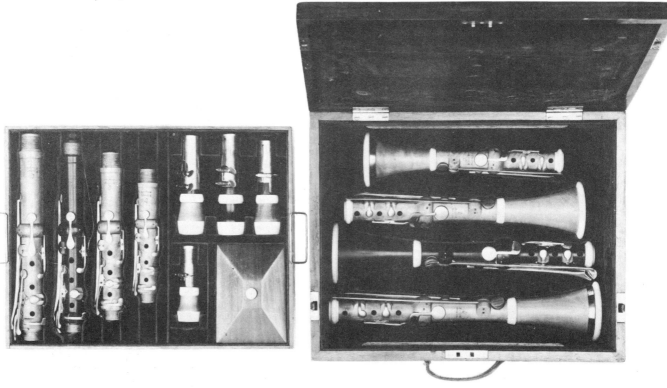

A set of four clarinets by Richard John Bilton, London, each stamped *Bilton, London, 93, Westminster Bridge Road*, *circa* 1840, lengths 26¾in (68cm), 25¾in (65.5cm), 23½in (59.7cm) and 19¼in (48.9cm)
London £1,100($1,870). 25.XI.76
From the collection of Mervyn Ward

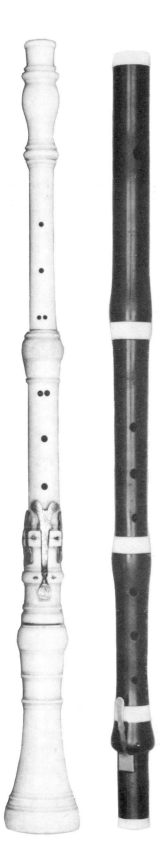

Far left
An ivory three-keyed oboe by Klenig, stamped *Klenig* within a scroll on each joint, second quarter of the eighteenth century, length $22\frac{5}{8}$in (57.5cm)
London £3,400($5,780).
25.XI.76
From the collection of Mervyn Ward

Left
A one-keyed ebony flute by Heinrich Gresner, Dresden, stamped on each joint *H. Gresner Dresden*, third quarter of the eighteenth century, sounding length $20\frac{15}{16}$in (53.2cm)
London £1,600($2,720).
12.V.77

A tenor viol by Frederick Hintz, London, branded *F. Hintz*, mid eighteenth century, length of back $17\frac{1}{2}$in (44.5cm)
London £3,600($6,120).
25.XI.76

Hintz is recorded in Mortimer's Directory of 1763 as 'Guitar-maker to her Majesty and the Royal Family; makes Guitars, Mandolins, Viols de l'Amour, Viols de Gamba, Dulcimers, Solitaires, Lutes, Harps, Cymbals, the Trumpet marine, and the Aeolian Harp'. One other viol by him is known, a bass dated 1760 now in the Victoria and Albert Museum

A violin by Antonio Stradivari, bearing its original label *Antonius Stradivarius Cremonensis Faciebat 1723*, length of back $14\frac{1}{16}$in (35.7cm) London £60,000($102,000). 16.VI.77

The 'Greffuhle' Stradivari violin, bearing its original label *Antonius Stradivarius Cremonensis/Faciebat Anno 1709*, length of back $14\frac{1}{16}$in (35.7cm) New York $170,000(£100,000). 5.IV.77 From the collection of the Carl E. Tannewitz Trust

The instrument's name originates from the Viscomte de Greffhule, to whom it was sold in 1882

Clocks, Watches and Scientific Instruments

A Venetian mirror clock, eighteenth century, diameter 2ft 4in (71cm)
Mentmore £15,500($26,350). 20.V.77

From left to right
An English gilt-metal chiming mantel clock, signed *E. White, 20 Cockspur Street, London*, height 1ft 2½in (36.5cm)
London £4,800($8,160).
29.IV.77

An ebonised basket-top bracket clock, signed *John Barnett Londini Fecit*, height 1ft 1in (33cm)
London £3,000($5,100).
28.I.77

From left to right
A William and Mary gilt-metal-mounted ebony bracket clock with pull repeat, signed *Dan Quare, London*, late seventeenth century, height 1ft 2in (36cm)
New York $5,900(£3,470).
15.I.77

An ebonised bracket clock, signed *Just. Vulliamy London*, height 1ft 5in (43cm)
London £2,700($4,590).
3.XII.76
From the collection of Anne Myers

A walnut longcase clock, signed
John Clowes Londini fecit,
height 5ft 9in (76cm)
London £3,200($5,440). 3.XII.76
From the collection of Anne Myers

A mid eighteenth-century Dutch
burr-walnut musical longcase clock,
height 8ft 8in (264cm)
Los Angeles $13,500(£7,941).
13.VI.77

A Louis XVI style ormolu-mounted
parquetry regulator, signed *F. Linke
à Paris*, late nineteenth century,
height 8ft 5in (231cm)
Los Angeles $22,500(£12,941).
25.X.76

A Louis XVI automaton picture clock, signed *Le Montjoye A Paris, circa* 1780, 3ft by 1ft 6in (92cm by 46cm) Mentmore £20,000 ($34,000). 18.V.77

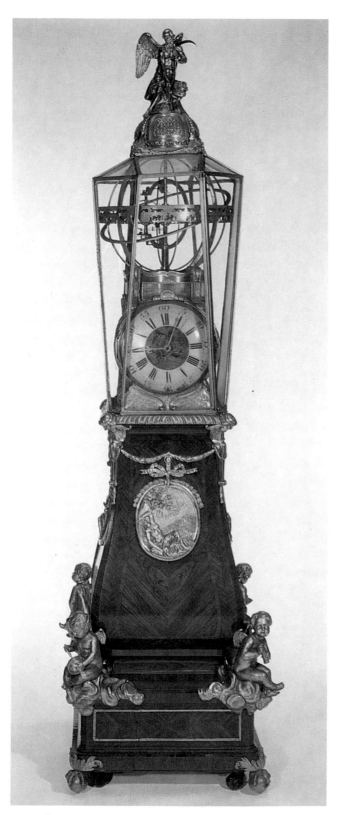

An early Louis XVI ormolu-mounted kingwood two-faced orrery clock, dated *1779*, height 7ft 11in (241cm) Mentmore £40,000($68,000). 18.V.77

A late seventeenth-century marquetry longcase clock, signed *Charles Goode London*, height 5ft 9½in (177cm) London £11,500($19,550). 29.IV.77

A detail showing the pendulum bob
temperature compensation. The pendulum
has brass and steel rods which slide one
against the other. With a rise in temperature,
the brass expands more than the steel and it
is so arranged that this difference causes the
bob to slide up the rod by the same amount
that the rod has lengthened due to the rise in
temperature

JOHN ELLICOTT
A mahogany month regulator, signed *Ellicott
London*, height 4ft 9in (145cm)
London £5,000($8,500). 3.XII.76.

Clocks for the 'transit of Venus'

Derek Howse

Twice every 113 years, the planet Venus can be seen from Earth passing in front of the Sun's disk. Simultaneous observations of this 'transit of Venus' from widely differing latitudes can be used to measure the radius of the Earth's orbit. As this fundamental quantity was not known with any accuracy in the eighteenth century, the transits of 1761 and 1769 resulted in scientific expeditions being sent all over the world to observe the transits. Indeed, one was to have a profound effect upon the history of the world: Captain Cook, sent to observe the 1769 transit in Tahiti, took the opportunity to explore and to claim for George III the two islands of New Zealand and the east coast of New Holland, now Australia.

To observe the transit, it is essential to have an accurate clock alongside the telescope. The regulator clock sold at Sotheby's was made, probably for one of these expeditions, by John Ellicott (1706?–72), a distinguished clockmaker who was also a Fellow of the Royal Society, the body entrusted with the organisation of the British contributions to these very early examples of international scientific co-operation. The clock was specifically designed to be transportable and easily set up when reaching its destination. Inside the case are wooden fittings designed to hold the pendulum and its heavy bob (having been detached from the movement) securely in the case while moving. The case is free-standing upon a separate folding cruciform stand whose four feet screw up and down, making the levelling of the clock particularly easy. Another feature is that it is fitted with a special kind of temperature compensation, invented by Ellicott, to ensure that, whether in the arctic or the tropics, the rate of going remains constant.

In 1760, Ellicott sold a clock for 30 guineas to the Royal Society, to be sent to Sumatra for the 1761 transit with Charles Mason and Jeremiah Dixon, who later gave their names to the Mason-Dixon line in America. Delayed by an attack upon their ship by a French privateer, they could not reach Sumatra in time and had to observe the transit at the Cape of Good Hope. The same clock was sent to Hudson's Bay, Canada, for the 1769 transit and was sold by the Society in 1771. Here record of its history ends and the question remains as to whether this example is the same one. There is another possible candidate, a clock once belonging to Admiral Lord Howe, also transportable and by Ellicott. Both can be seen today in the Navigation Room of the National Maritime Museum, Greenwich.

A walnut quarter-striking and minute-repeating perpetual calendar alarum month mantel clock, signed *Viner Invt Fecit 235 Regent Street London, circa* 1850,
height 9in (23cm)
Mentmore £30,000($51,000). 20.V.77

A silver-mounted and gilt-metal quarter-striking alarum candle clock, mid eighteenth century,
length 7in (19cm)
Mentmore £21,000($35,700). 20.V.77

A set of mathematical instruments by Dominicus Lusuerg of Rome, signed on a number of the instruments *Dominicus Lusuerg Mutinensis Faciebat Romae Ao. 1701*, length of box 18⅛in (46cm)
London £13,000($22,100). 3.XII.76

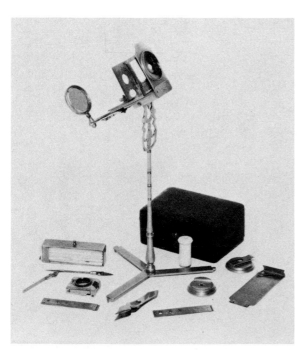

GEORGE LINDSAY NO. 90
A brass pocket microscope, signed on a silver plaque *Geo. Lindsay Inv. & Fec., circa* 1744, length of box 3⅛in (8cm)
London £1,300($2,210). 9.VI.77

An ebony backstaff by Edmund Blow, signed *E. Blow Fecit in Plow Alley at Vnion Staires Wapping May ye 10 1736*, and with inset ivory plaque inscribed *For Mr Thomas Hulcott 1737*, 1736, length 21¼in (54cm)
London £2,300($3,910). 29.IV.77

A gold and enamel verge watch by Richard Street of London, *circa* 1700, diameter 1¾in (4.3cm)
Zurich SF29,000 (£6,744:$11,465). 17.XI.76
From the collection of the late Sir Gyles Isham, 12th Baronet

A gold and enamel cased quarter-repeating musical watch by A. Chambery, signed *A. Chambery Avenier fecit An 1814*, diameter 2¼in (5.9cm)
Zurich SF26,500(£6,162:$10,476). 17.XI.76

A Swiss gold and enamel duplex watch, no. 323 by Bovet of London, circa 1810, diameter 2½in (6.3cm)
New York $15,000(£8,823). 13.VI.77

A gold and pearl set musical automaton watch, *circa* 1800, diameter 2½in (6.3cm)
Zurich SF57,000 (£13,255:$22,534). 17.XI.76

A gold and enamel pearl set verge watch, signed *Clary f.s. Breguet, circa* 1800, diameter 2⅛in (5.5cm)
Zurich SF11,500(£2,674:$4,546). 17.XI.76

A gold and enamel quarter-repeating Savonette watch, signed *Ratel, Paris* and numbered *2579*, nineteenth century, diameter 1⅝in (4.2cm)
Zurich SF8,000(£1,860:$3,162). 17.XI.76

BREGUET NO. 200/3668
A gold pair cased half quarter-repeating lever watch, the inside of the back with the casemaker's punchmark *LS* and the number *B200*, diameter 1¼in (4.6cm)
Zurich SF48,000(£11,162:$18,976). 6.V.77

An enamel and gilt-metal oxidised steel verge watch by Paul Bizot, signed *Paul Bizot a Paris, St. ger^m*, mid seventeenth century, 1⅜in (3.5cm)
Zurich SF100,000 (£23,255:$39,534). 6.V.77

A gold cased quarter-repeating Moses automaton cylinder watch, early nineteenth century, diameter 2⅝in (6.4cm)
Zurich SF100,000(£23,255:$39,534). 17.XI.76

BREGUET NO. 2093
A silver and gold mounted tourbillon watch, the cuvette inscribed *Pour le Prince Repnin en Novembre 1810*, diameter 2½in (6.2cm)
Zurich SF200,000(£46,511:$79,069). 17.XI.76

THOMAS MUDGE NO. 574
A gold pair cased perpetual calendar cylinder watch, hallmarked 1764, diameter 2¼in (5.7cm)
London £19,000($32,300). 3.XII.76

A silver-gilt bird-form watch by Choudens and Chauannes, probably Paris, *circa* 1650,
height $2\frac{1}{2}$in (6.4cm)
New York $14,500(£8,529). 27.X.76

Left
A musical striking quarter-repeating chaise watch, no. 1849, by Joseph Martineau Senior of London, the case signed with the initials *CH*, mid eighteenth century, diameter $5\frac{3}{4}$in (14.5cm)
London £16,000($27,200). 28.I.77

A gold hunting cased minute-repeating clockwatch, with perpetual calendar and split seconds chronograph, no. 8200, by A. Lange and Son, Glashutte, signed, diameter $2\frac{5}{8}$in (6.5cm)
Zurich SF210,000(£48,837:$83,023). 6.V.77

A gold hunting cased split seconds minute-repeating perpetual calendar keyless lever watch, no. 148-99, by S. Smith & Sons of 9 Strand, London, hallmarked 1899, diameter $2\frac{3}{8}$in (5.9cm)
London £8,000($13,600). 9.VI.77

Glass and Paperweights

An armorial goblet by
William Beilby, *circa*
1762-64, height $7\frac{7}{8}$in (20cm)
London £8,400($14,280).
20.XII.76

The arms on the bowl of
the goblet are probably
those of Henry Partis,
sheriff and alderman of
Newcastle in 1745, mayor
in 1752 and again in 1760,
he died in 1766

A Mount Washington magnum
chrysanthemum weight, diameter $3\frac{5}{8}$in
(8.9cm)
New York $1,100(£647). 1.VI.77
From the collection of Paul Hollister

A Gillinder white carpet-ground
weight, diameter $2\frac{7}{8}$in (7.5cm)
New York $1,000(£588). 1.VI.77
From the collection of Paul
Hollister

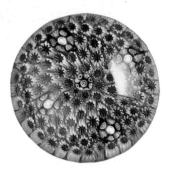

A New England carpet-
ground weight, diameter
$2\frac{5}{8}$in (6.8cm)
New York $1,100(£647).
1.VI.77
From the collection of Paul
Hollister

A St Louis sulphide and carpet-ground
weight, diameter $2\frac{3}{4}$in (7cm)
London £1,600($2,720). 4.VII.77

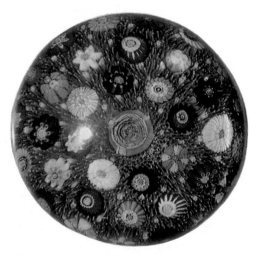

The celebrated Clichy moss-ground weight (two views illustrated), the reverse signed in
the centre *Clichy*, diameter $3\frac{1}{4}$in (8cm)
London £17,500($29,750). 4.VII.77

A St Louis green aventurine-
ground flat bouquet weight,
diameter 2¾in (7.1cm)
London £1,300($2,210). 4.X.76

A St Louis blue jasper salamander
weight, diameter 3⅜in (8.5cm)
London £1,800($3,060). 4.VII.77

A Clichy double convolvulus bouquet weight,
diameter 2¾in (7.2cm)
London £30,000($51,000). 4.VII.77
The maker of this weight has attempted to be
botanically correct in the modelling of the
convolvulous leaves, a feature not noted in
any other bouquet weights

A St Louis *piedouche* or pedestal weight,
diameter 3in (7.8cm)
London £2,000($3,400). 4.VII.77

A St Louis flat bouquet weight, diameter 2¾in
(7.1cm)
London £4,600($7,820). 4.VII.77

A Bohemian *schwarzlot* covered bowl decorated by Ignaz Preissler in black heightened in gold,
circa 1725, width 5¼in (13.4cm)
London £6,500($11,050). 7.III.77
From the collection of Major-General Sir Allen Adair, Bt

A Potsdam cut and gilt ruby-glass
royal armorial goblet and cover,
circa 1725-30, height 15in (38cm)
London £9,000($15,300). 13.VI.77

This unrecorded goblet is among the
most important ruby-glass objects to
have survived from the Potsdam
glass-house where the alchemist
Johann Kunckel had developed this
type of glass in the 1680s. The bowl is
gilt with the arms of King Frederick
William of Prussia as adopted in 1709.
He reigned from 1713 to 1740

A cameo glass plaque, engraved signature *Geo. Woodall*, cut title *Aphrodite, circa* 1885, diameter 10⅝in (27cm)
London £11,500($19,550). 10.III.77

Art Nouveau and Art Deco

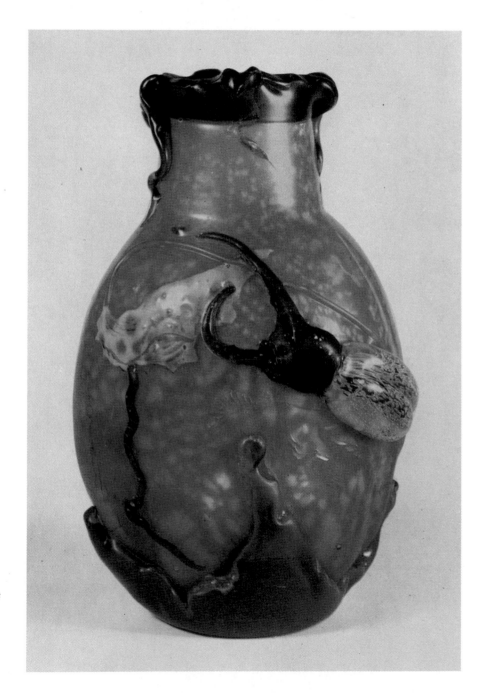

La Forêt Guyanaise
An internally decorated,
applied and carved glass vase
by Emile Gallé, the body
finely engraved *Gallé 1900*,
height 9⅛in (23.2cm)
London £22,000($37,400).
20.VII.77

An enamelled buckle by René Lalique, stamped *Lalique, circa* 1900, width 5⅜in (13.7cm)
Monte Carlo Fr26,000(£3,095:$5,261). 5.XII.76

A gold and enamel *parure de corsage*, designed by Alphonse Mucha and executed by Georges Fouquet, stamped *G. Fouquet 2873, circa* 1900, length 6¾in (17cm)
Monte Carlo Fr220,000(£26,190:$44,523). 5.XII.76

A Tiffany Favrile glass and bronze poinsettia hanging chandelier, impressed *Tiffany Studios New York 1523, circa* 1899-1920, diameter 26in (66cm)
New York $28,000(£16,470). 1.IV.77

Opposite
A detail of the doors of a lacquer cabinet by Gaston Priou, signed *G. Priou, circa* 1930, height 56½in (143cm)
New York $10,000(£5,882). 1.IV.77

The altar-chair from Queen's Cross Church, Glasgow, oak with horsehair fabric seat, 1897-98, height 2ft 9¾in (87.75cm) London £400($680). 10.XI.76

Charles Rennie Mackintosh photographed by Messrs Annan, Glasgow, *circa* 1900-1903

The Music Room at Hous'hill, *circa* 1905

Charles Rennie Mackintosh as designer

Philippe Garner

Charles Rennie Mackintosh was one of the most exciting architect/designers active in Britain at the turn of the nineteenth century. With a few notable exceptions his work was not well-received by his contemporaries. Apart from a very small group of enlightened patrons, Mackintosh inspired his strongest support abroad and, in particular, in Vienna, where Josef Hoffman and his colleagues of the Vienna Secession found in his work the materialisation of their own as yet imperfectly defined ideas. For a prophet who found little acclaim in his own land it was somehow appropriate that the first monograph on his work should have been a foreign production, written by Nikolaus Pevsner for an Italian publisher.[1] This short study published in 1950 was soon followed by Thomas Howarth's exhaustive *Charles Rennie Mackintosh and the Modern Movement*,[2] which is still the standard reference on the artist. These two publications heralded a slow re-awakening of interest in Mackintosh and the Glasgow School which seemed suddenly to gain considerable momentum in 1968 with the Scottish Arts Council's major exhibition, commemorating the centenary of Mackintosh's birth.[3] For the first time the work of Mackintosh and his colleagues was seen and enjoyed by a wide public. His outstanding talent is now seriously appreciated at an international level and he has received the homage of an exhibition of his remarkable designs for chairs at New York's Museum of Modern Art.[4]

For the historian Mackintosh's work is a fruitful subject for study. His output was limited as he only created furniture or objects in the context of specific commissions and never designed for commercial production, thereby making it possible to document fully every piece that emerges. Sotheby's have had the good fortune over the last ten years or so to handle the sale of a considerable variety of Mackintosh items, providing good examples of every phase of his work, and their own considerable enthusiasm for this artist has encouraged the rediscovery of certain works hitherto believed to be lost.

Charles Rennie Mackintosh was born in Glasgow in 1868. His architectural training began when, aged sixteen, he was apprenticed to the architect John Hutchinson. In 1889 he joined the practice of Honeymann & Keppie, an old established Glasgow firm. Here he befriended J. Herbert MacNair, fellow draughtsman and student at evening

[1] Nikolaus Pevsner, *Charles Rennie Mackintosh* (Milan, 1950).
[2] Thomas Howarth, *Charles Rennie Mackintosh and the Modern Movement* (London and Glasgow, 1952).
[3] *Charles Rennie Mackintosh (1868-1928): Architecture, Design and Painting*, Scottish Arts Council Exhibition, 1968.
[4] Filippo Alison, *Charles Rennie Mackintosh as a Designer of Chairs* (London, 1973).

The Blue Bedroom at Hous'hill, *circa* 1905, showing the cabinet sold in 1975 and the table illustrated in colour opposite

classes of the Glasgow School of Art. Mackintosh and MacNair in turn met and befriended the MacDonald sisters, Margaret and Frances, students at the School of Art who shared their ideas on design. The friendships flourished and led to a double marriage, that of Frances to MacNair in 1899 and of Margaret to Mackintosh in 1900. The 'Glasgow Four', as they became known, worked very closely and created a distinctive Glasgow style that blended a certain traditional Scottish austerity with subtle symbolist details and elegant lines derived from Aubrey Beardsley and the Dutch artist, Jan Toorop. The Glasgow style was significant above all for its emphasis on essentially simple forms, clean lines, attenuated verticals, a sparing use of colour and a full appreciation of the decorative value of the abstract elements of light and space. Charles Rennie Mackintosh was the leading figure in the group and his genius encouraged and gave direction to the talents of the others.

Mackintosh's first important commission was won in 1896 with his project, submitted in an open competition, for the rebuilding of the Glasgow School of Art. He worked on this project over a number of years and the resulting building is now often quoted as a key design in the development of modern architecture.

The Glasgow School of Art and the Queen's Cross Church, also designed in 1896, characterise Mackintosh's early phase in which the 'Scottish Baronial' tradition was still strong and in which he favoured sombre, dark-stained woods, most usually oak, for furniture and furnishings which were refined and austere and had not yet acquired the more precious features of his slightly later pieces. The Queen's Cross Church, recently threatened with demolition, has now been relinquished by the Church authorities to the care of the Mackintosh Society, though not before the oak

Oak table from the Blue Bedroom at Hous'hill, *circa* 1905,
2ft 6in by 2ft 1in (76.25cm by 63.5cm)
London £2,600($4,420). 10.XI.76

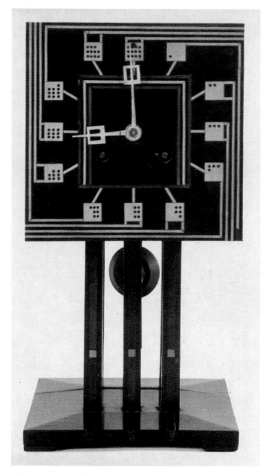

The 'Domino' clock designed for Derngate,
ebony, ivory and erinoid, *circa* 1917,
height 10in (25.5cm)
London £6,500($11,050). 10.XI.76

altar-chair and a pair of side-chairs had found their way into a Sotheby sale.[5] The Glasgow School of Art, however, and the majority of its original fittings are still in full use and, as far as can be traced, nothing from the School has turned up at auction.

Apart from the School and Church projects, 1896 was an important year for Mackintosh for another reason. He received his first commission from Miss Cranston, who, in giving Mackintosh a free hand in the designing of a series of Glasgow tearooms and, after 1903, the redecorating of her home, Hous'hill, encouraged the evolution of Mackintosh's more decorative vein. Public rooms for the leisured taking of afternoon tea had become very much a part of the social scene in turn-of-the-century Glasgow and no-one did more to promote this fashion than the energetic Miss Cranston. She shrewdly enlisted the help of exciting young talents to create the decorative schemes which were to make her rooms so especially attractive. Mackintosh worked in 1897 on schemes for her premises in Buchanan Street and Argyle

[5] Altar-chair, lot 72; side-chairs, lot 73, Sotheby's Belgravia, 10.XI.76.

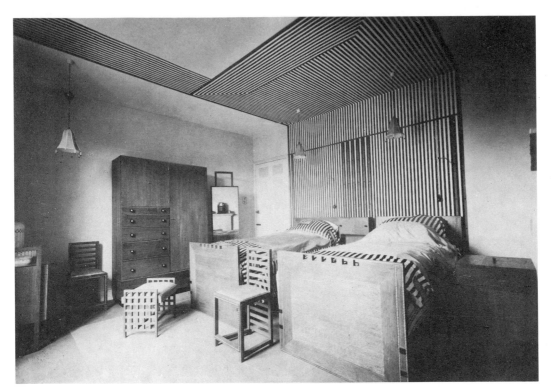

The Principal Bedroom at Derngate, *circa* 1916-17

Street, creating highly stylised friezes in the former and, in the latter, designing the first of what was to be a remarkable series of idiosyncratic high-backed chairs. This design, in ebonised oak with its attenuated uprights, oval panel with open-fretted motif of a stylised bird, and chequered horse-hair seat has become probably the most illustrated and best-known example of Mackintosh's chair designs. The artist's evident satisfaction with this design is borne out by its inclusion in the decoration of his own home and in the exhibit sent to Vienna in 1900. Sotheby's have sold several examples of this particular design. [6]

Miss Cranston's satisfaction with Mackintosh's first works for her is evidenced in the increasing responsibility he was to play in the design of her rooms. When, in 1904, she launched her new Willow Tearooms, Mackintosh and his colleagues designed every detail from the re-styled façade to the tableware. The Willow Tearooms incorporated several separate rooms of quite different character – in some Mackintosh used his favoured dark-stained oak in a variety of new designs, with clever partitions, plaster murals and geometric carpets. [7] The most exciting feature, however, was the Room de Luxe, the only room, incidently, to have survived virtually intact. Here could be seen Mackintosh's most precious and exquisite style in a setting designed for regular, commercial use. Double doors with sophisticated stained glass panels of Celtic *entrelacs* opened into it to reveal a frieze of mirror and lilac glass panels symbolising avenues of willow, a central decorative feature of a magnificent gesso

[6] Lots 133, 134 and 135, Sotheby's, 10.XI.70.
[7] See lots 55 and 56, Sotheby's, 9.III.70; lots 52 and 53, Sotheby's Belgravia, 3.IV.74.

panel by Margaret MacDonald Mackintosh and white furniture, tables and high-backed chairs upholstered in purple. Miss Cranston was Mackintosh's staunchest patron over a period of years, indeed, throughout his active Glasgow phase. Starting in 1903 Mackintosh, aided by his colleagues, completely redecorated her home, Hous'hill. Here also we find Mackintosh at his most refined. He created a brilliant Music Room, white, with a curved end wall, superbly counterbalanced by an openwork white-painted timber partition. Contemporary photographs show this partition and, standing before it, a supremely refined high-backed chair, its elegant uprights echoing the design of the screen, the sleek, dark-stained wood relieved with details of lilac glass.

After Miss Cranston's departure, Hous'hill changed hands several times and was finally demolished by the Glasgow corporation. Many of the contents had been removed by the second owner and were sold at auction on 18 August 1933. Howarth records [8] that 'armchairs of exquisite craftsmanship brought between £2 and £3'. This was the fate of the Music Room chair which subsequently emerged after decades of oblivion, to fetch a record £9,200 at Sotheby's in March 1975. [9] The previous Mackintosh record had been set at £8,000 in 1972 [10] by a set of four gesso panels, *The Four Queens*, executed by Margaret M. Mackintosh for Miss Cranston's card room in 1909. *The Four Queens* had suffered the same sad fate as the Hous'hill chair at the 1933 auction and the auctioneer, experiencing considerable difficulty in obtaining bids, had let them go at 25 shillings for the set. Other pieces from Hous'hill sold by Sotheby's include an upright cabinet detailed in leaded glass and mother of pearl [11] and an oak table identified from contemporary photographs as being from the Blue Bedroom, [12] and a pair of armchairs from the Card Room. [13]

Aside from his work for Miss Cranston and his designs for foreign exhibitions where he was not hampered by commercial constraints, the great achievement of Mackintosh's mature Glasgow phase was the design of the magnificent private house, Hill House, at Helensburgh between 1902 and 1903. Sotheby's have handled the sale of a wide variety of items from Hill House, including elegant ebonised chairs and tables and a hearthrug. [14]

Mackintosh's career was a comparatively short one for he rapidly grew disenchanted with the conservatism of a public which, with a few notable exceptions, failed to appreciate his visionary ideas. In 1914 he resigned his partnership and moved with his wife to London. The following years were restless ones for Mackintosh during which he found a certain solace in evolving a highly personal style of watercolour flower study. A number of these refined and highly graphic studies have been sold by Sotheby's over the last few years. [15]

The only serious patron to employ Mackintosh in this later phase was the wealthy toy-maker, William Bassett-Lowke, who commissioned him to refurbish his

[8] Thomas Howarth, *op. cit.*, p 116.
[9] Lot 53, Sotheby's Belgravia, 13.III.75.
[10] Lot 163, Sotheby's Belgravia, 16.XI.72.
[11] Lot 52, Sotheby's Belgravia, 13.III.75.
[12] Lot 75, Sotheby's Belgravia, 10.XI.76.
[13] Lot 136, Sotheby's Belgravia, 28.III.73.
[14] See lots 220 and 221, Sotheby's, 17.IV.67; lots 223 and 224, 2.VII.75; lots 237 and 238, 27.XI.75, both at Sotheby's Belgravia.
[15] See lots 161-66, 7.XI.73; lots 45-51, 3.IV.74; and lots 46-50, 13.III.75, Sotheby's Belgravia.

Clock-case designed for Derngate, ebonised wood inlaid with ivory and green erinoid, *circa* 1917, height 9⅜in (23.8cm) London £9,300($15,800). 20.VII.77

Thomas Howarth refers to this and the other clock sold this season in his discussion of the contents of Derngate: 'There were also two charming clock-cases about ten inches high made of ebony and erinoid in various colours – red, yellow, purple and white. The movements were French bought by Mr Bassett-Lowke in London and the cases themselves were made by German prisoners of war in the Isle of Man (*circa* 1917).'

Northampton home, Derngate. Mackintosh worked on this project between 1916 and 1919 in a quite distinct style, more rigidly geometric than anything he had done before. It was for Derngate that Mackintosh designed the two remarkable clock-cases that were sold at Sotheby's[16] during the 1976-77 season. These clock-cases encapsulate the style of Derngate, swan-song of this brilliant designer whose work is at last attracting the full respect it deserves and which, sadly, he failed to achieve during his own lifetime.

[16] Lot 74, 10.XI.76; and lot 130, 20.VII.77, both at Sotheby's Belgravia.

Jewellery

An emerald cameo of a Medusa head, Italian, *circa* 1840, the white gold mount later £15,000($25,500)
An antique gold and hardstone cameo brooch by Castellani, signed twice on the reverse with two 'c's
entwined, Italian, *circa* 1860 £900($1,530)
A gold, sapphire and enamel necklace in nineteenth-century renaissance taste, stamped *L & B*
£2,400($4,080)

The jewellery illustrated on this page was sold in London on 25 November 1976

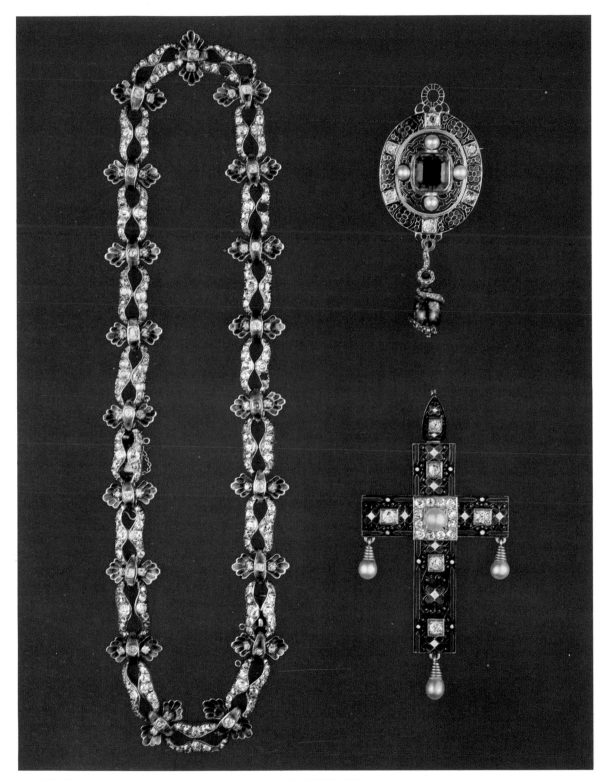

A gold, diamond and enamel necklet, *circa* 1830 £3,000($5,100)
A Holbeinesque brooch/pendant in gold, enamels, emeralds, half-pearls and diamonds, *circa* 1870, the drop earlier £6,000($10,200)
A Holbeinesque pendant in gold, enamels, pearls and diamonds designed as a Latin cross, English, late nineteenth century £1,600($2,720)

The jewellery illustrated on this page was sold in London on 25 November 1976

The Harley memorial ring

Diana Scarisbrick

Memorial rings have a long history. In his will of 1399 Richard II left 'one golden ring' to each of his executors, and the custom remained part of the funeral ritual in England until well into the nineteenth century. The circular form, symbolic of eternity, and the use of the ring at marriage ceremonies and hence its association with the emotions and affections made it more suitable for the purpose of commemorating the dead than any other jewel. By the end of the seventeenth century the memorial ring had come to assume a distinctive character, uniting macabre *memento mori* elements – skulls, skeletons, cross-bones, coffins, hour-glasses and the grave digger's pick and spade – with inscriptions recording the name and date of the deceased, and a relic of hair enclosed in a collet set with a crystal.

The Harley ring combines these symbols of mortality and an inscription, with a grandiose display of heraldry and a faceted emerald weighing approximately 5 carats. It is a monument in miniature to the loss and grief sustained by a family at the centre of the world of politics, literature and high society when the heir to their wealth and position died within five days of his birth. This is recorded in Roman

The Harley memorial ring, gold,
emerald and enamel, 1725
London £25,000($42,500). 25.XI.76

capitals on the outside of the triangular hoop, *HENRY CAVENDISHE LD. HARLEY, NAT. 18. OCT. 1725*, and the inside is inscribed in italic letters: *UNE VIE SI COURTE, UNE SI GRANDE AFFLICTION*. These inscriptions are set in a ground of white enamel, reflecting the tradition of wearing white vestments and mourning clothes at the funerals of children and unmarried persons. The octagonal bezel is set with a splendid emerald and at the back is an achievement, enamelled in *champlevé* and *en ronde bosse*, Quarterly, 1. Harley; 2. Brampton; 3. Cavendish; 4. Vere; the Motto *VIRTUTE ET FIDE* below, and the Supporters; *an angel Silver robed winged and crined Gold, and a lion rampant gardant crowned per fess Gold and Gules*. Around the sides of the bezel the crests of the Harley and Cavendish families alternate with crystal plaques enclosing the hair of the dead child, and flaming torches, discreet reminders of mortality.

The quarterings and crests record the dynastic history of the Harley family, their origins as Herefordshire squires marrying into the Brampton family, tenants of the Mortimers of Wigmore, in 1308, and the conferring of the oldest surviving earldom in England, that of Oxford, on Robert Harley (1661–1724), grandfather of the dead child. Robert Harley's political career, culminating in his leadership of the Tory Government 1710-14, owed much to the influence of his cousin, Abigail Hill, favourite of Queen Anne. Losing the support of these ladies in the struggle over the Hanoverian succession he was dismissed, impeached, and imprisoned in the Tower. On his release he lavished his political skills, his shrewdness and tenacity, and the large fortune he had made through investment in the South Sea Company, on the creation of a noble library. His son, Edward, 2nd Earl of Oxford (1689-1741), dedicated his life to the same purpose. The superb quality of the Harley ring echoes the munificent scale of his collecting. He married Lady Henrietta Cavendish, the only child of Margaret, co-heiress of the last Cavendish Duke of Newcastle, and the heraldry on the ring commemorates these two important heiress marriages. The death of their son, Henry, meant the end of the direct Harley succession and once again a daughter inherited the Cavendish fortune. This was Margaret Harley (1715-85), who married the 2nd Duke of Portland in 1734. When her father died she offered his incomparable collection of manuscripts to the nation, and so the Harleian Collection, purchased in 1751 with that of Sir Hans Sloane, became the nucleus of the British Library. Contemporary memoirs described the owner of the ring, Lady Oxford, as dull but worthy, and some of the literary characters who surrounded her husband considered her a great nuisance. However she was much liked by the celebrated and original Lady Mary Wortley Montagu, who, left a legacy by Lady Oxford, promptly spent the money on a ring engraved with both their names, Mary and Henrietta, as a reminder of the friendship that had survived all her years of travel and exile.

Besides evoking the personal ambitions and private sadnesses of those associated with the sparkling world of literature and politics the ring represents the high peak of achievement in English early eighteenth-century jewellery. Certainly no finer memorial ring survives, and it has remained in impeccable condition in the shagreen box lined with red silk, just as it was received by Lady Oxford 250 years ago to commemorate the tragically short life of her son, Henry Harley.

A cabochon sapphire weighing 73.58 carats SF75,000(£17,441:$29,651)
An Art Deco emerald and diamond brooch mounted in platinum by Cartier SF18,000(£4,186:$7,116)
A jade necklace of 198 beads graduating from 0.41cm to 1.02cm, the clasp set with a cabochon emerald SF160,000(£37,209:$63,255)

The jewellery illustrated on this page was sold in Zurich on 5 May 1977

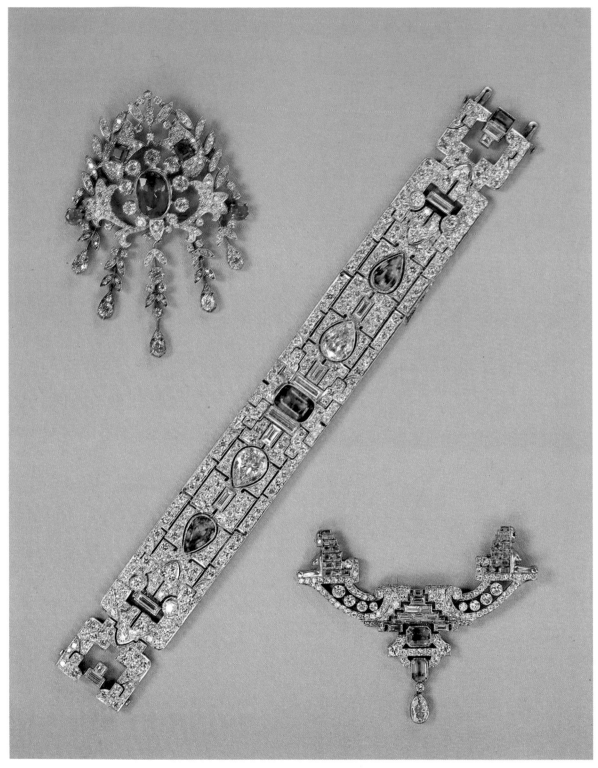

From left to right
A sapphire and diamond pendant brooch mounted in platinum and gold SF19,000(£4,418:$7,511)
An emerald and diamond bracelet mounted in platinum SF110,000(£25,581:$43,488)
An Art Deco brooch with emeralds and diamonds set in platinum SF9,500(£2,209.$3,755)

The jewellery illustrated on this page was sold in St Moritz on 18 February 1977

Above An Art Deco crystal, diamond and black onyx jabot pin by Tiffany & Co, set with 54 diamonds weighing approximately 2.15 carats $3,750(£2,205)
Left An Art Deco diamond jabot pin by Cartier, centring an old-mine diamond weighing approximately 4.25 carats $22,000(£12,941)
Right An Art Deco ruby and diamond jabot pin by Cartier, centring a ruby weighing approximately 3 carats $11,000(£6,470)
Below A diamond and ruby two-part clip by Brand-Chatillon $3,300(£1,941)

The jewellery illustrated on this page is from the collection of the late Joan Whitney Payson and was sold in New York on 13 October 1976

A ruby, diamond and emerald flower
brooch by Van Cleef & Arpels, centring a
ruby weighing approximately 4 carats
New York $21,000(£12,352). 8.XII.76
From the collection of the late Tilly Losch
Carnarvon

A gold, ruby, emerald and pearl pendant
London £10,000($17,000). 7.VII.77
From the collection of Her Royal Highness
The Princess Margaret Countess of Snowdon

An emerald and diamond brooch, *circa* 1830
London £68,000($115,600). 21.IV.77

A diamond brooch mounted in platinum
St Moritz SF180,000(£41,860:$71,162). 19.II.77

A pair of jade ear pendants finely carved in the
form of ripening pea pods, each loop set with
three diamonds
Hong Kong HK$125,000(£15,625:$26,562).
2.XII.76

A pair of diamond lily brooches by
Van Cleef & Arpels
New York $28,000(£16,470). 15.IV.77
From the collection of the late Dorothy L.
Silberberg

Above left and right
An emerald and diamond ring by Cartier, the platinum mount centring an emerald weighing
approximately 2.75 carats $46,000(£27,058)
An emerald and diamond ring by Van Cleef & Arpels, centring an emerald weighing approximately
7.25 carats $87,500(£51,470)
Centre
A diamond, emerald and natural pearl brooch, centring a heart-shaped diamond weighing approx-
imately 4 carats, *circa* 1910 $31,000(£18,235) From the collection of the late Joan Whitney Payson
Below left and right
A pair of emerald and diamond earclips, centring two emeralds weighing approximately
8.75 carats $26,000(£15,294)
An emerald and diamond ring by Bulgari, centring an emerald weighing approximately
9 carats $62,500(£36,764)

The jewellery illustrated on this page was sold in New York on 14 April 1977

A cultured pearl necklace by Van Cleef & Arpels, 135 graduated pearls measuring approximately 1 to 1.5cm
New York $140,000(£82,352). 14.IV.77
From the collection of the late Emily B. Guthrie

From left to right

A pair of sapphire and diamond earclips mounted in platinum SF210,000(£48,837:$83,023)

A sapphire and diamond bracelet by Van Cleef & Arpels SF85,000(£19,767:$33,604)

A sapphire ring, the step-cut sapphire weighing 44.29 carats, mounted with small turquoises in a ring of 18 carat gold wire SF400,000(£93,023:$158,139)

A sapphire and diamond ring mounted in platinum SF190,000(£44,186:$75,116)

The jewellery illustrated on this page was sold in Zurich on 18 November 1976

From left to right
A diamond necklace by Harry Winston, set with 284 diamonds weighing approximately 147.5 carats
$210,000(£123,529).
A pair of diamond earclips, platinum mounts set with 24 diamonds weighing approximately 18.5 carats
$60,000(£35,294).

The jewellery illustrated on this page is from the collection of the late Harriet A. Ames and was sold
in New York on 15 April 1977

1. An emerald-cut sapphire (approx 44.5 carats), New York $290,000(£170,588). 13.X.76
2. An emerald (approx 19.32 carats) and diamond pendant, New York $310,000(£182,352). 15.IV.77
3. A cabochon sapphire (approx 16 carats) and diamond ring, New York $80,000(£47,058). 17.V.77
4. A sapphire (approx 28 carats) and diamond ring, New York $60,000(£35,294). 15.IV.77
5. An emerald (approx 18.35 carats) and diamond pendant/ring, New York $520,000(£305,882). 14.IV.77
6. A step-cut emerald and diamond ring, London £23,000($39,100). 21.IV.77
7. An emerald (approx 3.5 carats) and diamond ring by Cartier, New York $41,000(£24,117). 18.V.77
8. An emerald (approx 29.9 carats) ring flanked by two baguette diamonds, New York $450,000(£264,705). 14.X.76
9. A rose-coloured octagonal step-cut diamond (9.97 carats), Zurich SF460,000(£106,976:$181,860). 5.V.77
10. The de Waal diamond (1.58 carats), Johannesburg R25,000(£16,666:$28,333). 18.IV.77
11. An alexandrite (6 carats) in diamond cluster mount, Hong Kong HK$200,000(£25,000:$43,010). 17.V.77
12. An oblong and step-cut diamond, mounted as a ring, London £31,000($52,700). 25.XI.76
13. A red spinel (approx 24 carats) and diamond ring by Van Cleef & Arpels, New York $19,000(£11,176). 15.IV.77
14. A black opal (approx 3.6 carats) and diamond ring, New York $9,000(£5,294). 15.IV.77
15. A ruby (7.25 carats) and diamond ring, Hong Kong HK$340,000(£42,500:$72,250). 17.V.77
16. A diamond (approx 9.25 carats) and ruby brooch, New York $125,000(£73,529). 18.V.77

A diamond ring, centring a cushion-shaped
diamond weighing approximately 54.15 carats
New York $520,000(£305,882). 14.IV.77
From the collection of the late Emily B. Guthrie

A diamond ring, centring an emerald-cut
diamond weighing approximately 38.10 carats
New York $850,000(£500,000). 13.X.76
From the collection of Bernice Chrysler Garbisch

An emerald and diamond brooch, centring an emerald-cut emerald weighing approximately
7.15 carats New York $210,000(£123,529). 14.X.76
From the collection of the late Joan Whitney Payson

A necklace in rubies and diamonds, the rubies weighing 100.28 carats, the diamonds weighing 39.27 carats
Hong Kong HK$400,000(£50,000:$85,000). 2.XII.76

Collectors' Sales

A Paillard, Vaucher & Co *Sublime Harmonie, Plerodiènique* interchangeable cylinder musical box, number *9735*, Swiss, *circa* 1890, height 41in (104cm)
London £13,000($22,100). 29.VI.77

The Plerodiènique type of cylinder musical box was invented by Albert Jeanrenaud of St Croix, Switzerland, in the early 1880s and the American patent granted to M. J. Paillard & Co on 31 October 1882. This unusual movement consists of two pinned brass barrels mounted on a common axis; as one plays, the other shifts laterally and changes tune, the result being an uninterrupted musical performance of considerable length

Above left
A tinplate clockwork Mickey
Mouse organ grinder, probably
by J. Distler, German, *circa*
1930, length 6in (15cm)
London £1,800($3,060). 15.VI.77

Above right
An Edison home phonograph,
model *D*, serial number
371004D, American, *circa* 1904
London £270($459). 26.X.76
From the collection of John
Carter

Detail of a magician and musical
monkeys barrel-organ
automaton, the musical
movement concealed in a
mahogany case below, French,
mid nineteenth century, height
36in (91.5cm)
London £4,000($6,800).
21.XII.76

A two-inch scale live steam coal-fired model double-crank compound road locomotive, length 38in (96.5cm)
London £2,000($3,400). 21. XII.76

A mechanical, painted tin, two-decker paddle-steamer named the 'Star', length 14½in (37cm)
New York $1,600(£941). 1.XII.76

A Jumeau doll, with kid body and original wardrobe, marked *Medaille d'Or*, height 24in (61cm)
New York $1,500(£882). 30.XI.76

The Archie Stiles Collection of toys and dolls

David Redden

PB-84 has often been the stage for unusual and interesting sales. But no sale in recent years has generated as much attention from both the news media and the buying public as the pre-Christmas auction of dolls and toys belonging to Mr and Mrs Archie Stiles of Myersville, New Jersey. Newspapers and television stations were fascinated by the story of Archie's 'Resale Shop', a sort of private junkyard in northern New Jersey where Archie Stiles had accumulated a vast collection of bygones over the years.

Archie had a generous interest in whatever came his way, though his special affection was reserved for toys, and as the truckloads of odds and ends passed through his yard, he put aside the cast-iron engines, the trains, the rocking horses, and the clockwork carousels. He put the toys on shelves around his living room, he put a cabinet of toys in the kitchen, he paraded them in rows along the windowsills, he began piling them in the porch. When the PB-84 experts went out to look at the collection, the ground floor of the house was almost impassable, and Archie stood there grinning, later confessing that as a child, he had felt deprived of the toys he had wanted.

Amateur psychologists might call Archie's accumulation a case of overcompensation, but the newspaper reporters and the television crews seized on the fact that Archie was about to make a killing. His collection of toys and dolls alone was worth, we told him, about $100,000 and the news media could not make enough of that. Here was a man, perhaps a little too colourful to be taken seriously as an astute investor, who was literally sitting on top of a fortune in toys.

In fact, toys and dolls have, over the last two decades, become a phenomenally popular field for collecting, and Archie Stiles was one of the beneficiaries. Men and women with plenty of time and money to spend on their whims have fallen easy victims to the mechanical ingenuity and innocent artfulness, the gay colours and the liveliness of penny banks and clockwork aeroplanes. These memories of childhood, after years of neglect and abandonment, have passed suddenly onto drawing-room shelves and into carefully-guarded cabinets. Again they invoke the spell with which they once captured the awe of children, and this time it is the adults who yield.

The range of toy-collecting is very wide and part of the fascination of the Stiles Collection was that it covered the entire field. In this eclectic accumulation were cast-iron, tin, and wooden toys, trains, bisque, china and composition dolls, bicycles, sleds and even a magnificent carousel horse. There were over 2,000 items and a large part of our task was grouping them appropriately.

The first day, 30 November, was devoted to dolls. Toys and dolls are not bought by the same collectors, the distinction between the purchasers being entirely one of sex. The women were given their opportunity first, and with a television camera crew jammed in the back of the room, the sale began with two hundred lots of dolls, dolls'-house furniture and dolls' carriages. As anticipated, the most sought-after items were the turn-of-the-century French and German dolls with heads moulded in bisque porcelain. A 24-inch Jumeau with kid body and original clothes fetched $1,500 (£882), an Armand Marseilles 253 'Googlie', $475 (£279), and an Armand Marseilles 258 'Fanny', unstrung and missing limbs, $1,600 (£941). The automata did well too, a 33-inch tall clockwork tin ferris wheel, hoisting eight gondolas and seating a total of sixteen bisque dolls, brought $1,000 (£588).

On 1 December, a largely male audience gathered for the toys. First were cast-iron toys from American factories, dating primarily from 1880-1920. This group typically included a large number of horse-drawn fire pumpers, fire patrols, hose reels and hook-and-ladder trucks. Of great rarity was a magnificent 28-inch 1908 Hubley four-seater brake, its four multicoloured horses pulling a full load of eight articulated passengers. It was knocked down for $5,750 (£3,382). A hansom cab, bereft of driver, passengers and horse, brought $1,200 (£705), as did a 7-inch bell toy in the form of 'Victory' astride a shell-form chariot. A small group of cast-iron mechanical banks were also sold, among them a 'Monkey and Coconut' for $550 (£323), and a Smyth 'X-Ray' for $900 (£529), although there was nothing of outstanding importance in this most expensive of the toy collecting categories where prices can easily exceed $10,000 for a single bank.

Tin toys also fared well and there were many of them. Here, condition was crucial, for tin collectors, whose toys are often more recent and more plentiful, are less prepared to accept the chipped paint, lost parts and cracked metal that cast-iron buyers acknowledge as the price of their interest. Among the tins, the outstanding toy was a $14\frac{1}{2}$-inch mechanical two-decker paddle-steamer named the 'Star', which looked more like some intricately-worked piece of folk art. This manufactured toy was so unusual that despite its decayed state, it brought $1,600 (£941). Clockwork toys from the German Lehmann factory were sought after, with 'The Powerful Katrinka' bringing $425 (£250).

Two large automated marionette shows, an amusing Santa Claus's workshop and a New Orleans Jazz Band, sold for $950 (£558) and $1,200 (£706) respectively. But surely one of the most appealing items in the sale was the final lot, a handsome, prancing carousel horse, which went to a collector of folk art for $4,000 (£2,353).

Archie Stiles had stayed with his toys throughout the exhibition and afterwards watched each lot go up for sale. He sat motionless in the back of the room, and later admitted the experience had affected him greatly. Those who watched him occasionally noted a tear falling across his cheek. Archie was toyless again. But with almost $100,000 in sales over the two days, he was not a poor man.

A Hubley cast-iron four-seater brake, 1908, length 28in (71cm)
New York $5,750(£3,382). 1.XII.76

An American hand-carved
carousel horse, height
46in (162cm)
New York $4,000(£2,353).
1.XII.76

Left
A mid eighteenth-century Dutch silver
corkscrew, length 4½in (11.3cm)
London £290($493). 3.V.77

Far left
Charles Hull's patent Presto corkscrew
London £195($331). 8.XII.76

From left to right
Grande Champagne Cognac, Spéciale Réserve 1810 (one bottle) London £90($153). 29.IX.76
Château d'Yquem 1921 (one bottle) London £110($187). 3.V.77
Grand Marnier Centenaire 1827-1927 (one half bottle) London £30($51). 3.V.77
Sherry Lonnergon 1855 (three bottles) London £50($85). 3.V.77
Maraschino Luxardo, glass seal embossed *IMP. R. P. EPREMIATA DI G. LUXARDO, ZARA* (one bottle)
London £25($42). 25.III.77

Wine Sales

The Wine Department has completed a very successful season with net sales reaching £1,301,466 ($2,212,492). Twenty sales have been held in the United Kingdom and four overseas. The total value of the sales in Amsterdam, which have now become well established and popular with buyers from Belgium and Holland, was Fl 708,669 (£170,947:$290,610). In March 1977 a sale of over 5,000 cases of the Estate wines of South Africa, on behalf of Stellenbosch Farmers' Wineries at Nederburg, netted sales of R230,283 (£153,522:$260,987), with all lots sold. For the first time fine and rare wines were included in a series of successful sales held in December in Monte Carlo in collaboration with the Societé des Bains de Mer.

By far the most popular wines are still Red Bordeaux, or Clarets as the British know them. The latter half of the season has seen the greatest rise in prices and in several instances the peak of the market in 1972-73 has been surpassed for the rarer bottles. Vintage Port has steadily recovered and the rise is likely to continue and even accelerate. Opening prices of the recently declared 1975s will be about £50 ($85) per dozen duty paid to retail buyers in Britain. This compares with about £16 ($27) the dozen for the 1970s in 1972. At an auction price of £55 to £65 per dozen, the outstanding 1963s seem cheap.

Many bargains are still to be found among the Burgundies, Hocks and Moselles. Great Domain and Estate bottled wines are sold at well below the cost of replacement.

The undoubted quality of the sales has attracted more and more new buyers to the London saleroom. About 70 per cent come from the United States and others from Switzerland, Holland, West Germany, France, Hong Kong and Australia.

Auction will always remain the best medium for the redistribution of wines of all styles and qualities in large or small quantities. The Department's team of experts has an ever-increasing fund of knowledge and experience of the market, which enables sellers and buyers to obtain the most up-to-date advice.

Among the more interesting items sold during the season were: one bottle of Berncasteler Doctor Trockenbeerenauslese 1921, Estate Dr Thanisch, £360 ($620); one jeroboam Château Petrus 1955, £360 ($620); one imperial Château Haut-Brion 1918, £300 ($544); one double magnum La Tâche 1952, £160 ($275); one bottle Napoléon Brandy 1820 presented to the vendor's family by Feodor Chaliapin the renowned Russian bass, £100 ($172); one bottle Madeira 1797, £130 ($224); one bottle Château d'Yquem 1921 from the cellars of Mentmore, £110 ($187). From a remarkable cellar near Lyons; 'Progue Marne' 1806, Fr700 (£87:$149); Tokai 1825, Fr600 (£71:$121); Ermitage 1832, Fr500 (£59:$101) per bottle, sold in Monte Carlo.

CORNELIUS KRIEGHOFF
The sleigh race
Signed, 12in by 18in
(30cm by 45cm)
Toronto $29,000
(£17,059). 9.V.77

FRANKLIN CARMICHAEL,
OSA, RCA
Evening, north shore,
Lake Superior
Signed and dated *1930*,
30½in by 36in
(76.3cm by 90cm)
Toronto $36,000(£21,176).
9.V.77

Sotheby's first decade in Canada

Geoffrey Joyner

On 31 August 1967 Brigadier Stanley Clark, OBE, head of the public relations firm of Clark, Nelson and now a Sotheby director, sent a cable from London to Toronto which stated, in part, 'Sotheby and Company's decision to . . . stage a week of sales in Toronto from October 16 through October 20 is an extension of its continuing growth . . . they have now confirmed planning a forthcoming series of auctions in Toronto, the first Sotheby's have ever held outside Britain.' A decade has passed and Sotheby Parke Bernet now conducts auctions throughout the world.

It was perhaps auspicious that the first sale was held during Canada's centennial year just as the young nation was about to step into its second century. Collectors, dealers, investors and museum curators were becoming substantially more aware of the importance, in fact obligation, of protecting Canada's art history and began to exude a greater interest in the burgeoning art market centred in Toronto. Sotheby's, at this time, was about to commence its 224th season and only three years earlier had acquired Parke-Bernet Galleries in New York. In March 1968 a permanent Canadian office was officially opened in Toronto by Sotheby's Deputy Chairman, Lord Westmorland, at which time it was announced that the new company would conduct specialised sales of Canadian art each spring and fall. These auctions represented the first occasions at which major catalogue sales concentrating on Canadian pictorial material had been held by an international firm and jointly they produced a gross total of just over $400,000. Art critic and historian Paul Duval wrote that the arrival of Sotheby's introduced a strong new catalyst into the Canadian art scene, 'The Sotheby sales have brought not only a heightened awareness of the variety and quality of Canadian art, but also introduced a much greater security and stability into the market place.'

The Robert W. Reford Collection sold in 1968 offered some of the finest early topographical material to appear at auction. Other significant collections and estates to fall under the gavel have included consignments from the Hon Madame Georges P. Vanier, the Late Rt Hon Vincent Massey, Lady Henrietta Banting, John A. MacAuley and the Hon Lady Aitken. A tremendous growth in collecting Canadian art has occurred during the past ten years and consignors and purchasers now come from many countries to participate in the Toronto sales. Despite the fact that approximately 90 per cent of the lots sold go for under $2,000, the annual turnover in 1976 from two auctions was well over double that of 1968 and is now approaching one million dollars a year.

Notes on Contributors

John Ayers is Keeper of the Far Eastern Section at the Victoria and Albert Museum, London. His publications include the four volumes which comprise the *Catalogue of the Baur Collection of Chinese Ceramics* (1968–74); *Oriental Ceramics: The World's Great Collections, Vol 6 The Victoria & Albert Museum* (1975), and the recently published *China for the West* (1977) written with David Howard.

Charles Beare is a director of J. & A. Beare Ltd, London, dealers, makers and restorers of violins.

Wendy Cooper is Assistant Curator at the Museum of Fine Arts, Boston. She compiled and catalogued the exhibition entitled *Paul Revere's Boston: 1735-1818* which was held at the Museum in 1975. Her articles on the American decorative arts include those in *Antiques Magazine* (February 1973, April 1973, July 1975) and *The American Art Journal* (November 1977).

J. B. Donne is a former Professor in the School of Art, University of Washington. His many articles on African art include those in *The Connoisseur* (June 1972, April 1974, February 1977) *The Antique Collector* (October 1975) *The Collector* (March 1975) and *Man* (April 1973).

Mary Henderson is a former correspondent of *Time and Life*. She has contributed articles to *Apollo, Country Life* and *History Today*. She is the wife of Sir Nicholas Henderson, GCMG, British Ambassador to the French Republic and previously Ambassador to the Federal Republic of Germany and Ambassador to Poland.

Frank Herrmann is the author of *The English as Collectors* (1973). He is currently at work on a history of Sotheby's.

Derek Howse is Head of Navigation and Astronomy at the National Maritime Museum, London. His publications include *Greenwich Observatory: the building and instruments* (1975), *The Sea Chart* (1973) written with Michael Sanderson, and the series of articles now collated under the title *The Clocks and Watches of Captain James Cook*.

Terence Mullaly is art critic of *The Daily Telegraph*. He was a personal friend of the late C. R. Rudolf whose collection he discusses.

Roger Pinkham is Research Assistant in Ceramics at the Victoria and Albert Museum, London. He has written on Limoges enamels for the Museum (1974) and also catalogued its collection of De Morgan pottery (1973).

Diana Scarisbrick is London correspondent of the Italian magazine *Bolaffiarte*. She has recently published the *Catalogue of the Harari Collection of Gems and Finger Rings* (1977) in collaboration with John Boardman, and is at present working on a catalogue of the Fortnum Collection of post-classical finger rings at the Ashmolean Museum, Oxford.

Justin G. Schiller is an antiquarian bookseller in New York specialising in historical children's literature. He is also a lecturer and appraiser on this subject and has recently co-edited, with Alison Lurie, *Garland's Classics in Children's Literature*.

Sir Francis Watson, KCVO, is a former Director of the Wallace Collection, London, and Adviser to the Queen on works of art. His publications include *Louis XVI Furniture* (1960), *Catalogue of the Furniture in the Wallace Collection* (1970) and vols 1–5 of *The Wrightsman Collection Catalogues* (1973). He is currently preparing a volume entitled *French Furniture 1660–1790*.

The 8th Duke of Wellington, MVO, OBE, MC, DL, is President and founder of the Anglo-Belgian Waterloo Committee which is concerned in safeguarding the battlefield and its monuments. He is Colonel-in-Chief of the Duke of Wellington's Regiment.

The following contributors are experts at Sotheby Parke Bernet's offices: Roy Davids, Philippe Garner, Derek Johns, James Miller, Julien Stock and Jane Strutt (in London), Mary-Anne Martin and David Redden (in New York) and Geoffrey Joyner (in Toronto).

Index